Don't you hear the H-Bomb's Thunder?

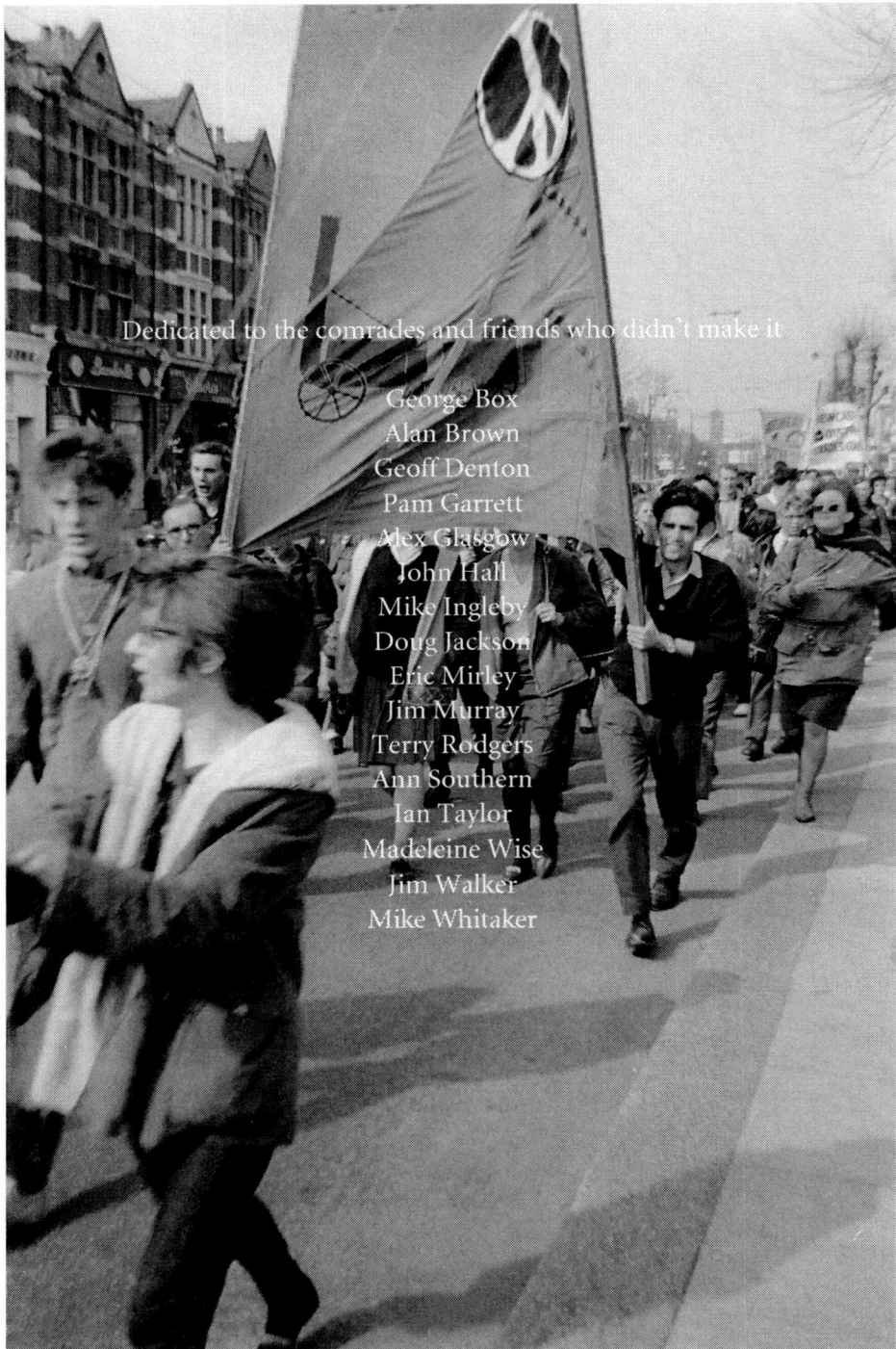

Dedicated to the comrades and friends who didn't make it

George Box
Alan Brown
Geoff Denton
Pam Garrett
Alex Glasgow
John Hall
Mike Ingleby
Doug Jackson
Eric Mirley
Jim Murray
Terry Rodgers
Ann Southern
Ian Taylor
Madeleine Wise
Jim Walker
Mike Whitaker

Don't You Hear the H-Bomb's Thunder?

Youth & politics on Tyneside in the late 'fifties and early 'sixties

John Charlton

NORTH EAST LABOUR HISTORY

MERLIN PRESS

Published in 2009
by North East Labour History
in association with
The Merlin Press Ltd.
6 Crane Street Chambers
Crane Street
Pontypool
NP4 6ND
Wales
www.merlinpress.co.uk

ISBN. 978-0-85036-699-0

British Library Cataloguing in Publication Data
is available from the British Library

Printed in the UK by Imprint Digital, Exeter

As Soon As This Pub Closes[1]

I could have done it yesterday if I hadn't a cold,
But since I've put this pint away I've never felt so bold.
So as soon as this pub closes, as soon as this pub closes,
As soon as this pub closes, the revolution starts.

I'll shoot the aristocracy and confiscate their brass,
Create a fine democracy that's truly working class.
As soon as this pub closes, as soon as this pub closes,
As soon as this pub closes, I'll raise the banner high.

I'll fight the nasty racialists and scrap the colour bar,
And all fascist dictatorships and every commissar.
As soon as this pub closes, as soon as this pub closes,
As soon as this pub closes, I'll man the barricades.

So raise your glasses, everyone, for everything is planned,
And each and every mother's son will see the Promised Land.
As soon as this pub closes, as soon as this pub closes,
As soon as this pub closes... I think I'm going to be sick.

Alex Glasgow, *Close the Coalhouse Door.*
(Permission granted by Paddy Glasgow)

Contents

Introduction

The 'sixties' has been subjected to adoration and abuse. The adorers remember the demos, the festivals, the music, the clothes, and the sense of 'answers blowing in the wind.' The abusers cite the challenge to authority, the lack of discipline, the promiscuity. All think they know what they are talking about. 'The sixties' is a value, a happening, a portmanteau, as well as a space in time. And, it only loosely corresponds to the actual ten years: 1960-1969. If pressed, many would say it didn't start till round about half way through the decade and perhaps went on almost to the strident arrival of Margaret Thatcher in office. It has now been written about a lot and its most luminous icons have become much featured in TV and radio documentaries.

Although it is perhaps just becoming fashionable fifty years on, the 'fifties' has appeared a dimmer place of lesser interest, somehow lingering just beyond vivid memory. It seemed like an undiscovered country about which we know a little, say; Bill Haley and the Comets, the Suez Crisis, and for Geordies, the last time Newcastle United won the Cup – three times too! Only a few historians or film-makers have ventured to its shores. Historical accounts are sparse. Yet it is an important territory, containing the sixties' pre-history, central to which were seismic changes in the history of Britain. In just a few years the economy embarked on a long boom. With company order books full, working class people began to enjoy rapidly rising living standards. Tax revenues allowed massive investment in housing, education, health and welfare. A bulging job market appeared to banish unemployment and to breathe confidence into workers. The situation remained uneven, perhaps especially in the north east where poverty, slum dwellings and poor educational opportunity continued for many.

Boom conditions were destined to last no more than a couple of decades but whilst they did, the generation of people born in the ten years or so after 1935, shaped their world at work, home and leisure, quite differently from their parents. This book explores that world from the perspective of a number of north easterners by birth or adoption, temporary or permanent. They are people who in their teens and early twenties turned to the left, engaging in a range of activities, political and cultural. The book is a collective biography strongly based on interviews with over thirty participants and it could not have been attempted without their active participation. However their story is given broader context by using other available sources which together illuminate a small piece of north east history that would otherwise disappear from view as so much of the region's rich radical past has already done.

A health warning

A reader of the first draft of this book said, 'this is autobiography disguised as history.' In reply I posed the question, 'how do you get yourself out of a book that you are in?' It is a rhetorical answer because I don't believe this to be desirable, let alone possible. I am in the book in two ways. First, I use chunks of personal biography hopefully to illuminate some points. My parents and grandparents are there as part of my attempt to explain where I came from. I do not this could be contentious. I am also there as the story teller. I was there at the birth of the 59 Society, Newcastle West Young Socialists and the International Socialists. These are personal accounts into which I weave other accounts. They may also be uncontentious except in some details; others may recall it a little differently. I was not in the Kings' College Socialist or Communist Societies, the Durham University Socialist Society, the Communist Party(CP), the Young Communist League (YCL) or the Socialist Labour League(SLL). And though I was present and involved in many of the Campaign for Nuclear Disarmament (CND) activities I was not the organiser of any of them. For my accounts of these organisations and activities I rely on what others have told me. I have quoted as accurately as possible and built a narrative from their accounts as faithfully as possible. The interpretation however is entirely mine.

The set of political ideas I embraced in the early sixties have remained my credo though I hope I behave with a good deal less intolerance than I once did towards those who do not share my perspective. I don't apologise for my angle of vision but I hope that readers will see enough that they recognise in my description of a world we once shared fifty years ago not to throw my offering into the dustbin of history.

It is necessary to issue another caution. People commmonly register their own youth as a golden time. One of those interviewed uses this specific term. The author as participant is specially vulnerable to wearing specs with rosy tints. It is my contention that something special did happen on Tyneside in the few years round 1960. I do not claim that Tyneside was unique. Yet again, at least one of those interviewed believes that the youth upsurge 'bounced off the democratic decay' that derived from the 'one party government' that characterised much of the region. The same person wonders if the language of protest had 'an echo of the great Tyneside music hall and folk music tradition.'

We shall have to look at these propositions. However the available evidence demands modesty. It seems that Glasgow and parts of London, at least, shared the moment and that several other places experienced elements of it. But there is apparently no detailed study of any other area so comparison is difficult. There is some patchy anecdotal evidence of interest. An activist who went to Sheffield in 1964 found no comparable movement beyond a strong Communist Party rooted in the engineering industry and the surrounding pits and a small New Left Club based on the University, though a much younger crowd was soon to emerge. Sheffield born Joe Cocker had started to perform in the clubs in 1961.[2] In Manchester, where the CP was also strong, the folk scene was already celebrated through the reputation of Ewan McColl but there seems to have been no vibrant youth movement before the mid-sixties. On the other hand, Glasgow and parts of London were probably at least on par with Tyneside. Glasgow had a working class socialist youth culture which found expression in the 1960 apprentices' strike in ship building and engineering and in early Ban the Bomb marches.

Mike Down was active in London before arriving in Newcastle in 1959. He wrote, 'I went with some sixth formers to the second Aldermaston march in 1959 – the first one FROM Aldermaston. Beforehand we went to the Partisan, the left-wing coffee shop in Soho run by *Universities and Left Review*, sleeping in school halls and Quaker meeting houses en route. I met people who later became very familiar to me – Peggy Duff, Canon Collins, Bertrand Russell. It was intensely exciting. We believed nuclear war to be a real and present threat to mankind and were protesting not just against the bomb but against the core values of the society which sanctioned it.'[3] In the St Pancras and Soho areas there were anarchist and socialist groups operating round the Partisan Coffee House, Jimmy the Greek's Café and Cy Laurie's Jazz Club in Ham Yard. Large contingents from this milieu were present on the 1959 and 1960 Aldermaston marches.[4] There are some very interesting research projects possible with the enormous advantage that many participants are still available!

Acknowledgements

This book could not have been researched and written without the active help of more than fifty participants in the Tyneside left of the early nineteen sixties. They are mainly acknowledged in the section entitled, 'Where have all the marchers gone?' A few of them have done extra duty in allowing themselves to be subjected to repeated interrogation! John Creaby has the memory of an elephant and an enviable good humour. Additionally he has kept a detailed journal of his very active life which ought to be published in its own right. Guy Falkenau and Lucy Nicholson have similar memories for detail. They keep turning up new stories, keep an open door and an ever ready coffee pot. Their generous taxi service has kept a little group together for years. Jim Nichol and

Jim Hutchinson are life time comrades in the International Socialists (IS) then Socialist Workers Party (SWP) who have been exceptionally concerned for me to get facts right. Jim Nichol brings many anecdotes to the story and Jim Hutchinson even remembers what happened on particular nights. Jim Walker, another life long friend from school days, was in at the beginning, full of encouragement for a task which he would have undertaken with more sparkle and wit. It is very sad that he is not around to see the result. Likewise Geoff Denton, another school friend, who died before I could talk to him about those days. He would no doubt have been merciless in criticism but from him I would have learnt some long forgotten tales.

Several people read drafts and offered comments. They were Roger Hall with whom I first stood on the door step seeking support for Arthur Blenkinsop and who has been around my life for more than fifty years. Willie Thompson gave the book his customary meticulous attention. John Mapplebeck cares a lot about getting it right and how things are said, like the very fine journalist he is. Dave Harker challenged the very basis of the project, but it is from such challenges that, hopefully, better work comes. Ian Birchall was an early reader who has an unparallelled knowledge of the often Byzantine workings of the British left. Sean Creighton's keen eye for detail and possible missed avenues, raised new questions. Kris Beuret made important suggestions on structure and omissions. Sally Mitchison gave it the final read and managed to find many little ways to do it all better. Finally I must thank Tony Zurbrugg of Merlin Press who took my project on very late in the game and managed to get it out very quickly indeed.

Thanks are due to everyone who was grilled by questionnaire, letter, email, interview and follow up phone calls. They are: Maggie Anwell, John Baker, Jennifer (Piachaud) Bartholemew, Jeremy Beecham, Jane (Lu) Bell, Albert and Joan Booth, Ann Berg, Colin & Lillian Boyd, Margaret (Dick) Brecknell, Marian (Campbell) Charlton, Mary (Feinmann) Chuck, Fiona (Scott Batey) Clarke, Brenda (Ingleby) Corcoron, John and Margaret Creaby, Ronnie & Doreen Curran, Sam Dodds, Mike Down, Brian Ebbatson, Linda (Potts) Ebbatson, Guy Falkenau, Trisha (Sorbie) Fitzpatrick, Lindy (Howard) Genton, Moira (Woods) Gray, Roger Hall, Wal and Gladys Hobson, Jenn (Scott) Holder, Jim Hutchinson, Pat (Marley) Johnson, Ann Kane, Dave Leigh, Irene (Edwards), Lovell, Pat (Duffy) MacIntyre, Vin MacIntyre, John Mapplebeck, Jean Mortimer, Jim Nichol, Lucy Nicholson, Maggie (Boyd) Pearse, Dave Peers, Sandra Peers, Norman Ridley, Harry Rothman, Walter Ryder, Barrie Scaum, Brian Sharp, Dorothy Simmons, John Smith, Anna Tapsell, Jane (Owens) Wadham, the late, Jim Walker, Marge (Wallace), Nina (Johnson) Watson, Terry Watson, and Mike Worrall. Please note that after this listing, and the first endnote reference, people will usually be named in the text by the name they are best known by today.

I am grateful to the following for permission to use material:

The editors of the *Evening Chronicle* and *Newcastle Journal* for clippings from the papers.

Local Studies, Newcastle City Library.

Chapter one: Just before 'the sixties'

For much of the nineteen fifties World War Two remained an important reference point in the minds and conversation of working people. After all, many of the men had spent their own youth in the services, from Salisbury Plain to the River Kwai. In 1945 they voted Labour, picked up their 'demob suits' from Wembley Stadium and headed home. Single women joined the men in service, though not in combat, or joined the Land Army. Married women entered the labour force in unprecedented numbers on Tyneside though most were dispatched to the kitchen at the war's end. Though minds were inevitably broadened by dislocation and dispersal, Tyneside remained an insular world where even 'the French onion man was a figure of mystery.'[5]

The Labour landslide in the General Election of July 1945 had apparently opened the door to a gale of change. There was a sudden influx of young people to the Labour League of Youth, fuelled by rising expectations. Yet, only six years on, Winston Churchill could fill the Newcastle City Hall and the Baths Hall next door, with hundreds left on the street. The party of political dinosaurs amazingly captured the concept of 'setting the people free'. The small voices warning, 'Yes. Free for millionaires,' were drowned out. Labour had apparently wantonly burnt the seed corn of change and large and small 'c' conservatism re-colonised the streets and minds. This is well illustrated in the success of the Lord's Day Observance Society's campaign to keep Newcastle's cinemas closed on Sundays till the mid-fifties.[6]

Nevertheless, the prohibition of Sunday cinema was just the small change of conservatism. The big freeze was sustained by the Cold War. Churchill had cast his shadow again with his often cited Fulton Speech in 1945 declaring that, 'an iron curtain has descended over Europe.' He had a worthy successor in Ernie Bevin, the docker-cum-Labour Foreign Secretary. The Berlin Airlift and the Korean War shaped attitudes to socialism as did a bi-partisan colonial policy. On the domestic front the essentially egalitarian policy of rationing basic provisions was submerged by a press barrage of hostility intensified by cartoonists and radio comedians.

Conservatism was also reinforced by National Service. From 1945 to 1959 all men were conscripted on reaching 18 years of age, though a system of deferred entry was available for apprentices and university students. After a short training period, some were launched into the combat zones of Palestine, Korea, Malaya, Kenya, Aden, Cyprus and the Suez Canal Zone to continue the imperial mission of their forefathers. Others might see 'eight hour day' duties in Nigeria, Germany or even Aldershot. In a period of domestic tranquillity only a few were likely to be radicalised by their experience. Perhaps the greatest de-politicising experience was being removed from 'normal' life in the late teen-age years.

Usually the most subversive aspect of the period of service 'captivity' was being subjected to the irrational stupidities of service routine and witnessing the incompetence of junior officers who were frequently of an age with the squaddies themselves. There were exceptions like the local League of Youth member,[7] appalled by having to kick doors down on patrol in Cyprus. Yet the rule was for young recruits to Labour to disappear from political life. Most would not return. Many of their female contemporaries disappeared too, into marriage and family life. However this situation was to change. Towards the end of the fifties the scope of deferrals from National Service was widened. This was soon followed by the end of conscription.

Anti-communism

Though nothing like so rabid as in the USA, anti-communism damaged progressive forces. The workplace could be an uncomfortable place for proclaimed socialists and 'He's a commie' was normally an unfriendly description. Many left wing activists were subject to black-listing by employers. Some of the worst problems came from inside the trade union movement, where right wing forces were organised to thwart left wing bids for union office. For much of the early post-war period communists and sympathisers were in a defensive stance which did not help recruitment. There was little new blood. Indeed that which there was often came through family connection: many new activists were the sons and daughters of active parents.

The conservatism of the times affected the Labour Party too. The Newcastle City Labour Party remained out of office for ten years till 1958 in a largely working class city though Manchester, Liverpool (Progressives), Leeds and Birmingham also experienced periods of Tory administration in the fifties. The councillors and party officers, usually men and a few women of over forty, were veterans of even more difficult times between the wars. Perhaps that landslide of '45 was felt as an aberration; normal life had returned. The emphasis was on maintaining respectability, affirming loyalty and keeping heads down.

The Bevanite rebellion in the dying moments of the Labour Government attracted some of the younger generation and gave an ideological home to older Socialist Leaguers and 'Crippsites'.[8] Bevanites argued for more public ownership, keeping medicine free, a more vigorous anti-colonial policy, a deeper criticism of the Atlantic Alliance and a softening in attitude to the Soviet Union. They carried out a spirited, if nationalistic, campaign against German re-armament and were among the first to try alert the public to the dangers of nuclear war. In Newcastle they even managed to run a lively monthly newspaper, the *Northern Star*. It was a short-lived revival however. The victory of Gaitskell in the leadership election in 1955, followed by Nye Bevan's own turn round on nuclear weapons was demoralising. The Labour Party lost the 1955 General Election but moved to the next election with some hope that the intervening Suez debacle would damage the Tories. But there was much trepidation. The latter sentiment was born out by Macmillan's 1959 triumph, based on the cynical, but successful, manipulation of the economy and his reminder that 'we've never had it so good'.

The Communist Party was in no shape to benefit from Labour's crisis. Despite the war-time alliance with Stalin, it was outflanked electorally by Labour's 1945 triumph. The Soviet Union's carve up of Eastern Europe and its representation in the British media, coupled with the firmness of Labour government's alliance with Washington, gave little space for a Communist offensive. Some roots were established in the unions and work places away from the public glare. The shop stewards' movement, the subject of so much hysteria in the right wing press of the 'sixties, grew but the pick up in the economy in the early fifties did not in general create a sympathetic environment for shop floor political agitation.

Such difficulties were magnified in 1956. First, in February, a secret speech by Stalin's successor, Nikita Khrushchev came to light. Khrushchev severely attacked Stalin for developing a cult of personality. The horrors of the Moscow Trials could be talked about. The British party leadership tried to clamp down on discussion and any signs of opposition. Then in October, the students and workers of Hungary exploded into open revolt against their Stalinist leadership. When Russian tanks arrived in Budapest with their guns blazing, British communists were shocked and appalled. The attitude of the British leaders was to try to batten down the hatches on discussion. The Hungarian rebellion was one of the first international crises appearing nightly on the TV screen. In twelve months it was calculated that a quarter of the membership left the party.[9]

So, the late fifties was a very low point for both Labour and Communist Parties. Labour experienced a temporary electoral revival immediately after the Suez fiasco[10] but it had vanished by the 1959 General Election.

On the other hand trade union membership prospered. A low level of unemployment was a novelty for Tyneside in the twentieth century. After the immediate post-war crisis, caused largely by war time dislocation and raw material shortages, the area moved into fast economic growth. There was a little renewed anxiety round 1956-7, when the Bank Rate soared, but demand for coal, iron and steel was strong and ship builders experienced full order books by 1960. The start of the National Health Service helped create a buoyant public sector and each of these developments stimulated housing demand and hence a boom in the building industry. This was good news for trade union recruitment and the closed shop became the rule in many sections of industry and services. This situation strengthened shop floor control and was the main explanation for the publication of the Donovan Commission Report of 1968[11] and the legislation which followed. However the impact of the shop floor on politics during the nineteen fifties was modest. Disputes over piece rates, hours and working conditions settled in the workplace or company, without bringing in the state, minimised political conflict. There were some exceptions but unlike the situation in the late sixties and seventies there was relatively little involvement by industrial workers in socialist politics. Engagement usually came from individuals attracted by ideas: opposition to the arms race, east-west relations, public ownership and imperialism.

Education and gender

So far this is a down beat account, a story of relatively little happening on the domestic political front. Political passivity from the working class is undeniable but it needs explanation. What is also true is that beneath the surface there were many tributaries which would feed the activity which surfaced round 1959-60 and which would create major upheavals from the mid-sixties and into the seventies. One such was created by the introduction of universal secondary education after the 1944 Education Act. That Act was soon seen to be deeply flawed especially in its pigeon holing of all state school children by the 11 plus exam. The critique of this was to lead into the ideologically charged debate on comprehensive education. But before that got underway an entirely new slice of the social structure was travelling through the system experiencing liberation, alienation or both. These were the children of manual and low status white collar workers who had themselves largely been denied education beyond the age of 14. The brightest, or luckiest, of their children passed the 11 plus and entered the Grammar Schools, the brightest or luckiest of *them* stepping on the escalator that might lead to universities and the professions. Such progress was by no means guaranteed in the madly hierarchical atmosphere of schools which prized conformity even above brilliance. In these little hot houses were produced the angry young men and though, generally much more muted, even suppressed, angry young women. The latter sowed the seeds for what was to become part of the new women's movement. These men and women were to supply a number of the lieutenants and rank and file of socialist parties, sects, and even the trade union bureaucracies a little later.

If broader entry to grammar schools was a welcome feature of the 1944 Act, the 11 plus exam was certainly a downside. For those who failed the exam, secondary modern school experience varied considerably. A small number of such schools, often those in middle class areas, offered a general certificate course and a second best route to the escalator. The others were often housed in relics of the first stab at state education for all, in 1870. They would frequently experience large classes staffed by underqualified and poorly trained teachers regurgitating a watered down academic curriculum quite useless for the children under their roofs. School days were to be endured not enjoyed.[12] One small consolation was the buoyant labour market. Jobs were largely available both before and after National Service. Work experience and National Service drew very few into socialist politics but the end of conscription in 1960 may have contributed to changing this situation. Certainly more non-Grammar school youths turned in this direction after that point.

Widened educational opportunity for some had another consequence. Grammar school youths going onto university and teacher training colleges on full maintenance grants were not restricted to their own town or region. Many came into the north east, to Newcastle, Durham, Sunderland and Darlington. Those attracted by socialist ideas became involved in action and a number stayed in the region to continue this activity beyond graduation. So, educational experience was important in feeding the new movement when it emerged.

I have touched upon gender. The position of women in the fifties is complex. On the one hand the north east had among the lowest ratio of women in the workforce anywhere in Britain. This derived from the nature of industry in the region. Coal mining, ship building, iron and steel manufacture were overwhelmingly male occupations. Social attitudes sprang from this. A woman's place was said to be in the home not the work place. In reality this attitude was breached in practice since working class women had long serviced the middle class as domestic servants and hotel staff as well as more generally as shop assistants. This continued after the war but there were other changes taking place that raised the demand for women workers. In Newcastle just after the war, the Ministry of Pensions and National Insurance opened enormous premises at Longbenton. With it came a great demand and opportunity for female labour. But this site was merely the biggest part of an enormous expansion of state and municipal employment in all aspects of welfare and education. The growth of the retail sector as living standards rose had a similar effect. It also led to the gradual abandonment of the convention that women left the work force at marriage. This came from a delicate interplay between the needs of the economy and women's desire to have a career outside the home.

The fall out from the H Bomb

In the mid-fifties information began to creep into the public domain of the true effects of the Atom Bombs dropped on Japan in 1945 and especially the new features of warfare: truly mass destruction and radiation which could affect survivors and future generations. It was followed by the dissemination of scientific information branding atmospheric testing of H Bombs, let alone their use, as acutely dangerous. The issue was taken up initially by small numbers of scientists, writers, minister of religion, Quaker meetings and a tiny group of left-wing socialists. The focus was on the British Bomb and the need to give a moral lead to the world. Following a large public meeting in London in February 1958, the first mass mobilisation took place at Easter, when four thousand people marched to the nuclear weapons site at Aldermaston, Berkshire. The north east was represented by a small contingent. One year later a few hundred from the area joined the much larger march to London. The issue had caught the imagination and nightmares of young people. The little CND symbol was appearing on countless jackets and jumpers. Weird sounding phrases like Strontium 90 and 'half-life' entered the vocabulary of protest. Civil Defence prescriptions, sandbags and brown paper, were both terrifying in their banality and risible. The process of protest, marches, symbols, songs and the additional prospect of sex, was simply thrilling.

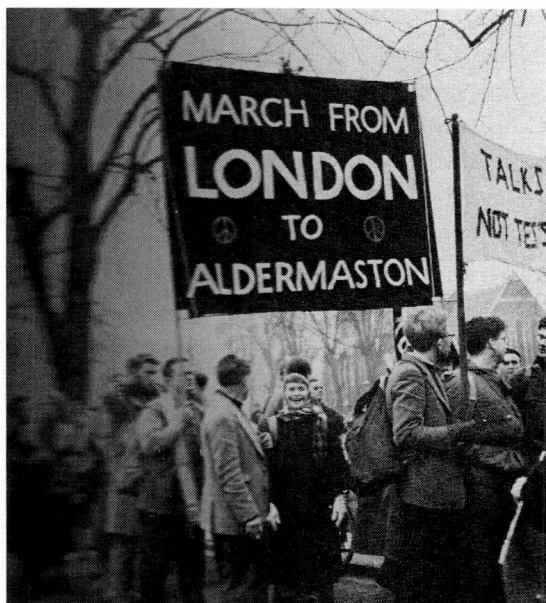

Little thought was given to how unilateral nuclear disarmament could be achieved. Yet some thought about it. Since the authorities would not listen to moral persuasion maybe non-violent direct action could force the government to capitulate to good sense. This was immensely appealing to the young and, from 1961, hundreds sat down at Holy Loch, Wethersfield, Fylingdales and Whitehall. By the time it was obvious that governments would not be swayed by that either, the moderate leadership of CND was taken up with the possibility that a new Labour government would provide a solution through diplomacy. Some of the rank and file shifted their focus to concentrate on a more radical political solution, the overthrow of capitalism. Before the late sixties they could be probably be numbered in hundreds. Some stayed with the Labour Party but probably the majority went to college, went to work, and made babies.

Winds of change

The anti-bomb campaigns were the biggest attraction for rebellious youth but not the only ones. Many were enraged by the situation in South Africa and the supine attitude of the British government towards it, in vetoing UN resolutions of censure. Oddly though, the eruption in South Africa in the spring of 1960 may have emanated from a speech by a Tory. During the previous year the two leading resistance organisations the Pan African Congress (PAC) and the African National Congress (ANC) were vying for position in the campaign against the Pass Laws. The PAC was calling for a campaign of non-violent civil disobedience.

Prime Minister Harold Macmillan arrived in South Africa in February 1960 where he made the speech which marked a shift in British policy away from underwriting the policy of apartheid. He said, 'The wind of change is blowing through this continent. Whether we like it or not, this growth of national consciousness is a political fact. As a fellow member of the Commonwealth it is our earnest desire to give South Africa our support and encouragement, but I hope you won't mind my saying frankly that there are some aspects of your policies which make it impossible for us to do this without being false to our own deep convictions about the political destinies of free men to which in our own territories we are trying to give effect.'

It may be that this speech and the curt reply it received from South African leader, Hendrik Verwoerd, acted as a stimulus to the growing opposition to the Pass Laws. A month later on 21st March, 69 black South Africans were killed and 300 injured at Sharpeville when a peaceful protest against the pass laws was fired on by the police. A howl of revulsion sounded round the world. Protest meetings and marches were widely held including a large one in Newcastle. The massive assault on black South Africans continued throughout the early sixties. It included an intensification of repressive laws and the trial and imprisonment of the leaders of the ANC, the PAC and the white student movement. It provided a strong and continuous focus for the new socialist youth movements which were deeply involved in the campaign to boycott South African goods.

Though occurring far from the north east, the so called 'race riots' in Notting Hill and Nottingham in the summer of 1959, evoked memories of the 1930s' fights against fascism when it became clear that Mosleyites were involved. Although the north east's industrial structure meant there was a low influx of commonwealth migrants to the area, the socialist youth groups were very alert to racist behaviour especially in relation to hotels and boarding houses operating a colour bar.

A tiny tributary surfaced from the 1956 crisis in the Communist Party. Leading CP intellectuals E P Thompson and John Saville raised the opposition standard inside the Party around their journal *The Reasoner* and, when they were excluded, outside with *The New Reasoner*. A second small initiative launched *The Universities and Left Review*, the two uniting in 1960 as the *New Left Review*. There is little evidence of support for this venture among CP industrial workers, but on Tyneside their socialist humanism agenda was picked up by non-CP shop stewards from Vickers and Parsons and some Labour Party young socialists, the first meeting being held at the Bridge Hotel in December 1959.[13] The Newcastle Left Club provided a new forum for committed Marxists who did not have to defend Washington or Moscow and were strongly interested in the idea of workers'control. It met intermittently over the following two years. By autumn 1961 it contained the core of what was to become the International Socialists.

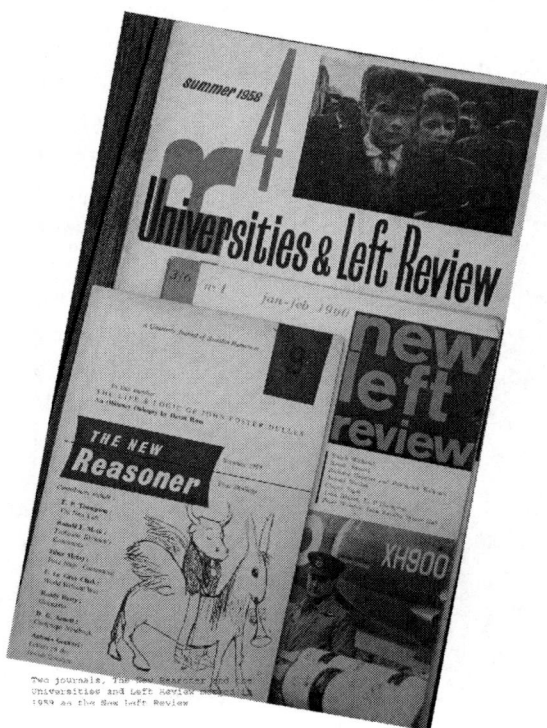

Two journals, The New Reasoner and the Universities and Left Review united in 1959 as the New Left Review

The Brasilia of the North?

The Labour Party was a stream rather than a tributary. Along the Tyne there were several Labour Parties, corresponding to the local authority or constituency areas. Newcastle was the regional hub upon which many political campaigns were focussed. After the flush of victory had abated by 1950, conservatism reasserted itself in local Labour Parties. But there were some stirrings of radicalism. In Newcastle the Bevanites were reinforced by the recruitment of some of the remnants of end of the war Trotskyism associated with the great Tyneside apprentices' strike of 1944. The leader of this group was T Dan Smith, who had been a Wallsend activist since his teens in the late thirties. The son of a Durham miner, Smith claimed that blacklisting drove him, straight after the war, to start a one man decorating business with bike, ladder and paint pot.

Less than two years after being accepted into LP membership Smith was elected onto the council soon followed by two of his far left comrades, Ken Skethaway and Jack Johnson. Small business life made Smith financially independent. Council membership gave him good contacts. From his first year on the Council in 1950, his firm bid successfully for decorating contracts each year into the next decade. This was to prove his nemesis. But Smith wanted more than to accumulate wealth. He truly wished to change the face of the town and region. He built alliances with other Labour left wingers but also with other modernisers. In a short time he had captured the Labour Group, albeit precariously.

T Dan Smith, 1960

When the municipal elections of 1958 were narrowly won, Smith's group was ready to drive through their modernising and modernist project.[14] 'Development' became the watchword; a new Town Hall, a new city centre, a radical road system, accelerated slum clearance and council house building, a new Central Library, new schools and comprehensive education all by the mid-sixties and, a little later, a new Metro system. In a show of hubris he coined the phrase, 'the Brasilia of the north.' This was a rather unfortunate image implying development on a virgin site, like Brasilia itself. Unlike Brasilia this would involve the wholesale destruction of the existing town. The alternative metaphor, 'the Venice of the north' was a fanciful reference to the idea of separating pedestrians from vehicles by building a system of linked high level walkways in concrete. It was not a bad idea in itself, but the partially completed result did not adorn the city. Nevertheless this was a remarkable municipal agenda.

By the end of the fifties there was a new socialist movement engaging several hundred young people under 25. Yet very few of them were drawn to Dan Smith's project. Few became local councillors. Over the river in Gateshead, and down river both sides, the new YS grew in the first five years of the 1960s and there was a similar pattern of weak involvement in the Labour Party's local agenda. Smith's evocation of poetry in concrete held little attraction for the youth movement. Although he was not yet tainted by financial corruption, young socialists could see the construction company vultures circling overhead. It offered little to a youth movement enraged by the Bomb, oppression in South Africa, US attempts to unseat Fidel Castro and, a bit nearer home, Transport's House's[15] serial attempts to stifle opposition. It was perhaps the unkindest cut of all that Smith the visionary and his epigones throughout the region had to rely for support on the grey careerists among the post war's first adult generation. Most of the young visionaries turned out to have other business.

This book tells the story of this generation of activists up to the arrival of Harold Wilson's government in 1964. There are perhaps unsurprising findings. The improvements in housing, education and employment opportunities, referred to above, helped to foster considerable social mobility. The same factors began to have an impact on the prospects of many women. Then, many of these activists took up politics at a conjuncture between the attitudes and mores of the fifties and those of the sixties. The book's argument is that this represented a unique historical moment.

Chapter Two: Before 'we' arrived[16]

Research through multiple interviews has thrown up some unexpected themes. The personal interviews led to discussion of the cohort's parents' generation. With a few exceptions, the parents were born in the decade 1910 to 1920, their children from 1935 to 1945. Both were therefore babies or small children during the twentieth century's two world wars. This offers the opportunity to compare the impact of those conflicts on the formative years of each generation and of the very different post-war worlds in which the two generations were reared.

Of more than fifty parents whose histories are known, there are only three fathers who were of military service age in the Great War. A small number of parents were born just after the conflict ended. The rest were infants or children during the war years. Very few seem to have escaped some kind of trauma in their early years. There was loss of fathers, or other close relatives in combat, wounding, disability and chronic sickness including the effects of gassing in the trenches. There was loss of mothers in childbirth or from tuberculosis. There were single mothers, a consequence of desperate war time relationships, abuse of servant girls and abandonment with a heavy dose of moral disapproval thrown in. The consequences for children could be dire: fostering across or outside families already stressed by war, grim living conditions, rapid changes in location and accommodation, scant care and deficient diet.

My father was born in 1915. His mother was an unmarried woman of 30. She was the second youngest in a large rural family from Gunnerton, on the North Tyne. She had left school at 12 and entered domestic service as a parlour maid. She moved round a succession of houses of the Northumbrian country gentry, arriving in Newcastle shortly before the Great War where she worked as a waitress at the Royal Station Hotel. She then sought higher wages as a post-woman when the service was opened to females at the start of the war. Unable to support her child without working, she fostered him out to three consecutive families in Newcastle. He was rescued by his aunt who was also working in Newcastle. She took him to their eldest sister in Gunnerton when he was three years. His mother had married towards the end of the war. He visited her, rather than lived with her, and suffered regular violence at the hands of his stepfather. He only joined his mother permanently when he left school at 14 and was able bring money into the home.[17]

Fred Marley hardly knew his father who left the home while Fred was a small boy. He was born in Elswick in 1912, near Armstrong's factory. His mother struggled to keep the family of five children above the poverty line.[18] Colin Boyd was born in Stanley just after the war ended. His father had survived the war but was seriously injured on the Somme. His disablement meant chronic sickness and long stretches of unemployment through the childhoods of his children which put enormous stress on their mother.[19] Bryce Nichol was born into a family distressed by loosing a boy of 18, his uncle, at Gallipoli in April 1915.[20] Margaret Dick's grandfather went to war with the Black Watch. She says, 'he survived but his marriage didn't. My grandmother left. I don't know why but it may have been lack of money, or the loss of two infant children.' Margaret's father was sent to live with a grandmother in Fife. He got an apprenticeship as a plumber but like many in the thirties was sacked at the end of it. He moved to Beadnell and worked on the buses as conductor and driver. Blindness in one eye exempted him from war service but he worked as a maintenance fitter on Acklington aerodrome during the war.[21]

One of the older parents, Alex Watson, was born in Ayrshire in 1892 in very straitened circumstances. His father, a miner, had left his family of six children. His mother died soon after, in 1895, and the children were placed in the workhouse. He was apprenticed to a cobbler at 12, but soon was sent down the pit. He was old enough for conscription in 1914, and was wounded at Paschendaele in 1916. He was invalided out to a poorly paid storeman's job at Armstrongs, Scotswood. Don Edwards lost his father, a seaman, at the Battle of Jutland in 1916. His mother died less than two years later when he was just six. He spent his childhood being fostered resentfully around his Merseyside family.

Harry Rothman's Uncle Tom was a victim of the war. 'He went off to war in 1914 with the Manchester Regiment returning wounded and shell shocked to spend the rest of his life impaired and hospitalised. He lived till 82 and as a child I remember visiting this strange amiable man in hospital, as it were, "hidden from history." '[22]

Lucy Nicholson's mother, Grace, was born just after the war and out of wedlock, like her older sister. Her mother, a Durham miner's daughter, was shuttled between middle class households, as a maid servant and was the victim of predatory employers.[23] Wal Hobson had similar exploitation in his family. One grandfather went to war in 1914 as batman to Lord Kitchener. He never returned to the family, surfacing after the war as butler to a titled lady whom he eventually married. His wife returned to her family to assist in the pub which her father had acquired through his marriage. Wal's other grandmother had gone as a maid to a Newcastle ship owner's family. At 19 she was made pregnant by a son of the family who was then dispatched to South Africa. She perhaps had her revenge by giving her child, Wal's father, her employer's surname. He was brought up by a stepfather permanently invalided by a gas attack in the trenches.[24]

When Jessie (Rowlands) Anwell was just months old her father was killed in Egypt in 1914. Her mother was plunged into grief. She survived a suicide attempt but had her children removed. As a tiny child Jesse was split up from her siblings and shipped off from Wigan to family associates in a mining village near Bishop Auckland. This pitman's family lived in the most abject poverty, lacking proper sanitation.[25]

Jessie (Ross) Scott-Batey was born in 1918. She was the only child of two older parents who were 53 and 38 at the time of her birth. Her father had two sons by a previous marriage, one of whom was killed in the War, the younger right at the war's end, just weeks before Jessie's birth. The second son was severely injured and died a few years later. Her father was to die when she was only eight. Both her parents were in domestic service on an estate in the west of Scotland but Jessie was brought to Sunderland as a child to live in the same house as her rather severe school teacher aunt.[26]

Jeremy Beecham's father Lawrence, was born in London's East End. His parents were Jewish refugees from the pogroms of eastern Europe in the 1890's. They were extremely poor. Jeremy recalled his father describing his father, sleeping on two kitchen chairs pushed together. They had tried emigration to the USA but it did not work out and they returned to London before Lawrence, as a young man headed to Tyneside to work as a furniture salesman.[27] Dave Leigh's family moved from Lithuania round the turn of the century and both his parents were born in poverty in east London.

Mis-Education?

Then there was school. Most of these children entered the education system during or shortly after the war. The word 'education' might be a misnomer since the school diet was rote learning in basic literacy and numeracy, tales of the British Empire and large dollops of moralism aimed at watermarking the children's minds with their subordinate status in the hierarchy of life. The system of moral terrorism was reinforced by routine physical punishment: the cane and strap.

The schools and, for the most part the teachers, were relics of late Victorian England which had enforced compulsory school attendance from the age of 5 to 12, or 14 years. State secondary education in town and country had existed since the Education Act of 1903 and scholarships were available. School fees were levied till 1946. The munificence of local authorities or churches determined the availability of grants for uniforms, books and travel though none were available for maintenance. All this ruled out secondary education for all but a few. Even passing the scholarship exam was no guarantee of progress. Head teachers might advise parents against taking the financial risk involved. For many parents, even if desired, it was not an option. The meagre wage of a 14 year old could be a vital part of the family economy in the unstable inter-war years. And even entry into the grammar school could be brought to an end by economic necessity. Part-time education from 10, common in the mill towns of Lancashire and Yorkshire, was less common in a north east dominated by mining, ship building and engineering – though it could happen in rural areas during harvest time.

There were a few exceptions to this dismal story. Relatively secure clerical work for a parent might just allow for a child's progress. A benign head teacher or class teacher might offer encouragement to a bright child. Some report memories of a warm and sympathetic teacher at some point in their school days though this could be snatched away like my father's young female teacher, who died prematurely of TB, or Lionel Anwell's favourite, who seemed to have been 'just moved on.' A particularly determined child might pursue education beyond school in local authority night schools or even, for a few girls, commercial colleges. A very small number indeed actually made university. 'I was lucky,'was the often cited opinion of the few who were educationally successful.

Education forms such an important part of the consciousness of that generation but, perhaps the right way to look at it, is a perceived lack of it. This is sometimes tinged with a degree of bitterness. I saw this in two generations. My maternal grandmother often pointed out that she had been top girl in her school, pushed into X7, as she called it, at the age of 10 and set to teaching the other children their three 'r's. The bitterness came from being denied the opportunity to become a pupil teacher at the age of 13, because her coal mining family could not afford for her to stay at school. Domestic service was her lot and she was sent off, she said, as a farm servant the day after leaving school at 13. This was in the late 1880s. My father was similarly aggrieved. He was in the top class a year early in his village school at Chollerton in the early 1920s. A scholarship to the grammar school at Hexham beckoned, till the Head Master informed him that his family could not afford the fees and upkeep and he would not therefore even enter him. The greengrocer's delivery bike in Newcastle's west end was his reward in the summer of 1929, his country childhood summarily ended.[28]

Wal Hobson's father passed for the Grammar School in South Shields but was unable to go because of parental poverty. John Baker's mother Mollie had this experience too. Instead of going to high school she collected money door to door round Byker and Walker, for the East End Coal Company.[29] Brian Sharp's father was another child bright enough to pass the scholarship exam. 'He went to Gateshead Grammar but had to leave and get work at 14 in the steel works because of parental poverty.' Brian's mother, Nicolina, also ended her school days early. 'Her family were Andaluccis, recent immigrants from Italy, living in deep poverty in the Teams. At 13 she was working in the family ice cream 'factory' making it, then selling it at the end of Redheugh Bridge. She had to stay there till, she sold out.'[30]

Harry Rothman's Dad (Benny) was a very bright man who had passed for the grammar school though he had left school early to work in a garage to bring in income. He was self educated pushing himself to night school after the working day to study a wide variety of subjects. He became a socialist, perhaps influenced by an Uncle Arthur Solomon, an old ILP treasurer, involving himself early in the Workers' Sports Federation and the Young Communist League.'[31]At 18 Benny became famous as the leader of the Kinder Scout Mass Tresspass. Harry says,'He was imprisoned and his family were shocked and disapproved perhaps nothing like they were when he married a non-Jewish mill worker, my mother. In fact this latter act led to ostracism by his family, his sisters firmly believing that by marrying out he had blighted their chances of marriage.'[32]

Fred Marley's experience was similar. He got a scholarship to Rutherford Grammar School in 1925 where he excelled academically and at sport. However he always remembered the annual humiliation when in front of the whole school he and only three other boys were handed a sum of money. They were expected to be grateful. He would take it home to his mother who would then be able to buy clothes for his sister. He had to leave school at 16 in 1931, a very bad year for getting work. He got a job as a street sweeper for the City Council. He held it till he had a stroke of luck. He obtained a job as a cleaner at the Rediffusion workshops when his best friend who worked there was taken on as a junior player by Newcastle United. He stayed with the company for the rest of his working life, ending as Regional General Manager.[33]

Lionel Anwell's[34]educational frustration was compounded by being blind from birth. He was deposited in the Royal Victoria School for the blind in Benwell, during the war. Blindness was more than a disability. It was often seen as a mark of stupidity too. He felt he was saved by the arrival of a caring and informed teacher in his early teens till she disappeared without explanation. Before that he recalled being changed into institutional clothing when his parents had supplied perfectly good clothing themselves, having his fingers jammed in the piano lid for striking a wrong note and eating off dirty plates. It was assumed that blind children would not be aware of the state of the plate. But his worst felt indignity was being informed that he could not proceed to the London College for the Blind, though intellectually equiped for it. He had read Dickens, Thackeray and

Shakespeare before he was 15, an achievement shared by only a tiny number of sighted children. The reason given was a lack of parental funds. His immediate destination at 16 was the workshop for the blind and a career of mat-making, a task which damaged his finger tips and interrupted his enthusiastic piano playing. He was not daunted however, undertook voice training and a semi-professional career as a concert singer.

Lionel's friend, Peter Wallace, had been blinded in a childhood accident. He too was sent to the school for the blind at Benwell. Unlike Lionel he graduated to Worcester College, Oxford where he studied law. Educational disappointment came later for him when his parents' income fell disastrously. He was compelled to leave college and return, in the late twenties, to the workshops for the blind. Basket making replaced legal text books. Later he travelled for the workshops and finally acquired his own shop, in Newcastle's Grainger Market.[35]

Not everyone's educational experience was unremittingly negative. Lillian Boyd, a poor miner's daughter, at the height of the depression passed the scholarship exam for Stanley Grammar School. Her disappointment was to have to leave at 15 for shop work. In a sense she had her dignity restored in the 1980s when she became Chairman of the school governors at that school. That followed a life of self education. Her husband Colin was not so lucky. He went straight out of school to the pit, briefly, then into a succession of unskilled jobs which made demands much below his obvious ability.[36] Don Edwards, parentless from two years of age, did well at school acquiring his City and Guilds Certificate in electrical engineering in the late 1920s.

Jesse Anwell educational story is astonishing. At 11 she passed the entrance exam for Bishop Auckland Grammar School. Her daughter Maggie, said, 'Encouraged by her Communist Party adopting family, she had to appear before the Charity Board. In her presence the Chairman said the application was denied. The vicar's wife intervened asserting that she should be given a chance, as an experiment with the very poor.'[37] Attitudes were both discriminatory against girls and patronising. Jesse's career must have astonished everyone. She went to the grammar school, doing a daily milk round to supplement the family budget. She went on to the sixth form, getting top marks in her Higher Certificate. Presumably raising further grants, she went on to Durham University, graduating with First Class Honours in Modern Languages, and added a Teaching Certificate. No teaching jobs were available in Durham in 1936 so this pitman's child went off to the Sorbonne in Paris and returned to Oxford in 1940 to complete a PhD.[38]

Dorothy Simmons said of her father, Harry, 'He was from a family from Norfolk which had moved up to Newcastle to work in munitions. He passed for the grammar school but could not go because his parents could not afford to pay for his uniform. He went to night school and worked hard. I have a photo of him in his work coat as an apprentice in the smelting industry. He got his HND, so he did very well.'[39]

Margaret Dick's mother , Violet, also overcame a background of poverty. Her mother's family were agricultural labourers from north Northumberland. Spotted as a bright child at her village school at Belford, she was retained as a pupil teacher which she continued till her marriage at the start of World War Two. Although she would not be recognised as qualified she was later able to take up teaching outside the state sector. [40]

For the children of the manual working class, and, especially the girls, there was hardly a glimpse of opportunity. It was highly unusual for schools in the mining communities to offer anything but the pit for boys and domestic service and shop work for the girls. Lillian Boyd was exceptional in getting to the grammar school though, as mentioned, it was shop work that was open to her at 15. For some of the middle and lower middle class families the lottery aspect of education might still apply. Such families were still vulnerable to war-time trauma and economic instability. Harry Simmons and Tom Howard both had shaky starts due to their parents' war time experience. Both had fairly dismal school experiences and both chose to make up lost time at technical colleges before pursuing their careers. Roly Scott-Batey also had an unstable childhood. Born in 1912, his father was 'in business' but often in straitened circumstances largely due to alcohol. Roly made it to the grammar school and then, remarkably, to university.[41] His wife to be, Jessie Ross, passed for the high school and managed to get to teacher training college in Newcastle to study domestic science.[42]

The Jewish children in the group, first or second generation migrants, had difficult starts. They experienced financial hardship though the strength of family traditions offered some protection. Working in father's or close relative's businesses was often the alternative to grammar school or college. Leslie Feinmann was an exception to that. His father, a small scale textile manufacturer, put him successfully through grammar school and medical school. However his career was one of the few leading to a main stream profession.[43]

A dismal labour market

For most, the labour market in the late twenties and early thirties drew them in prematurely. It was probably the worst moment to be starting since the industrial revolution. Because they were a source of cheap labour, young people might find something. Fetching and carrying, delivering, cleaning and kitchen work was available. Boys could, and did, go down the pit at 14 though they were as vulnerable to unemployment and lock-out as their fathers and uncles.

Sons of apprentices could hope for places in the yards, in engineering, joinery and building trades. Indentures might have offered some marginal protection to youths but once out of their time the grim years of the depression took their toll.

For the unskilled, life was even more uncertain. Picking up odds and ends punctuated serial and often unsuccessful visits to the National Assistance Board. Roger Hall's father, also Roger, was a delivery boy helping a man with a horse and cart before getting a job in the City Lighting Department as a lamp lighter. Turned down by the army because of deafness, he worked through the war in the fire service. Roger's mother, Elsie, worked in a family greengrocer's shop. John Baker, senior, started work round 1932 in semi-skilled work as an electrician at Parsons, hanging on with low wages till the War.[44]

Leaving the area in search of work was a common experience. Eddie Hutchinson had many jobs after leaving school: the Co-op, Hawthorn Leslie, Parsons and British Engines. They were punctuated by unemployment and National Assistance. In the late thirties he went south to train as a sheet metal worker. There was no job available in that trade when he returned. He was dogged by ill health, his asthma being exacerbated by factory work. Unfit for military service, he secured a job on the new Team Valley trading estate labouring in an aircraft parts factory.[45]

Migration abroad was a possibility for some. Newcastle City Council even had a council sub-committee dedicated to the business of opening up such opportunities. It was by no means a benign process, especially when applied to the children of the poor and unemployed. But some people pursued that route voluntarily. One of Wal Hobson's great uncles, Charles Willis, when serving in the Royal Navy in the War, met American sailors whilst docked at Cherbourg in 1917. He returned to Shields after the War, 'possessed of the notion that America was the land of opportunity.' In 1922 he set off for Detroit and a bar job before heading for California where he settled, only returning to England on vacation in the 1950s.[46]

The lower middle class fared a little better than industrial workers in the depression years. Nurses, teachers, clerks and even shop workers could have more job security, a regular income and a higher one. Jesse Ross qualified for teaching in 1938.[47] Some craft workers like John Mapplebeck's father, an engine driver for the North Eastern Railway, avoided the severe privations of the depression, though he perhaps had a lucky break. He had gone down a Durham pit at 14 but his height made the work intolerable, so he got out.[48] Many workers aspired for these marginal improvements for their children too but it was not till after the Second World War that such desire could be realised in large numbers.

A roof over the head

Housing was also a miserable experience and a sphere which would have to wait for another world war for progress to take place. Colliers' housing was notorious for its primitive conditions. Cottages would commonly have only two bedrooms, one for the parents and the other for however many children there were. Division by sex was accomplished by extra beds in living rooms. Beds would be rotated shift by shift. The need for independence and space encouraged early marriage. Shared outdoor toilets and zinc baths were universal, indeed it was the late fifties before they were largely eliminated. Jim Nichol remembered, 'in the mid-fifties (in Westerhope)[49] my older sister paid me 6d for emptying the zinc bath in the yard after my Dad had his bath.' Pit head baths were still rare and largely confined to new collieries opened in the late thirties. Social facilities such as miners' welfares did not exist before the mid-thirties.

Conditions in the private rental sector where most working class families lived were little better, at least at the bottom of the housing market. Skilled workers, especially from families of several generations in their trade, had benefited from steady incomes and the housing boom on Tyneside in the two decades before the Great War. In Elswick, Benwell and Scotswood in Newcastle's west end, in Heaton, Byker and Wallsend in the east end, then Percy Main and North Shields and along the south bank of the Tyne from Blaydon to South Shields, neat and better appointed terraces of Tyneside flats had sprung up for ship-yard and engineering worker families. They were finely differentiated socially: foremen classically occupied the superior end terrace. Nevertheless lack of bathrooms and outside lavatories was still the norm. John Baker's parents lived in a flat in Byker which even after the war still had gas lighting and a water tap only in the yard.[50]

Pitmen had one valuable compensation, much rarer for townspeople: a garden. This was invaluable for feeding the family. However, many working men kept allotments, a first World War innovation which survived the war's end. Compensations there might be, but accomodation was still pretty basic, as Lucy Nicholson recalled at her grandparent's Craghead cottage, 'the midden men would come on Wednesday. They would empty the toilet by releasing the black metal trapdoors at the back. The whole of the back lane stank. Shit and ash and urine trapped in the closed walls of the cobbled streets. The men laboured under the weight of the wet claggy mess. Heaving it onto a horse and cart they carried it away to goodness knows where.'[51]

The kitchen was very much the woman's sphere. Miners' and rural labourers' cottages usually had the cooking facility in the only living room with perhaps a small scullery at the rear containing a low, china sink. Water had to be boiled on the stove and carried. In fact carrying was a regular part of the woman's labour:

carrying water, carrying laundry, dry and wet, carrying coal or wood, carrying provisions and, of course, carrying small children. In the Tyneside flats there was the added burden of stairs for the tenants of the upstairs flats. Several of the people interviewed, like Lucy, recall visits to grandparents' homes as children where these conditions pertained. For many they carried on into the post-war period. Only a few came from homes where labour saving devices such as vacuum cleaners, electric washing machines, irons and fridges were obtained before the late 1950s.

Lucy Nicholson remembers being surprised and a bit overawed when she visited the homes of middle class professional members of the Communist Party in the late fifties where such appliances were in use. My mother was truly excited and proud of the twin tub washing machine she acquired round 1960. Her mother, then over 80, thought it would never get the clothes clean! Previously in my childhood, my mother had an electric tub machine with a wringer perched on top which still involved a lot of physical labour, dragging the wet clothes out and struggling to get them through the wringer before taking them out to the clothes line.[52]

Council housing, more spacious and with indoor toilets and bathrooms, appeared in small numbers after the short lived 1924 Labour Government's Housing Act. A few ambitious councils like Gateshead, Felling and Newburn took advantage and small estates with gardens appeared. From the mid-thirties economic recovery fuelled by re-armament increased levels of employment and stimulated the building of the classic three bed-roomed semi-detached estates. In the north east their spread was not so rapid or extensive as in the South but estates were built in High Heaton, Kenton, Denton Burn, Walkergate, Low Fell, Tynemouth and Whitley Bay before the outbreak of war. They were occupied by clerks, school teachers, local government officers, draughtsmen, lower management and shop-keepers. Only a few manual workers arrived there before the war. They represented an aspiration only realisable in the boom years of the nineteen fifties.

Impact of war

With very few exceptions all the parents were born in the first two decades or so of the twentieth century, and mostly between 1910 and 1920. Again, with very few exceptions therefore, the fathers were too young for service in the First World War. They were babies or small children and therefore subject to the disruption and dislocation of their lives brought on by the cataclysm of war and its immediate aftermath. As Wal Hobson says, 'that war did amazing things to families and communities. Ours was touched in so many ways.' Lindy (Howard) Genton's father was one of the few in this group to have fought in the

First World War, as a teenager from Glasgow. He subsequently arrived in the north east, marrying a Gateshead woman.[53]

The north east of England is often represented as a distinctive region somewhat isolated from the rest of the island. It certainly has distinctive dialects and some particular cultural forms like the great miners' galas. It also arguably been specially vulnerable to economic storms. Of the major urban areas of the UK it has become home to the fewest number of post-Second World War migrants from the former Empire, rendering it apparently more ethnically homogenous. Yet the north east's population has been constantly modified by comings and goings. From early times Tyneside and Wearside have been recipients of an enormous traffic in people. In the eighteenth century Newcastle became a print centre second only to London. Writers and book sellers gravitated towards the town lending it a cosmopolitan touch.

Both Merchant and Royal navies brought people from many parts of the world. Many stayed and settled in the area. The habit of rapidly demobilising sailors at the conclusion of conflict deposited many men into the town. In August 1815, for example, two royal naval frigates dispatched nearly six hundred men on the town quayside at the end of the French wars, many of whom sought work on the Tyne. The development of the coal economy with a proliferation of coal mines, docking facilities, a highly developed railway system and rapid urban development attracted miners and construction workers in droves. They came from rural districts, Scotland, Ireland and further afield. Teesside, a rural backwater till 1860 became an urban industrial area in the twenty years that followed. Workers of diverse backgrounds teemed into the area.

Economic down-turns and war ejected people from the region in thousands. Some never returned but many did and they, like thousands of newcomers, brought widened experience and variety to the localities in which they settled. Each of these developments had an impact upon social, cultural and political life.

The 18th and early 19th Century radical movements in the north east had been boosted by migrants to the area, the former by Scottish free church members and skilled craftsmen, the latter, by Irish labourers. A leading light in Newcastle Chartism, Thomas Ainge Devyr, was a journalist from Ireland. At the end of the century Scots and Irish workers arrived as heavy industry boomed on Tyne and Wear. Some, like the future MP and Minister, Arthur Henderson, became involved in the trade union and labour movement. Later the Labour and Communist Parties, and especially the ship-building and engineering unions were boosted by incomers. Many sought work in the relative prosperity of Edwardian days and the First World War. Rural Northumberland and Durham, the Lake counties, Scotland and Ireland were the most common source of migrants to the urban areas.

Newcomers

Don Edwards, blacklisted on the Mersey after youthful militancy, arrived on Tyneside in the mid thirties, a really unpromising moment. He had just married. An electrician by trade, he worked in maintenance at the Royal Victoria Infirmary before starting union building at the North Eastern Electricity Board's new Carrville Power Station. He was later to become an Electrical Trades Union regional officer.[54]

Jeremy Beecham's father, Lawrence, arrived in the twenties to work at British Home Stores' furniture Department. He was a little older than most of the parent group having been born in 1903. His family were recent Jewish migrants from the pogroms of the Russian Empire. His mother was a political activist in east London in the pre-war forerunner of the Communist Party, the British Socialist Party. That family had tried to make a new life earlier in the United States, an experience which had not gone well. Beecham was soon busy in the furniture trade and active in the local Labour movement.

James (Jim) Mortimer, an accountant by profession, arrived in Stockton from Aberdeen in the thirties and served as Labour Party organiser on Teesside for twenty years till his premature death in 1959.[55] Pete Johnson, a cub reporter on the *Reading Star,* was relocated by his newspaper group to Ashington in the late thirties. The outbreak of war took him back to the south east into factory work not the forces, because he was not deemed physically fit for military service. After the War he soon headed back to the north east, to North Shields, journalism and political activity. He brought his wife and two children and a third was born in the town.[56]

Approach of war...again

I was born in November 1938 in a downstairs Tyneside flat in Beaconsfield Street in the west end of Newcastle, close to the General Hospital and St James's Park football ground. This was the area my father had lived in since leaving school in 1929, as well as during school holidays, since 1919. When I was born he was driving cabs for Slaters' Taxis out of the Central Station. He had taken this job after marrying my mother in the spring of that year to make more money than he could get from as a time-served motor mechanic for the same firm. He had met my mother, Mary Lee when driving Slaters' Horse box to the Morpeth Hunt in the autumn of the previous year.

Just a month before my birth, Prime Minister Chamberlain returned from Munich to announce, 'My good friends, for the second time in our history, a British Prime Minister has returned from Germany bringing peace with honour. I believe it is peace for our time...Go home and get a nice quiet sleep." The day after my birth was Kristallnacht when the first major pogrom of German jews was carried out the streets of Germany. I don't know how my then apolitical father related to these enormous events. The most I can say is that both my parents would have been relieved by Chamberlain's optimism, as so many people clearly were.

Meanwhile my parents were keen to move to what they saw as a more salubrious neighbourhood. In 1938 they had put £10 deposit down on a new bungalow at Denton Burn which when finished would cost £220. Whilst waiting completion, they secured the tenancy of a further ground floor Tyneside flat, off Highbury, near West Jesmond Station. This was a street of clerks, school teachers, local government officers and police officers. It is just possible that they had West Jesmond school in their sights, as a school with a high reputation. However the country was sliding towards war and whilst my father carried on his employment as a cabby, he must have been thinking about his options. With the declaration of war in the summer of 1939 their caution, born of earlier hardship, led them to forfeit the deposit and give up the house.

My father chose to volunteer in 1940 to get his choice of Service, entering the RAF before the end of the year, as a motor mechanic. In his 25 years he had never been further from Newcastle than a charabanc day trip to Blackpool. This was typical for working class Geordies. In five years of service he was to see Iceland, Holland, Belgium and Germany as well as several parts of the UK but he never 'saw a shot fired in anger'. On the other hand he saw occupied Germany as he followed the invasion force into Europe in the spring of 1945. He talked, though not often, of the sight of German people begging in the streets of Hamburg. He said he felt pity rather than animosity for those ordinary people. His horizons were certainly broadened by war service even without actual combat.[57]

Even travelling by train across Britain was a novelty, but a passage to India, via the Mediterranean, the Suez Canal and the Red Sea was simply staggering. Roly Scott-Batey tasted India and Burma with the Oxford & Bucks Light Infantry, his already socialist perspective reinforced by the experience. Lucy Nicholson's father, Ted, just missed serving in the war but went to India in 1946 on National Service, straight from completing his engineering apprenticeship. He was there during the independence celebrations. He was radicalised by the experience, joining the CP on his return.

Eric Walker was another for whom military experience proved to be a life changing experience.[58] He was called up before the war ended finding himself in Palestine during the emergency in 1947. He was actually present in Jerusalem when the King David Hotel was blown up. Eric's partner, Doreen (Walden), went from Sandyford to Egypt as a WAAC. Taking leave, she travelled alone from Alexandria to Palestine in 1947 and was also present during the last days of the British occupation. She too was disturbed by Zionist terrorism, finding the treatment of the Arabs appalling. They both supported the Arab cause then and continued to do so, visiting Arab friends made then in the 1980s and 1990s. Eric said that he decided to become politically active by joining the Labour Party, 'on the train back to Newcastle,' recruited by the MP, Arthur Blenkinsop, a family friend, though his left Fabian parents had given him a socialist perspective already. As a teenager, he had collected pennies for Spanish Refugees on Grainger Street, Newcastle.

Jimmy Walker had a most harrowing war. As a twenty two year old he was evacuated from Dunkirk and sent for retraining to a beach near Skegness. Six months later he was dispatched to the far east, arriving in Singapore, in his own words, 'just as the RAF was leaving.' Captured by the Japanese, he was put to work on the Burma railroad, moving up the Malayan Peninsula, 'lodging' in three camps. In one he wrote, edited and distributed a subversive underground

Of Rice and Men

jJimmy Walker had a terrible traumatising war in three Japanese camps. This is a sketch of a cartoon he produced for an underground paper at Iruka Camp in 1945

After the sketch made in Iroka Prison Camp 1945

Jimmy Walker No 291

MORE SKWOSH (mo skosh)

93

newspaper, *The Tropical Times*, an offence punishable by death if caught. He saw dozens of friends and comrades die, largely of disease and malnutrition. In 1943 he was taken off the railway and sent to Japan where he laboured as a slave in a copper mine and factory till the war ended with the dropping of the Atom Bomb on Hiroshima. He developed a strongly cynical attitude to all authority but also felt he was in a sort of distant trance for a long period afterwards. He said that he had no idea how to relate to his young sons who were seven and five when he returned.[59]

That is not to argue that war service for those who escaped capture was any kind of picnic. Those serving in the far east could return with malaria, a debilitating start to life in peace time. It took my uncle five years to shake off the effects of this, putting great stress on his marriage. Others were scarred by horrors witnessed or, in the case of many sailors, horrors feared. Perhaps all the service personnel, and particularly the married ones suffered the often unspoken agony of separation from wives and young families. Like Jimmy Walker, several returned at the war's end feeling like strangers unable to settle into normal routines and not necessarily wholly welcomed by wife and children.

There were also problems for those who stayed at home. Even married women were turned into single mothers. For often quite inexperienced parents there was a strong reliance, where that was possible, upon their own mothers and aunts. Bombing raids in the industrial areas led to official and unofficial evacuations. Jim Walker's mother was pregnant when shipped out to the Co-op nursing home at Gilsland in Cumberland whilst his father was on the way to the Far East. After a near miss in a raid over Jesmond and Heaton, my mother decamped to Morpeth with two babies. She was slightly more fortunate because her parents could take her in. My father was on a convoy bound for Iceland.[60] The Baker's first house, in Scarborough Road, suffered bomb damage in a German raid in 1941 while both John's parents were out, his father on fire watch. A deep mark on a large clock's case was the visible evidence of this raid, throughout John's childhood.[61]

There was another penalty for men who were deemed physically unfit for service. Roger Hall's father, Roger, suffered from deafness and was turned down for service.[62] Jim Hutchinson's failed the physical examination because of asthma. Whilst close family might 'breath a sigh of relief', as one person said of her mother, young men out of uniform could be harassed and made to feel guilty. There were no white feathers in the Second World War but there was certainly a 'white feather attitude' in working class communities. Two ILP brothers had a cycle shop on Brighton Grove in the West End. I remember passing it with my parents just after the war when I had got a 'trike' for Christmas. I must have asked if they got it there because I was told not; that 'conshies' lived there. I had no idea what it meant till much later. We went elsewhere for bikes.[63]

Single women were recruited for war service as non-combatants in the Land Army or in other specialised activities. Early in the war, Jessie Ross took responsibility for a group of eight children evacuated to Keld, a remote village at the head of Swaledale on the Pennine Way. She married Roly Scott Batey in 1942. After her new husband went off to India, she went to work for the Ministry of Food as a demonstrator of cooking 'from a ration book'. She described her work as 'preparing imitations of traditional food, sometimes with the aid of cartoon figures, Potato Pete and Carrot Pete.'[64]This took her round villages in the area. She had rather a good war as an attractive, intelligent woman enjoying a freedom not experienced before.

Remittances from service husbands and some new state benefits coupled with the rationing book provided a basis of economic security unheard of before the War. Nevertheless, the situation could be emotionally fraught. Anxiety about the fate of husbands abroad was constant and in certain areas at certain points there was the fear of bombing. This became reality in Newcastle, Gateshead and North and South Shields in 1941 and 1943. For many of the Jewish parents there was the worry over the fate of relatives left in Central Europe, then at the war's end confirmation of the very worst: death in the camps. The Beechams, Russells, Landaus, Leighs and Falkenaus all had experience of this to relate. Guy Falkenau's father, Rène, lost his parents from occupied France. Guy's grandfather sat tight when he could have escaped, believing that his first war service in the French Army had proved him a patriot. He was taken with his wife to Auswitch in 1943. His son risked his own life by working in the Resistance, specially charged with finding and hopefully liberating Belgian citizens from occupied and Vichy France. Several other members of Guy's father's family were wiped out in the camps.[65]

War also brought men into the north east. Raoul Piachaud was a medical officer in the RAF. In 1942 he was sent to Acklington, the Northumberland air base. His was an unusual background. He was born in Ceylon of French-Dutch planter parents. He trained as a doctor in the thirties and was attracted to the Communist Party, a loyalty which did not survive the forties. He decided to settle in the north east when his war ended in Holland in 1945.[66] Pete Johnson also returned to the North East with his family after the war to work on the *Shields Gazette.*

Civvy Street

The war over, people by no means returned to a world of calm and comfort. Despite the arrival of a Labour Government with its several promises, our parents' generation struggled with the legacies of their youth in the twenties and thirties as well as with different ones of war. They could fairly be said to have lived turbulent lives, some, extremely so. It was lived experience which left its mark in many ways. My own parents never felt secure, always mistrusting the signs of stability and improvement in their lives. In many cases improvements were slow to come in any case. War had seriously damaged an already severely inadequate housing stock. Council house building did not start properly for five years after the war. Temporary accommodation was only a partial solution and many people found themselves 'living in' with relatives or, in desperately overcrowded situations.

For those who were physically fit, work was available and in some cases men were able to shift careers and ultimately improve their lot. Jimmy Walker, back from a Japanese prison camp, joined the civil service. His problems were psychological rather than material. On the other hand, Eddie Hutchinson's chronic sickness remained a handicap and great sacrifices were made to see three sons through university education in the following decade.[67]

Looking back, it is obvious that after 1950 the economy entered a long boom though few interviewees record memories of their parents being aware of it at the time. The availability of Hire Purchase brought a range of consumer goods into the reach of working and lower middle class households for the first time but many people were cautious about using the facility and even reluctant to admit using it. It was still thought somewhat immoral to voluntarily take on debt which was how the 'never never' was seen with memories of 1930s insecurity only a decade or so away. Pennies were still counted in most households.

It was the generation coming to adulthood after the War that began to cast care aside, often to the disgust of their elders. 'Pride will come before the fall,' my own grandmother warned. 'Wait till you can afford it.'

Chapter Three: From 1945

With the war over most parents, still young adults, had to set about re-orienting themselves in a different world from the world of 1939. On the personal front there was difficult adjustment, change of direction, new opportunities or an apparent return to the past. Those who had fought in the war returned to elect the Labour Government in the landslide victory of 1945. [It is a common assumption that the service vote was a crucial factor in producing the labour landslide.] In the November local government elections of that year the party gained control of Newcastle City Council for the first time too. There were exciting prospects. In a short time the Government had put the NHS in place, got the 1944 Education Act up and running and nationalised a number of key industries. With all but three of the region's 27 constituencies returning Labour MPs, the two County Councils, all the borough councils and most of the district councils under Labour Party control, the north east looked, and no doubt felt, like a Labour citadel.

Yet there was a sense of unease. Internationally, the idealistic aura round the creation of the United Nations was tempered by the onset of the Cold War and the rise of hostility towards the war-time ally, the Soviet Union. To a degree this was orchestrated by a Labour Foreign Secretary, Ernest Bevin. The Labour Administration apparently raised no criticism of the decision to use the Atomic Bomb on Japan or US involvement in China propping up the corrupt regime of the Nationalists and supporting their control of Formosa (Taiwan). At home the government struggled with fuel and food shortages, devalued the pound savagely, attacked strikers and failed to make a satisfactory start to housing the homeless or clearing the slums. The Tory press soon recovered from the immediate demoralisation of the 1945 defeat and led the campaign to shift public opinion against the LP. In the north east the LP lost control of the City Council in 1948 after only three years. By 1951 the Tories were in office, nationally and locally.

Politics on the ground

Defeat on both fronts polarised the Labour Party, as scapegoats were sought for defeat. Right-left divisions appeared in local parties throughout Tyneside. The divisions were to continue through the fifties, sixties and beyond. The strength of each side can usually be gauged from the political complexion of the MP. The right wing dominated. Out of sixteen Labour seats on Tyne and Wear only Morpeth, Jarrow, Gateshead and two Newcastle Constituencies elected members who could be described as 'on the left. Morpeth, which embraced a large part of the Northumberland coalfield elected the fellow traveller, Will Owen. Ellen Wilkinson, the famous left wing MP and Minister of Education, died in 1947 and was replaced by another left winger, Ernest Fernyhough. Apart from Ellen, the best known of the left wingers was Konni Zilliacus who suffered de-selection for his views from his Gateshead seat in 1950.

The bulwark of the right wing was Newcastle West Constituency, under its MP Ernest Popplewell, and the key organisation man, Bob Brown, a full-timer for the gasmen's section of the General and Municipal Workers' Union. They were aided by the acerbic old suffragette, Connie Lewcock, a party activist since World War One. From 1945 to 1952 Central Constituency was represented by the lawyer Lyall Wilkes, who had been on the left as a young man in the thirties and who was a critic of the Attlee administration. However there was a loyalist core in that party and when Wilkes resigned in 1952, in somewhat mysterious circumstances, they secured the nomination and election of Ted Short, the Blyth Head Teacher and, briefly, deputy leader of the Labour Group on the Council. He was to become Deputy Leader of the Labour Party in the 1970s. East constituency was represented by Arthur Blenkinsop, also a left winger in the nineteen thirties, supported by his mentor, Charles Trevelyan. After '45, Blenkinsop, a junior minister, was a middle of the road loyalist, but in the late fifties a supporter of CND. Though largely right wing in Labour terms, his local party was tolerant of dissenters. Leading left-wingers, Dan Smith, Ken Skethaway and Ted Fletcher had their party bases there. There was a strong right wing Roman Catholic base there too led by Party Secretary, Benny Brennan. He had been active there since the early thirties. The remaining Newcastle Constituency was North which never elected a Labour MP and was the most consistently left wing of the four. Here the Scott-Bateys, the Feinmanns, Peggy Murray and Eric Walker, were prominent left wing activists.

Across the river, Gateshead Borough and Felling Urban District both had Labour MPs and Labour councils with large majorities, as did Blaydon further west. The Gateshead Party was pretty factional throughout the fifties, following the removal of Konni Zilliacus. Alliances shifted between the factions according to issues but the key group was the Trade Union section, based on the railway sheds and led by the prominent left winger, Alec MacFadden of the NUR. He was usually in alliance with Jim Murray, Roman Catholic, town councillor and shop steward at Vickers Armstrong, Elswick.

Murray was a key figure in the Tyneside Labour left, as a youth, aligned with Zilliacus, then the Bevanite group. Keep Left, the New Left, the International Socialists and CND. Fascinated by ideas, he was a true Tyneside worker intellectual. Also in the Murray group were two veteran women activists, Rosa Pearson and Mary Bell, who had cut their political teeth in the era of the General Strike. They had been active in the Socialist League after the 1931 debacle, and the various campaigns round the Spanish Civil War. A third group were the Roman Catholics. Gateshead had a large Catholic population which was reflected in LP and council membership. Probably influenced by Jim Murray, they usually voted with the left. The right wing, which also included Catholics supportive of the LP national leadership. This group was strongly represented on the Aldermanic Bench and ran the council. The leading figure was the Secretary Agent, Harry Luxton, who was one of the very few prominent LP figure anywhere to support the rabid anti-communist Christian group, Moral Re-Armament. The Felling Party was the fiefdom of Andrew Cunningham, the Regional Secretary of the General and Municipal Workers, who was eventually to be imprisoned for corruption in the 1970s.

In Newcastle the body responsible for the selection of Council Candidates was the City Party, a delegate body from the four constituencies and the trades unions. This was the most public face of the Labour Party in town. The arithmetic of delegation made it a leftist body. It was run by the full-time Secretary, Joe Eagles, the Chairman, Roly Scott-Batey and councillors like Smith, Fletcher, Gladys Robson, a veteran of the women's suffrage movement and pre-war trade union activism, and the formidable Doris Starkey, councillor, Co-operator and May Day organiser. Peggy Murray, an old thirties left-winger, was another important part of this leadership. It also enjoyed some support from the NUR, the Boilermakers, the ETU, USDAW (shop workers) and CAWU (clerical workers) though the three biggest union delegations, the T & G, the G & M and the AEU were usually made up of right wing loyalists.

It was the City Party that initiated the Bevanite monthly newspaper, the *Northern Star,* which survived for five years in the early fifties featured discussion round nationalisation, NATO, Test Ban Treaties and German re-armament. So the lines were drawn basically between those who saw defeat as a consequence of going too far and those who argued the party had not gone far enough. The City Labour Party left was determined to regain power by devising a radical programme of change in transport, housing, education and culture. In this they were supported by figures not associated with the left, Ted Short, Bob Brown and Nobby Bell. Dan Smith was certainly the visionary and driving force. The first enemy to defeat in this project was the Party itself. The victorious local party of 1945 was controlled by a pre-war junta of councillors some of whom had served since 1912. They were so used to defeat that in victory they were ill prepared and, perhaps like the party nationally, were actually surprised to win. They were deeply conservative and overwhelmed by the imagined glory of the Mayor and Sheriff's regalia and the rigid formalities of office. They maintained their hold of the party in the Council for a further five years before illness, incompetence and death removed them.

As Chairman of the party in the mid-fifties, Dan Smith wrote a pamphlet with Arthur Blenkinsop, *Peril in the city* which set out a plan for dealing with the serious housing crisis. Initiatives on education, town planning and transport followed. It all created an excitement in the party and in the media. The opportunity to fulfil promises came with the May Council elections of 1958 when Labour came to office, narrowly, on the casting vote of the Lord Mayor. The generation born between 1910 and 1930 were running the city.

The 'in between' generation

By the mid-fifties, people born in the late twenties and early thirties were helping to shape local politics. Many were too young to have served in the war though might have entered the labour force at some point during it. They were also mainly too young to vote in the 1945 Election though some launched into political activity then. A key arena of activity was the Labour League of Youth which experienced a great upsurge in membership after the 1945 landslide. Albert Booth, later to serve as Secretary of State for Employment in the 1970s, and his wife Joan, have clear memories of this moment. Booth was an apprentice engineer at North Eastern Marine, Wallsend, in 1945. He remembers the shock of winning. He knew no one who expected it.[68] His friend, Ronnie Curran, a young coal mining electrician, later to become a union official and his future wife Doreen, at school at the time, shared the experience. [69]

Following the surprise, came the excitement. From Labour families they were reared with the awful memories of the betrayal and disaster of 1931, it seemed that the massive parliamentary majority could lead to a major transformation of society. Coupled with the Labour victory, and perhaps they thought, explaining it, was the sense of a 'people's war' led by key labour leaders like Attlee, Bevin and Morrison. This spirit could lead to big improvements in housing, education, welfare and employment prospects. It was around such hopes that the League of Youth grew across the north east. The Tynemouth/North Shields branch recruited widely among young working people: miners, engineers, shop workers, civil servants and senior school pupils. They held political meetings, public speaking contests and a range of social activities: dances, sing songs, hikes and camps. They also became foot soldiers at election times, campaigning with boldness and excitement. In Newcastle they joined a youth parliament and some supported the *Northern Star* newspaper. Hugh White, an activist in Newcastle North and the future Lord Mayor who welcomed President Carter to Tyneside in 1977, was an enthusiastic member of the parliament as were two members of the Elliot family of Birtley.[70]

The Elliots were heavily involved with the League of Youth. Pete Elliot described the way politics, music and week-end holidays all melded into one, building South Birtley Labour Party League of Youth, 'there were a real nice bunch of lads and lasses who joined with us, albeit from different backgrounds and different standards of education....we had some great bank holidays together...we went to Amble, Warkworth, Unthank, Whitburn, Allenheads and Crimdon Dene...I'd take my guitar along as we had no canned entertainment on holiday in those days, and many the nights of singing we'd have around the old sea coal fire.'[71]

League of Youth growth was short lived. It began to tail off from the time of the General Election defeat of 1951. Labour's defeat damped enthusiasm for political activity. Indeed the opposite occurred with the revival of the Young Tories which would rise to its apogee on the backs of three consecutive election victories. In retrospect we might also offer the start of the long boom in the economy and the fall in anxiety about employment as a brake on recruitment to socialist youth organisations. Some tenacious individuals like the Booths and Ron Curran and his brothers in Tynemouth, Hugh White and Walter Wilson in Newcastle and Jimmy Murray in Gateshead carried on. The League of Youth was wound up in 1956 in a flurry of bans and expulsions though these were not much experienced in the north east. Individuals like these were to form a bridge to the next upsurge at the end of the decade. Many aligned with Bevan and the Labour left and were active in the peace movement, the anti-German rearmament campaign and the demonstrations against the British and French invasion of Egypt in 1956.

Full employment

For the three decades after 1940 most of these people would be in full employment. Structural change and rising expectations could bring an occupational variety to the individual that could never have been enjoyed by most of their own parents. Relative material security was experienced widely though psychological insecurities fashioned in their own childhood and youth was not so easy to expunge. They could have repercussions on relations with their own children. This is a difficult area to explore. It raises sensitivities about what people feel able to say about relationships and some might argue that there is an inevitable clash, anyway, between parents and children. That may be so but it may well be that First World War childhoods, inter-war deprivation and Second World War disruptions exacerbated that potential inter-generational antagonism.

Very few parents had formal education beyond the age of 14. The school leaving age was raised to 15 only in 1945. Some had attended Workers Education Association, National Council of Labour Colleges or local authority evening classes. Others had participated in educational facilities provided by the forces. In civvy street some had used such qualifications to change direction. Those with a self-educational drive could have books and magazines around the house[72] and might belong to book clubs like the Left Book Club or the Readers' Union. A belief in the value of education was often firmly held. For example a miner in the cohort pushed his daughter towards a scholarship at a direct grant school. Another put his son through correspondence courses run by the National Council of Labour Colleges.

It was men and women like these who had aided the Labour landslide in 1945. If there was a 'group' belief it was secular: in education, welfare, council housing and public ownership. This appeared to be true of the wider group of parents, as well as those parents who were active in the LP, the CP, the unions and the Co-op. Religious observation was very low apart from the odd Methodist, Quaker and, a few who remained practicing Roman Catholics. Jewish parents were most often non-religious and socialist rather than Zionist. Their formative years preceded the emergence of the State of Israel and their activity and attitude was rooted in the discrimination against their own parents and anti-fascism during the 'thirties. This picture would have been much less true for the society at large which was altogether more conservative.

For the most part the recruits to socialist activism were from socialist or labourist homes. This applied strongly to the first occupational group, the professionals. The parents were Fabians, active in the Labour Party or in pre-war communism. Guy Faulkenau's father had been an anti-fascist fighter in Belgium before arriving in Britain in the early part of the war. As we have noted, he had returned to the resistance movement in France. Nicky Landau's father, in the 1950s, a prosperous businessman, came from a third generation Tyneside Jewish family. He had been active in the anti-fascist struggles before the war and was a firm Labour Party supporter later.

The father of one of the student incomers, Lu Bell, had been a CP activist joining at Cambridge though he had become alienated from communism in the fifties. Likewise Jennifer Piachaud's father was a former communist sympathiser. Fiona Scott-Batey's father and mother were deeply involved in LP activities before and after the war, as were Pat Johnson's and Mary Chuck's. Their political philosophies had been formed in the inter-war period when the capitalist system's inequalities and instabilities brought mass unemployment and the threat or reality of fascism.

Before the excesses of Stalinism were widely known or understood, the Soviet Union appeared to offer an attractive alternative to capitalist Britain. This was a view shared by both Communists and sections of the Labour left, the latter sometimes steering clear of the CP because they believed its impact in Britain was too marginal. For many there had been passionate commitment to the Spanish Republic. A sometimes guilty attachment to its martyrs was a strongly surviving strand in leftist thinking. While none of these parents had fought with the International Brigade or the POUM, a number had been teenage helpers of the solidarity campaigns. For these people Spanish holidays were impossible while Franco lived, despite the high profile and low cost of holidays offered there by the growing travel industry in the late fifties.

This world view, built out of pre-war experience in their youth was shared by manual and white collar working class parents who were part of the movement. To it was added a belief and involvement in trade unions and the Co-operative movement. In both case these were beliefs with a material basis. Steady pay rises, job protection and improved working conditions flowed from trade union involvement. The Co-op was an expression of mutuality and the place you went for the essentials and even the luxuries of life with the dividend thrown in. The Co-op features in most of the accounts. For some it was just as the major retail experience but other joined in its regular social activities, outings, sports days and children's parties.

The women

The gender ratio in north east industry was heavily weighted towards men, a tendency also strongly reflected in white collar work and the professions. The bias probably had its roots in the nature of industrial work: mining, heavy engineering, ship building, merchant shipping and deep sea fishing. If there was a material basis, there was certainly also a strong cultural imperative for wives to stay at home. This was generally true of middle class wives too.

However in working class families the attitude was usually breached in practice by involvement in the retail sector, clothing manufacture and a variety of cleaning functions, both industrial and domestic. Men would defend this by stating, 'Aye. She just does a bit of part time work. For the extra, you know.' It is significant that when asked in interview about their mother's work, several started by saying, 'she didn't work.' Then, when pushed they began to recall a different story. It was of part time work, almost, of odd jobs. A sentence might start with. 'She just…' There was also the idea that women took their political cue from their husband. One of the author's earliest political experiences was on the door step in the 1959 Election where it was not uncommon for a woman answering the door to say that her husband was out, or she would have to ask him how they were voting.

In political or trade union circles it was common for a man devoted to political or trade union activity to leave his wife at home, apart from occasional social events. Of course these are stereotypes founded on truths. However, one of the significant features of this cohort is that women from politically active families were much more likely to have their own views even if that usually meant sharing them with their partner. A number of them had met their partners in political or related activity. Several mothers in this narrative defy the stereotype, coming across as strong and independent women.

This certainly applied to Lily Rothman. 'She was bitter about her limited education and being obliged to leave school at 14 to support her family. Stress led to a breakdown at only 18. She became a Communist, and co-operator. She believed strongly in the Co-operative movement and was active in the Co-op Guild. For her it was a working example of working class mutuality. She was an avid reader of fiction and even the dictionary gave her pleasure. She was a very hard worker. She had 19 jobs in her life, serving as a shop steward in the mills and stayed in the cotton industry as long as there were jobs. She believed in the adage that 'hard work never killed anyone' though in her case, it probably did. Her father had been a free thinker, a committed atheist which she had 'inherited,' though she was not with out a deep layer of superstition, possibly deriving from the Irish side of her family.'[73]

Several other mothers were political activists. Jesse Scott Batey subscribed to the Left Book Club from her late teens. She said, 'I was very impressed by *The Road to Wigan Pier* and John Strachey's books. I read them as they arrived (monthly) and some of my friends did too.'[74]On moving to Jesmond straight after the war, she and her husband Roly, just back from the Far East, 'looked for like minded people who wanted to do something.' They were soon building the Labour Party in a very Tory area. One of her friends was Tess Owens. Both of them successfully stood for the Council in the mid-fifties. Also part of the small but active Jesmond socialist community were Sylvia Feinmann and Olive Marley. Though neither were councillors, they were active in the Labour Party, the peace movement and other left campaigns during the fifties whilst their children were growing up. In Tynemouth, Nell Johnson campaigned for the Communist Party, helping to build a branch along the Coast. Pat Duffy and Lillian Boyd were working class women who were driving forces in their local Durham Labour Parties and the Co-operative movement. Significantly they were politically active mothers of *daughters,* thereby providing strong role models for their offspring.

Origins

The majority of the youngsters we know about had at least broadly socialist politics in their biographies. Several did not. It is difficult to be certain why, because the sample is so small. However it is possible to make some sense of it. Without evincing any socialist convictions, parents could hold views rooted in class antagonism. My father and uncle voted Tory in 1945 but both were very antagonistic to employers, citing episodes of patronising and authoritarian attitudes. The former felt marked for life by a headmaster's decision not to enter him for a grammar school scholarship in the 1920s on the grounds that his parents could not afford the cost of that education. The latter, perhaps buoyed by democratic discourse in the RAF in India during the war, even as an old man, would recount the tale of his own father being summoned by his employer in 1931 who announced a wage cut and told him that 'we must all tighten our belts.' Such class attitudes in the home would help to shape the outlooks of the offspring.

A few of the cohort remembered coming from Tory voting homes. My parents and grandparents were all Tory voters during my childhood although my father swung sharply to the left later in life. Both grandmothers, servants with rural backgrounds, were strong deference voters. My paternal grandmother was excited at getting a ticket to hear Winston Churchill speak in Newcastle in 1951, though her lowly status was marked by her ticket being for the overflow meeting where you heard the 'great man' through loudspeakers, but did not see him. They were strong in the belief that Labour did not have the breeding to govern, blind to the fact that many members of the Attlee government were public school and Oxbridge types anyway.[75]

Linda (Howard) Genton remembers asking her mother why they voted

Tory. 'Because we do not dirty our hands at work' was the reply. Her father was a meter reader for the Electricity Board who harboured a number of right wing attitudes, including the belief that 'Hitler was right.' Linda's mother was taken up, perhaps obsessed, by the problems of having an autistic elder child. Her pursuit of solutions included trying various religious sects into which she drew her younger daughter. As she got older Linda was left to her own devices, developing a growing sense that her family's behaviour was 'all a bit weird.' Meeting an active left wing boy friend at the Paletta coffee bar in Newcastle when she was 16 clinched the separation from her family's values.[76]

Other parents behaved in an authoritarian or belittling manner in seeking to enforce their own values and practices upon their teen-age children or mercilessly deriding the young person's enthusiasms. Marian Campbell's father was derisory about her vegetarianism, her activities in the peace movement and especially her friendships. A sense of cold war paranoia shows through in his claim that a CP couple who lived in an apartment over-looking the sea at Tynemouth were signalling to Russian trawlers out on the North Sea. In Marian's mid-teens he enforced church attendance.

Other parents tried to strictly regulate dress, hair style and musical taste. The presence of these attitudes and practices, which were pretty widespread, of course did not guarantee the offspring beginning a journey to left politics. Neither did belonging to a strongly socialist home and family. However so many young people did just that when it had not been true for their immediate seniors in what I have called 'the in between generation'. This strengthens the argument that there was a special moment round the dawn of the 1960s.

Chapter four: home and school

Family traditions and history are clearly important in shaping individual outcomes. This is strongly suggested in the narratives of family, related by participants in this account. They are so often marked by rich detail. Of course, access to almost all the parents' lives is second hand and therefore coloured by the child's perspective which in this group is almost entirely benign. The material offered is also influenced by the questions posed. None of this need invalidate family history as an explanation for individual behaviour. 'I became politically active because I came from a family of activists,' is an explanation which satisfies many people. It may remain valid even if siblings went in quite different directions. Siblings might actually relate a different family narrative. The key to explanation may be found in the *experience* of the individuals as they grew up in the places they lived, the schools they attended and the friends they made.

Home life

Though several people remark upon the living conditions of grandparents, only a few of those featured in this study experienced serious housing problems themselves. Some contrast the old and the new; the move from inadequate housing to new estates. One who suffered really poor housing conditions was Pat (Duffy) MacIntyre. Her mother, Mary, was widowed in the war when Pat was just seven. She recalls it as a savage blow affecting their lives in many ways including their accommodation. 'Our living conditions were horrendous: a two-up, two-down house with no bathroom, no hot water, no electricity and an outside lavatory that was always breaking down. We had no carpets, only cheap lino on the floor downstairs and nothing at all to cover the rotting wooden floor upstairs. Window frames were not quite attached to the walls, so when it rained, it rained in. Water ran down the kitchen walls and flowed in rivulets onto the hearth where it sizzled on contact with the hot stones. One of the two bedrooms was completely unusable because of damp so, since my Nana slept in the downstairs front room, Mam and I shared a bed and my brother slept in a single bed at the foot of ours. That arrangement lasted till I left for college at 19. My brother was 17. You did not need to climb the stairs to see into the bedroom. There was a big hole in the wall because the structure was crumbling away. You could see into the room from the foot of the stairs. In 1955, our landlord (who always ignored pleas to do repairs) charged 10/- a week rent. That same year he sold our house and six others for the sum of £140---£20 each. In 1956, after a long campaign by my mother, our house was declared 'unfit for human habitation' and most of the rest of the houses around us were also cleared.' [77]

Jim Nichol recalled the cramped conditions of a miner's cottage with an outside toilet. He remembers going into Newcastle, from Westerhope, by bus as a teenager, passing the multi-storey blocks going up in Elswick and thinking, 'I'd love to live there.' [78] His close friend, Sam Dodds, remembers the poor state of those cottages and feeling sorry for Jim, because, when he was a small child, his coal miner father had managed to get hold of a Council house on a new estate nearby. 'A bath, an inside w.c., my own room and a garden were pure luxury.'[79] This was Linda Ebbatson's experience too. Her family moved from Walker to a new council house on Benton Estate, 'It was great: three bedrooms, inside bathroom and toilet and a big garden to grow vegetables in.'[80]

John Baker remembered the excitement when electricity came to their house in Scarborough Road, Byker in 1953, 'We no longer had to climb on a chair to turn the gas mantle on.' Four years later they were off to a new house on Longbenton Estate and 'inside toilet. Utopia with a garden.' It is a story of life improving in stages. He says a diary entry from 1953 has him remarking, 'I saw a TV working in a shop in town'. They soon had theirs, 'supplied by Rediffusion,' and they enjoyed a holiday in Blackpool.[81]

John Creaby brings out another feature of a world fast disappearing. He lived in Gateshead in an area of Tyneside flats. 'Several bits of my family lived in the same or nearby streets; uncles, aunts and grandparents. On Sunday everyone would congregate for dinner at noon. The grown ups would crowd round the table first and then the children would follow. If the weather was OK my Grannie would bring hot potatoes out to us children on the step.'[82]

Several people shared Sam, Linda and John's experience of moving 'up in the world' during childhood. The parents of working class children tended to rent Tyneside flats from private landlords or council houses. The latter were spreading like a rash round the suburbs of Newcastle and Gateshead in the 1950s. This shift would effectively disrupt long established family connection though one of the mothers travelled right across town to her former neighbourhood church on Sundays and on Wednesdays for the Mothers' Union branch. She was to continue this from her twenties for the following sixty years as did her sister and a niece.

Linda Ebbatson's family travelled from Benton to Bensham (Gateshead) every Saturday for an extended family meal at her grandparents. This practice may have contributed to the commonly held view that the move to council estates in this period effectively fractured working class communities which had grown organically over generations. Linda remarked that the Bensham neighbourhood contrasted with her Benton one in that it had community organisers, though they were certainly not referred to in that way. These were women, like her grandmother and her friend, Mrs Fenwick, who kept an eye on the neighbourhood's sick or those down on their luck and also organised an annual trip or a street party. At Benton much of that was missing although her mother's generation tried to keep some of it alive.[83]

Brian Sharp's family provide another example of the sometimes ambivalent nature of the move out to new estates. Brian says, 'we moved to Low Fell (from Teams) when I was14 and at the Grammar School. I was really pleased because it took me near to many of my school friends. My mother though really missed her close Italian family and went back every day, yes, every day. I had to go from school to my grandmothers after school because that's where my mother was.' It is not surprising that his parents lobbied to get away from Low Fell and down to Bensham, nearer the Teams and family, giving up the superior Low Fell accommodation.[84]

Many of the middle class children grew up in three bedroomed semi-detached houses built between the wars in suburbs like Denton Burn, Kenton and Low Fell. A paradox was that although there was more physical space it could be accompanied by more restriction created by the intrusion of lower middle class values of restraint, respect for property, muted speech and judgemental comparison with neighbours. I certainly felt some of this when chance and my father's employment took us, as tenants, into the owner occupied semi-detached land of Kenton. Summer holidays delineated social difference. My mother once reported, from a coffee morning she attended that Mrs (they referred to each other as Mrs) Taylor was 'doing Bournemouth this year as Whitby was becoming common.' Our holiday, no less enjoyed, was a bike ride to our grandmother's near Corbridge. My home provided open access to my middle class friends while it was very common to get no further than the front step of their homes when calling on them.

The source of social snobbery was probably rooted in the fact that the people who voiced or acted out their superiority were often themselves the children of manual workers. The war had beneficial effects for some like the former hotel porter in my street who had done emergency teacher training in 1947 enabling him and his family (his wife had been a shop assistant before marriage) to take a step up the housing and social ladder. His children were sent to a Direct Grant Grammar School. This family was also quietly Conservative in voting behaviour and quite disdainful of the few Labour supporters on the street. As a late teenager I was increasingly alert to such attitudes. It probably helped to propel me to the left.[85]

There were some explicitly political homes. The Feinmann's in Osborne Avenue must at times have felt like occupied territory for the children. Left wing students lived in the house and their friends dropped round to paint banners, write leaflets and talk. Mike Worrall lodged there and remembered the visit of the South African Cricket team to the County Ground opposite in 1960. 'I got hold of some black and white gloss paint and painted a dustbin lid with the Anti-Apartheid symbol and propped it up in my window overlooking the cricket ground in the hope that the crowd and players would see it.'[86]

The Feinmann's daughter, Mary remembers that,.'It was just the home I grew up in. My memories are of a busy family life, very much focussed on survival day to day! Six children, who saw little of a father who was totally committed to everything he did – his medicine and the extra work that he did with the Ship-builders Union over mesothelioma – the Labour Party – CND – and his family when he was at home, and a very hard-working mother, who was at least as committed as my father, but had less opportunity to develop her politics. There was a lot of talking – real talking – about politics. But it wasn't just about politics. It was about philosophy and ideas generally. Also art was important, theatre, music, dance. I remember CND marches and 59 Society meetings, but also the Quaker Meetings, so that we encountered religion, and the *Messiah* in the Town Hall and the People's Theatre – and I know mum and dad went on to be involved with the Poetry in the Morden Tower.[87]

The Marley's house was a bit like the Feinmann's with people coming and going. It was a port of call for travelling national speakers. Pat Johnson recalled going into the kitchen after school one day and seeing a figure doing a handstand, her skirt enveloping her head. 'Don't worry,' she called. 'I'll be down in a moment. I'm just restoring my menstrual flow.'[88] It was Pat Arrowsmith, Britain's best known direct action advocate, on her way to Holy Loch.

Brian Sharp remembers Lucy Nicholson home in Benton as, 'A place where you were always welcome. You just walked in. It was full of interesting people who talked about the world. Very exciting!'[89] Lucy's parents were both active CP members, her Dad, Ted an engineering shop steward and Newcastle East CP Branch Secretary. She was on Party business from the age of 12, handing out leaflets. Branch meetings were held in her house which was also provided a lodging for itinerant speakers passing through Tyneside and even refugees like the Iraqi Abdul Torfuq, a twenty two year old communist who had escaped from the purges following the February 1963 Baathist Coup. Lucy says, 'he turned up 'on the doorstep one night with a letter of introduction and stayed for ten years. He became one of the family.' Lucy thinks her parents, Ted and Grace, 'were idealists who believed in everyone's basic goodness. They never locked the door. Ted was totally unmaterialistic. He bought an old car, a Humber Super Snipe, to help in Party work but could not learn to drive. One night a man knocked on the door and asked how much he wanted for it. He said, oh, empty your pockets. The man tipped out a pound and some small change. That'll dee, said Ted and the man drove it away.'[90]

School days

In the late forties or early fifties members of this cohort entered secondary education. There were three routes: the direct grant grammar and high schools (independent), the local authority grammar and technical schools, including Roman Catholic, and the secondary modern. Before the 1944 Education Act little distinction was seen between independent and state grammar schools. In working class circles they could be equally remote and very few children of the manual working class entered them. Entry to both was by examination. After 1944 all pupils took the 11+ whilst the direct grant schools had their own entrance exam at 11. One of the most significant differences between the pre and post war situations was that many more parents could afford the upkeep of their children through high school and, aided by grants, possibly beyond. Though several youths who passed the 11+ were obliged to leave at 16, there are no cases in this sample of a failure to take up the place for financial reasons.

Unlike the situation two decades later, there was no moral imperative discouraging labour movement activists from using private schools which in any case were heavily subsidised by direct grants from public funds. Local authority and school scholarships were available for the Direct Grant schools though attending one of those was still an expensive business requiring considerable sacrifice from parents. Expenses could be similar for the local authority grammar schools. In both cases uniforms were obligatory, as was equipment for games, cooking and handicrafts and the purchase of musical instruments. Both types of school might offer school trips which also needed to be financed by parents.

Over twenty activists in the youth movements attended independent schools. Some found the experience irksome. Fiona Scott-Batey felt she was sent to the Central High School because her parents were Labour activists. Her city councillor mother was the spokesperson for the Labour Party's campaign to turn Newcastle comprehensive and her parents feared she might be persecuted at a High School threatened by change. Indeed the anti-comprehensive campaign was led by the vindictive head of Heaton High School, Dr Henstock. Fiona found she could not avoid being noted as the child of dangerous lefties in her school anyway. She was sheltered to some extent by the fact that there were a number of girls from left wing homes already at the Central High School.[91]

Also perhaps, independent schools felt pretty secure in the 1950s. Although there was a left wing attack on the public school system, the direct grant schools were seen as having some relationship with the local authority and therefore different. It seems mildly ironical that a Labour Mayor, and Chair of the Education Committee, Gladys Robson, presided over Lord Mayor's Day at the Royal Grammar School in the late fifties and was cheered by the pupils, perhaps also ironically, when she awarded a day's holiday!

If Fiona felt she was at the independent school for political reasons, this probably did not apply to the other children. The Marleys sent their daughters to the Church High School from the nursery department through to the sixth form. Fred Marley was so bitter about his own education that he was determined that his own children would have no such problems.[92] Dan Smith, leader of the Labour Party and a strong left wing public figure sent his daughter to Dame Allen's. This school had a number of girls who were openly left wing, involved in the Labour Party and the Peace movement. Brenda Ingleby's mother was able to pay the fees and support her daughter out of compensation received from the death of her husband whilst working for an oil company in the Far East. Dorothy Simmons's parents just thought it would give her a good start in life. Margaret Anwell felt her father and mother did not agree about her going to that school. Her mother, who was teaching French there, prevailed. Linda (Potts) Ebbatson says, 'I decided to take the exam because I heard another girl in my class say she was taking the exam for Dame Allen's. My parents just went along with my wishes.'[93] Jennifer Piachaud's medical consultant father, with a non-British colonial past was not sensitive to the English class system anyway so would be unlikely to have thought of any other course of action.[94] Jeremy Beecham had to pass the scholarship exam to get into the Royal Grammar School whilst his brother, who did not, went to the state grammar school after passing the 11+.

Among those who went to the direct grant schools the Dame Allen's girls most were positive about the experience. Several point to a socialist teacher, Mrs Williams, as a strong influence and feel that the school in general encouraged enquiry and independence of mind. Linda Ebbatson shared these views but registered a negative experience too. Her father was a boilermaker, an active trade unionist and a socialist and she lived on a council estate. She was acutely aware of class. She found the first two years at school very difficult, struggling with her feeling that, 'I spoke a different language', and that 'even some professed socialist school mates looked down on her.'[95] It seems possible that such feeling reinforced a socialist perspective absorbed at home from early childhood. Nicky Landau, a very rebellious young woman, by her's and others' accounts, hated the school. She found it very boring and played truant frequently, from about 13. She was a bit brazen in volunteering that on one absence she was attending a peace march. That her parents apparently supported her action probably did not help. She was asked to leave.[96]Pat Marley had an unhappy time at the Church High. She said, 'it was a bit difficult in that high Tory environment to be a girl from a socialist atheist family.' Unlike Nicky, however, she just decided to relate to a few friends and 'get on with it.'[97]

Most of the boys in the group who passed the 11+ exam went to the state or Roman Catholic high schools. A decent level of literacy was required to pass the 11+ and expectations were low, especially when grammar and technical school places were so few. Passing was not necessarily a satisfactory experience. The schools had just ceased being fee paying after the war and old attitudes died hard. Wal Hobson said, 'the Grammar School (South Shields) in 1950 had masters and boys from when it was recently fee-paying. They did not like kids from bottom end working class families on grounds of hygiene, clothing and shoes. They were much happier with the middle class kids. Some younger teachers were OK but there was a horrible atmosphere. We knew we were the working-class kids. A lot had to leave school at 15. My pal from my street was one. His father had deserted the family and his mother could not afford for him to stay.'[98]Ken Appleby also found South Shields Grammar stifling and discriminatory, bitter sarcasm a regular part of the teachers' armoury.[99]

Terry Watson said, 'I was surprised to pass. I wasn't expected to.' Once into the Grammar School the working class kid could drown. Many did. They were usually heavily streamed and the working class primary schools filled the D stream where the children were treated by the school culture, as thick, sometimes reciprocating by playing 'thick.' But some swam. John Creaby remarked that, '(the) whole period at Grammar School was not a happy one. The class distinction amongst the grammar school students and often from the staff had an impact on my social awareness development.' Terry Watson's experience was common for working class children passing the exam, 'I was isolated from the kids I grew up with. I was lonely, but I just had to get on with life.'[100]

Wal, Terry, John and Ken, though performing very well academically, all left school at 16 largely due to parental finances. John Creaby said, 'My father had left the sea to work in engineering and the shipyard, when I was 12 years of age. After just less than two years working "on land", he had a serious accident at work, from which, he was told he would never work again. But being the strong character that he was, he did obtain work after a long period of self-rehabilitating. The economic pressure at home must have been extreme, although I was not consciously aware of it.'[101]

At Heaton Grammar School less than a quarter of the school year stayed on for sixth form and, of those who did, most lived in the owner occupied areas of Kenton, High Heaton and Jesmond. Most parents were in lower middle class occupations. Few Heaton, Byker and Walker boys carried on after 16. Yet, unlike their grandparents in the twenties and thirties their parents could just about afford the cost up to 16. And also, unlike them, if their offspring left school early, they arrived in a buoyant labour market. The five Heaton pupils who became somewhat active politically in CND or the YS were all from working class families.

Staying on at school beyond 16 was a big choice for many especially for those who were the first in a family to do so. It meant a call on the family income for a further two years with a possible further three stretching beyond that. Some parents already making a financial sacrifice would encourage extending school days into the sixth form. Working as a bus conductor, then chauffeur after the war, my father was on a very low income where strict accounting was needed. A lost pair of football boots or a torn blazer could eat into very modest reserves.

Brian Sharp and his close friends Mick Paxton and Malcolm Scott all passed the 11+ and went to Gateshead Grammar School. All were from working class families. Brian and Mick's fathers were on very low wages while Malcolm's was a station master and a little better off. Brian's home was always short of money, his father a poor manager of meagre resources. He stayed on at school, because, 'my mother was determined I should. She worked at the rope works and the glue factory and used the pawn shop. My Dad's suit would go in on Monday and be redeemed on Fridays. My mother paid for my uniform and sports kit and when I sustained a serious knee injury playing rugby she paid for a private physiotherapist. As working class kids you were aware of difference. When the school made a trip to Paris Mick and I stayed at home. Not even my mother could pay for that.'[102] Nevertheless, Brian seems to regard school as liberation – opening doors to a better life.

In school, sixth form experience itself could be quite different. Superior class attitudes from teaching staff to pupils miraculously disappeared and would be heard no more. There was a presumption that sixth form pupils would head for college and would therefore be joining a club to which the masters and mistresses already belonged. Friends were made and lost along the way. Close mates at primary school were dropped after selection and something similar happened at 16+ as most of the school year entered the labour force.[103]

The select nature of the group encouraged intellectual posturing and there was plenty of that. Theatre and concerts, a stroll round a gallery, hardly ever experienced by the working class kids before 16, heightened the sense of difference. Teachers became more outspoken about work affairs and the odd leftie made himself known. There was even a *sotto voce* suggestion that the *Daily Worker* might be of interest. Even this was a risky act at a school where a pupil had been temporarily excluded for trying to sell that paper in school. Teacher opinion was significant in the autumn of 1956 when the government went charging into Suez. Jim Walker recalled his English and Latin master telling the class that we were living through, 'one of the most shameful days in this country's history.'[104]

Seventeen and eighteen year olds in 1956 felt personally about the Suez escapade because the threat of spending the next summer in the desert was pretty real. I am sure my mother, conservative in inclination, opposed the Suez venture because of what it might mean for her son. Certainly Suez was the first big political event to cause serious anxiety and provoke serious thought for these young people. Coming from a working class Tory home, I wobbled on the issue but subjected to firm opinions at school, from staff and friends, I became quite clear: it was a bad idea.[105] A group from Heaton joined an enormous demonstration at the Bigg Market on a Sunday night during the crisis and heard Nye Bevan for the first time, hammering the Eden Government at the Connaught Hall.

The liveliest teachers were usually allotted the sixth form 'elite.' Theatre, concerts, Art Galleries were suggested. Dame Allen's teachers encouraged visits to the Literary and Philosophical Society. Maggie Anwell remembers thinking it 'as the most beautiful place in the world.' Jim Walker's quip, 'Libraries?' We practically lived there,' refers to the Public Library and, especially the Victorian Reading Room at Newcastle Central Library.[106] This was the recommended place for the state Grammar School pupil.

Some sixth forms fostered discussion and encouraged listening to classical music. Names like Kingsley Amis, John Osborne, Brendan Behan, Dylan Thomas, Jack Kerouac and Jean-Paul Sartre crossed the radar. Minds tapped into discussions on atheism, existentialism, Angry Young Men, Hidden Persuaders[107]...Suez, Budapest...the H Bomb's thunder. From there, for some, it was not a big leap to action: the local Labour Party, the Campaign for Nuclear Disarmament and Anti-Apartheid. The critical point was that involvement came from engagement with ideas, not at all from class struggle. This would apply equally to those who came from middle and working class homes, from socialist and none socialist homes.

Those failing the 11+ could face serious difficulty. In his lively biography, *Geordies—Wa Mental*, Dave Douglass described his 1950s Felling school experience. 'Without exception. The teachers hated the 'C' stream. We were a stupid, illiterate, violent, stubborn and sometimes dirty morass of rudeness... Teachers were aggressive foes, or else soft shites whom we could bait in retaliation...the Headmaster was a small, wiry, non-dialect Geordie who at times could look into the dead eyes of feigned ignorance and keek like a detective for signs of intelligent life. At other times he was capable of monumental violence...a show trial before the school, four boys dragged from the ranks...

dragged by the hair, dragged to the stage…air charged with sick violence…the Head flaying like a cavalry officer with the stick across the legs…whacking with fearful thrusts, smacks across the sides of the head ringing through the hall.'[108]

It was not only the pupils who were considered second rate. Many teachers were poorly qualified. With teachers in short supply, they might even be formally unqualified. In my first job as a teacher in Newcastle's east end, the establishment was 12. I saw 27 men and women pass through the staff room in the school year 1959-60. They included a retired policeman, an art student with poor English, a visiting Australian tourist short of money and two or three mature teachers who apparently could find work nowhere else. Considerable violence was expected of teachers who were actually supplied with leather straps. A blind eye was usually turned to teacher fisticuffs. The building dated to the 1880s and there was a real shortage of equipment. It was a very tough situation indeed for children entering its doors.

Dave Douglass, who started work in a bakery then went down the pit, is unusual in being one of the few young industrial workers who became politically active on Tyneside in this period. The Labour Party Young Socialists, the Young Communist League and CND were largely white collar and student organisations. Dave survived his educational trauma, educating himself, attending Ruskin College and participating throughout his life in the labour and socialist movements.

Not all of the secondary modern schools were so bleak. Lucy Nicholson recalls that her head mistress at Longbenton was a Quaker woman dedicated to producing the best possible environment for the girls in her charge. She eschewed corporal punishment and gave art, music and drama a special place in the curriculum. Most of all she is described as encouraging self worth in children who had been marked as failures. Her school was a new school and well appointed for the time. Children could leave school with a fistful of GCEs, entering white collar jobs or craft jobs or further and higher education.[109] Guy Falkenau, in Gateshead, had a similar experience. He became the first pupil of his school to go to college to qualify as a teacher.

Work

Jim Nichol's traumas started earlier. He was shattered by the loss of both parents, his mother from TB, from whom he contracted the disease at 11, and his father from pneumoconiosis when he was 14. Family chaos at this point led to the humiliation of being lined up in a council office for selection for fostering and separated from his older sister. He felt fortunate to find warm foster parents. He was to return to his aunt's home for secondary school. At this point he hardly knew his youngest sibling who had lived with his father till his father's death.

Jim performed well at school and at 15 secured a job with the National Coal Board as a clerical worker. He knew that his father would have been relieved that he did not have to be an underground worker.[110] His friend Sam Dodds, also a collier's son, took a job in a hat shop. There was no question of Sam going down the pit. He was not keen to do so and was backed up by his parents. More than twenty boys from the local area joined Newburn Young Socialists. Most came from coal mining families but so far as is known, not a single one became a miner. It may have been true that in their parents' generation a similar antipathy to colliery life existed but the real difference was that from the late fifties two new factors weighed in.

Firstly, free public education was available. The newly built Walbottle Campus created a secondary school education which broadened opportunity for both working class children who aspired to higher education and many of those who did not. The second more important point was the increase in job opportunities. Of course this was not universally the case. The Newburn area was part of the Tyneside conurbation in easy reach of a diverse range of jobs and post school technical and commercial education. The same might not be true for youngsters in the more distant mining communities of Northumberland and Durham. And, as Dave Douglass' biography shows, there was a constituency of young people close to the river Tyne for whom the pit remained, if briefly, the most likely job destination. These were the boys battered, psychologically and sometimes physically, into low expectations and educational failure.

Among the females in the cohort, Irene Edwards went from commercial school into the civil service. This was a typical destination for girls who left school at 16. They were usually expected to be passive in the work place and, if they had opinions, to leave them at home. This was not case with Irene who quickly joined the union and became a union activist. Asked by Paul Foot to write a piece for *Labour Worker* while a very junior clerical officer, she felt obliged to show it to her Chief Executive Officer who proceeded to emasculate it beyond recognition.[111]

Indeed, most young people went to work, not college. This applied to grammar and high school youth as much as the rest. The grammar schools had very small sixth forms with perhaps as little as twenty per cent of the annual intake proceeding to college. Of that group only a handful would have fathers who did manual work. Terry Watson left St Cuthbert's Grammar School and got an apprenticeship in the laborotories at George Angus, the factory making oil seals for the motor industry. Here he met and became friends with Alec Comb, another young worker, of whom he says, 'He was an outgoing strong minded young man, already in the Young Communist League. I drifted into the left. It seemed like a natural evolution. Of course my family was left wing, involved in the Labour Party and I had an uncle in the CP. I lived in a left wing street in Scotswood where everybody was Labour.'[112]

Dunn's hat shop in Clayton Street, Newcastle was where Sam Dodds started work at 15. He was to stay there for thirty one years. He recalls that union membership was virtually non-existent in large parts of the retail trade, though he was an individual member it was not easy. 'Dunns was a Quaker firm with decent working conditions. The pay was not good but management was respectful and holidays were linked to service, going up from three, to four, five and eventually six weeks annual paid holiday. I always argued for socialism but it fell on stony ground with my work mates.'[113]

Marge Wallace got a scholarship for Dame Allen's school but left at 16 to work at the Newcastle Breweries. She wrote, 'my pay was £4 16s 0d a week, which didn't go far after I'd given my parents £2 a week for board. I worked a 35 hour week. I was a lab assistant, so we were considered "professionals" or white collar, so unions didn't apply. The two bosses were men (of course), but the head of the lab only hired women as lab assistants. I remember the worst part of my job was when I had to go to another building to get beer samples, and it entailed going through the cellar, which was filled with men (very rough types) who liked nothing better than to down tools and shriek and yell at anything in a skirt. I had to run the gauntlet here four times a day. In those days, of course, women just had to put up with it. The 6 or so women I worked with were friendly enough, but we didn't have enough in common to socialise out of working hours, except at Christmas. I got on better with a young woman who was a "blue collar" worker in the lab, washing glassware and the like, and she and I used to meet socially, and kept in touch for years afterwards.'[114]

Later she joined the civil service and was, 'assigned to the Ministry of Agriculture rather than the Ministry of Pensions where everyone else seemed to end up. The first thing I discovered was that women earned less than men for the same work, which annoyed me a great deal. My pay was somewhere between £5-6 a week, and we worked about 37 1/2 hours a week. I couldn't help noticing that all the top jobs were held by men, though there were a lot of women bosses in the lower ranks. Promotion beyond them seemed to be very difficult for women. I knew several very capable women who failed the promotion board time and time again.[115]

Marge went off to college in 1964 but returned to the Breweries as a vacation job. She said, 'I discovered that only the women did any work, and they were paid less than the men and boys. The boys spent most of the time larking about behind the piled-high crates. The work was very hard and tiring (I was lifting full crates onto a conveyor belt). When there was a lull in the work, we were given stupid things to do, like scrubbing the floor with long handled brushes, except the handles weren't long enough, so you ended up doing it bent double – excruciating! It would have made more sense if they had sent us home, but I suppose that would have meant cutting our pay, and the union wouldn't have allowed that. I liked the women I worked with in the factory; they were all very friendly, and one even invited me to her house. They told me they usually didn't like students, because they were "stuck up"; I can only assume my socialist background and ideas had something to do with the positive way I interacted with them. When my four weeks were up, the factory manager said he was really surprised I'd stuck it out.'[116]

Jim Walker's early work experience was varied. While his future career in journalism suggests that he was always moving in that direction, he explains that, 'most of my contemporaries became school teachers but I knew I'd be late every day – this time even more conspicuously-missing from the platform. So I started work as a gardener for Newcastle Corporation, thinking what fun it would be to squirt water on flowers that would afterwards bring traffic roundabouts and central reservations to life. But I failed to consider the achievements of Management. There's no job so fulfilling that they can't turn it into drudgery. So we, the gardeners, had to dash, bent double, watering ninety stems a minute till we finally hated the sight of a geranium. And we learned a dozen ways a minute to skive in order to keep ourselves sane. As the flowers began to wilt, the Chief Gardner could think of no solution except to appoint a suit filled by a Mr Renwick to supervise us. He failed because he knew nothing about horticulture and even less about skiving.'

Jim did not stay long at the Council. '(He) moved to a vulcanized rubber factory as a Progress Chaser, moving pieces of paper from one part of the reeking hangar to another. Snow melted, Spring came and went but the weather never changed inside that corrugated iron Limbo where 238 turners stood at lathes, making metal rings to fit inside oil seals. Some men had been there for more than a quarter of a century and had realized long ago that life's a thousand years too short for factory work but it was too late – they had mortgaged their unique and irretrievable lives. Eventually they'd get a marble clock, followed shortly by a marble slab.' Jim Walker's way of seeing has echoes of *The Ragged Trousered Philanthropists* sharply capturing some of the bare truths of work in a capitalist society, but there is another possible factor. The job market in 1960 was buoyant enough for him change jobs frequently. He was to have four in the two years before he arrived in his first media office, the *Northern Echo* in Darlington.[117]To treat such matters lightly was individual to Jim but it is harder to imagine such levity in the previous generation reared in the Depression.

I started work in September 1959, teaching in a secondary modern school in Byker. I was assigned that school by the City Education Department. This was the method employed with probationary teachers by some local authorities, although the Situations Vacant columns in 1959 ran to many pages of the *Times Literary Supplement.* Young teachers dissatisfied with their jobs could easily move on. So, the schools with the most difficulty were doomed to be staffed by inexperience and incompetence. My school was certainly difficult for a young teacher. I was immediately introduced to the recommended method of keeping order, a heavy leather strap, whilst one old stager gleefully brought in lengths of conveyor belt: rubber strips reinforced by wire cable. The aging head teacher kept a punishment book, encouraging staff to enter incidents of corporal punishment though in practice this hardly ever happened. The classes were large, usually in the low 40s. Maintaining discipline placed enormous demands upon any but the extreme sadists, of which there were a few. The result was demoralised teachers and angry, aggressive or passively resistant pupils. The sports field, miles away, was one of the few brighter lights for some pupils and the games teacher. Running the school football team and trying to assemble a cricket team was a saving grace for the year I was there. My desire to teach English and History was more or less put on hold. Time was left for active politics and the start of involvement in the branch of the National Union of Teachers.

Pat MacIntyre was sent to her first teaching job in a Roman Catholic primary school on Teesside where the conditions were primitive. She had to teach in a Nissen hut which leaked in wet weather, was freezing in winter and over-hot in summer. The winter conditions made her ill and she had to spend time off school. When she felt a little better, but not well enough to work, she went into school to let the Head Teacher know that her doctor advised her to tell the Head Teacher that her health would not stand up to continuing in that classroom. Out of sight of witnesses, the Head Teacher punched her, knocking her to the ground! She reported the incident to the NUT and to the parish priest. The union encouraged her to take the matter up with the police but the priest implored her not to and offered to settle her in a better school, which he did.

Ken Appleby left school at 16. He went from South Shields' Grammar school to Reyrolles, the switch gear firm at Hebburn. He said, 'I talked myself into the drawing office and then into an apprenticeship. I was actually the very first apprentice in the drawing office. It was quite a business. On the first day you were given a ticket for *Collars* [a Newcastle collar shop] where you had to go on the first Saturday afternoon-we worked on Saturday mornings – and present your ticket and the money – for which you got a box of stiff collars. You had to wear a clean one each day. It was a very strict office. In fact you might be reported for bad behaviour out of work.' Yet, in 1960 bad behaviour was not likely to lead to instant dismissal. Indeed Ken reports a general loosening of petty discipline in the course of his apprenticeship.[118]

Strike!

There were industrial disputes. In April 1960 an apprentices' strike began on the Clyde. Pickets travelled to Tyne and Wear and up to 5000 local apprentices followed suit. The strike lasted a few days, the employers made concessions and the strikers returned to work. Guy Falkenau and John Creaby, though only in their mid-teens spoke to the visiting apprentices. The Newcastle YCL was interested but when the Tyneside apprentices joined the strike they were apparently unaware of the socialists.

There was a much bigger unofficial strike of seamen in the Summer of 1960. This was nationwide and, although led from Liverpool, north eastern seamen were a bulwark of the action. Here the leading figure was Jim Slater of South Shields who was to achieve greater fame and notoriety in the 1966 strike when he was demonized by Harold Wilson and the media. In 1960 the seamen stayed out for five weeks, holding regular meetings, pickets and marches in each of the towns along the rivers. These events were headline news in the local media.

Both these disputes were typical of the period. They were unofficial. In the seamen's case Sir Tom Yates, the General Secretary, roundly condemned the men, branding their leaders communists. He was obdurate in his determination not to meet them or allow local branches to meet while the strike continued. Further, there was little intervention from the state. The nine policemen facing the apprentices' flying pickets outside C A Parsons were described as 'pushing a bit.' In the several press pictures of seamen's actions, including mass picketing of ships, there is no sign of a police presence.[119]

Very few of the new young socialists saw any relevance in the militant industrial activity of sections of the working class before the early mid-sixties. And few workers seem to have taken an interest in the socialists. Ken Appleby was an interesting exception. From a strong Labour and CP family in Shields, he tried the League of Youth but found it boring. 'They just sat around and talked. I wanted action.' When the apprentices' dispute was brewing, Ken tried to bring the young draftsmen on the river into it. 'Of course it was just about impossible to link up at work. You couldn't move around the factory without arousing suspicion. No. I discovered a lovely centre of agitation! The canteen at the Tech. More than a hundred of us were on Day Release. Twice a week we would meet in the canteen. There were lads from every workshop on the Tyne. It was easy to get to get information and pass it on.' He met up with the Clyde apprentices who came down to seek support. This was the start of his taking an interest in workers' struggle. He asked himself, and them, why the leading militants he met were all apparently political animals. This took him into active politics and to the far left. This passage became much more common in the late sixties.

The apprentices' and the seamen's strikes of 1960 were relatively rare events.

For the youngster who left school at 15 and took an apprenticeship, learning the craft and doing day release at the Technical College meant absorbing a culture in the workplace where full employment and job security were at levels unheard of before. There was little of the unrest and turmoil which fosters debate and possibly action. After work, with money in the pocket, there was leisure activity to engage with. Rock and Roll was in the air. New fashions grabbed attention. Active politics was way down the agenda. Of course there were exceptions, who, for quite personal, even eccentric reasons moved into politics. A strong family tradition, a family inured in socialist or trade union culture or an accidental friendship could be the spur. John Creaby went to catholic grammar school but left school at 16 to work at the Co-op. In his case perhaps the Co-op was the final ingredient to add to strong family connections. He chose to take an interest in Co-op education, graduating via the Co-op College to the NCCL, young socialist and CND activism.

Jim Nichol also had strong family motivation. He remembers 'a lot of politics' in his childhood. His father was an active member of the miners' lodge committee and had socialist views on the big issues: Suez, German re-armament, 'the Tories' as enemy. Jim was introduced to labour leader, Clement Attlee' at the Northumberland Miners' Gala in 1955, his Dad just saying that it was important. It seemed obvious to him to leaflet for the LP in elections and to take a public sector job when leaving school as a clerk in the NCB. His father had emphatically turned him away from going down the pit and encouraged him to take an arithmetic correspondence course with the NCLC. His father died from pneumoconiosis when only 39, though the death certificate recorded coronary thrombosis. An employer conceding an industrial disease as a cause of death risked a claim for compensation.

Many of the young people in this study came from politically conscious homes. Such homes were generally more critical of the status quo and probably more bookish that the average home. If we add the reverence for education among white collar and skilled workers we can see the advantage for those children in the educational lottery of the nineteen fifties where chance played a part on which side of the statistical line a pupil fell at 11. State grammar school places in Newcastle were available to only 14% of the school population. In Gateshead it was even lower.

We must not lose sight of the fact that the numbers moving into political action were small. At most there were a few hundred over a five year period from a population of perhaps 100,000 in the age group 15-25. By comparison in the five years round 1970 the figure would have been at least five or six times that number. This later period was the height of the student movement, the women's movement and most significantly the peak of workers' struggle with government. The late fifties was an altogether less actively militant time. Apart from the campaign round the Bomb, the only issue to excite demonstrations was the brutal behaviour of the white rulers of South Africa and these demonstrations were pretty small compared with what was to follow. The *Evening Chronicle* reported several demonsrations in the Newcastle town centre giving figures in the low hundreds. Despite the inclination of the press to underplay the impact of such events, the figures seem about right.

Chapter 5: Collective effervescence[120]

In the spring of 1961 a March from London to Holy Loch passed through Tyneside. It was noted only briefly by a largely hostile media but it made a great impact on anti-Bomb activists in the region. Some joined specific stages as it passed their town or village. A few locals even stayed with it all the way to Holy Loch. Many attended meetings in Sunderland and Newcastle and a large contingent travelled by bus two weeks later to join in, or support the sit down outside the gates of the US base at Holy Loch. Eight of the Tyneside contingent were arrested, charged and convicted. In that spring and summer mass involvement in the campaign peaked with the biggest of the Aldermaston Marches, two big events at Holy Loch and a sit down in Parliament Square.

Although the genealogies of the individuals involved were very diverse there can be no doubt of the unifying potency of the issue of the bomb. Whilst fear of extinction might have resulted in paralysis for some, it acted as a mobiliser for many. Mike Worrall was probably the first of his generation to become active on Tyneside around the issue. Mike was a conscientious objector (C.O.). He feels he was pushed in that direction by his experience at public school. He'd been sent there unwillingly, hating the regime of cricket and corps. 'I remember standing on parade being addressed by a Major General. He boomed, "all pull together chaps. I look forward

From Mike Worrall's activity diary 1958-65

to seeing you in a couple of years time." A little voice inside said, ' I don't think you will.' Registering as a C.O., Mike was sent into the hospital service at the Queen Elizabeth Hospital in Gateshead. He moved on to the Royal Victoria Infirmary where he met Dr Frank Farmer, a medical physicist who was an active Quaker. Dr Farmer introduced him to the Fellowship of Reconciliation.[121] Although there was some good discussion, it had a limited appeal for Mike since he was not religious. He soon found the Direct Action Committee (forerunner of CND) and though missing the first Aldermaston at Easter 1958 he went on a CND march in London in June1958. This was the first of over 80 marches, sit downs and poster parades in which he participated over the following seven years! [122]

A small north east contingent had attended the first Aldermaston March though their names are no longer known. That march achieved considerable publicity, surprising the organisers. Only a hundred or so started the march to Aldermaston but others joined and around 4,000 people reached the gates of the site. Until that point anti-bomb organisation was tiny and over-weighted with famous people including Bertrand Russell, Canon Collins, the writers J B Priestley, Sir Compton McKenzie, Doris Lessing and E M Forster, the sculptors Henry Moore and Barbara Hepworth, the composer, Benjamin Britten, actors Flora Robson and Peggy Ashcroft and the scientists, Julian Huxley and P M S Blackett. Some had been associated with pre-war campaigns including even one survivor of the Edwardian women's suffrage movement. Many of them were rather full of their own importance and, with some notable exceptions, usually absent from the protest events.

Locally CND was largely run by older people whose political memories

Dr Leslie Feinmann in later life

stretched a long way back. Will George was a bluff and rather pompous business man who lived in a grand house at Woolsington. He was nicknamed irreverently 'the table mat tycoon' having given the world laminated table mats. He tended to bring business methods to bear on organization adopting a command strategy. He was effective in building large public meetings. Grigor MacLelland was a Quaker businessman who had served in the Friends Ambulance Unit in occupied Germany. He had also been to Moscow and Peking on Peace delegations in the mid-fifties. He was a respected public figure on Tyneside and excellent on the platform, lending the movement a grave and attractively modest authority. He was generous in meeting the fines of those arrested on demonstrations, though humorously reminding one of the beneficiaries of his 'debt' of £5, forty years later. Other leading Quakers were Dr Frank Farmer and John and Mary Burt. John was Head Master of Whitley Bay Grammar School. Like Will George, Mary Burt opened their home in Whitley Bay for CND garden parties. Lesley Feinmann was a chest physician, gentle, agreeable and very encouraging of young people.

Fred Marley was Regional Manager of Rediffusion. He had worked his way up the company after joining it as a teen age floor sweeper. He had an expertise in electronics and would supply efficient loudspeaker equipment for events. Both he, and his wife Olive, had a lot of experience of political organizing. They had been at the centre of the unsuccessful campaign to re-elect Konni Zilliacus after his de-selection by the Labour Party in 1950. Olive, her friend Sylvia Feinmann and Enid Atkinson of the United Nations Association were vigorous and enthusiastic organisers in the Gosforth and Jesmond areas. Also from Gosforth were Frank and Nora Turnbull who were keen spiritualists. Mr Turnbull was Regional Manager of the Automobile Association.

Michael Campbell was a portly, argumentative Jarrow and Durham County Councillor. Bob Griffin, a tall balding ascetic school teacher, was also a stalwart of the Humanist and Fabian Societies. Jim Elder, a real eccentric, was a slightly built excitable City Planner who lived in a splendid

Jim Elder in 1963

house on the edge of Gosforth golf course. He had left the CP in 1956 after twenty years in membership. 'I can take anyone but the fucking trots,' he said in an early International Socialist day school in his house which was open to left organizations of many persuasions. Jack Lawther, the youngest of the famous miners' union brothers, was the most prominent of the working class figures in CND. He was a transport officer for the NCB and was often employed getting people to demonstrations. Ray Boynton, a shipyard draughtsman was on the GMC of the Newcastle West Constituency Party and one of the few outspoken left wingers in that party. Dave and Iris Atkinson were CP members from Kenton. Dave was Secretary of the Newcastle Branch of the Postal Workers Union and active since the 1920s.

The Tapsells, Anna and Mike, were younger – in their late twenties when they arrived on Tyneside in 1959. Mike, was a junior planning officer in Jim Elder's department. They brought a lot of political experience to Tyneside. Anna, had been London Regional Secretary of CND. Mike had been brought up in a CP home. His father Walter, editor of the *Daily Worker* had been killed in Spain in 1937 where he had been a political commissar for the International Brigade. Mike was in the YCL from childhood, but fell out with the Party in his late teens over the Soviet Union's treatment of Yugoslavia. He was involved in the new peace movement from its beginning.[123]

WEEKEND AT WHITEHALL

ike Worrall talks to the press at the C.N.D. 'sit down' outside the Ministry of Defence last weekend.
Following last week's letter to 'Courier', stating that local C.N.D. members remained seated uring the playing of the National Anthem, it is interesting to note that the British press can coax at least one of their number to his feet.

Mike Worrall and a reporter

Tactical clashes

From the start, nationally, there were clashes over issues and campaign strategy. The main division was over the attitude to the Labour Party. Some believed that the election of a Labour Government was an absolute priority and therefore counselled against activities which might damage Labour's electoral prospects. Others believed that the anti-nuclear struggle transcended main line party politics and argued for urgent non-violent direct action. The latter was probably the overwhelming position of the new generation activists with one qualification. They might also yearn for a Labour government but could not see how direct action would not enhance the prospect. The Blackpool Conference decision of 1961, reversing unilateralism, certainly damaged the Labour Party in the eyes of the young activists who swung towards direct action.

These tensions were played out on Tyneside but largely without the bitterness that marked the national scene. The young people were not much moved by leadership quarrels though Canon Collins was seen as a rather patronising figure. Although not everyone participated in direct action to the extent of sitting down and inviting arrest, there was general approval for the tactic. Some of the senior members of Tyneside CND's committee did not approve but neither were they especially obstructive. Those active in Labour politics like Leslie Feinmann of Newcastle North and Ray Boynton, encouraged the actions of the young activists. Other older CND supporters who were Labour Party activists like Councillors Doris Starkey, Ted Fletcher, Ken Skethaway, Jim Murray in Gateshead and even Newcastle council leader, Dan Smith, were no less supportive. It would probably have made little difference if they had not been, since even those young people who were active in the Young Socialists, like Jim Walker, John Creaby and Guy Falkenau would probably have felt more strongly about banning the bomb than electing a Labour Government. In any case several of the activists had no loyalty to Labour anyway, since they were Young Communist League members.

Mike Worrall's tactical notes

In Tynemouth, Nina Johnson, daughter of a CP District Committee member, Nell Johnson, organized the coast contingent for the second Aldermaston March in 1959. CND's equal criticism of both the Russian and American bombs had been a barrier to CP involvement with the new anti-nuclear movement in 1958. This was to change. Many young Party adherents, like Nina, and some older ones, Vera Kenyon, Barbara Davies, Rae Smith and Dot Bean, simply ignored the CP's policy and just got involved. A number of other Party members from the Tynemouth and Whitley Bay areas joined her. Nina says, 'No one at school seemed interested. Then Marian (Campbell) and I went up to school and ran a CND flag up the flagpole. It was a bit like *The Chalet Girls at School*. We went up on the Number 11 bus working out how a flagpole worked. The Head Teacher was furious but could never prove who did it. Marian had a very strong will. She was a stronger personality than me, was much more confident and extrovert. We were determined to go on the 1959 Aldermaston Easter March. Some of the YCL group came and were told off by May Smailes, from the District Committee. I just went off and booked a coach, to hell with the cost. We filled it, and then another. The coast CP group mainly supported CND.'[124] The Party's official policy change came in 1960. The post-1956 CP was in no position to ignore a burgeoning youth movement.

Guy Falkenau came to CND from the Labour Party which he had joined at 14. His grandfather, Peter Hancock had been the father of the Gateshead Council, having been elected in 1921. His Aunt, Bertha Elliott was the Labour Agent for Darlington. She lived above the Newcastle City Labour Party offices in Victoria Square. Bertha was an enthusiastic supporter of CND. It was at the newly formed Gateshead CND that Guy met John Creaby in the summer of 1958. A member of Young Catholic Workers, John had joined Christian CND. Like so many young people in the late fifties CND soon became the centre of their lives. They saw the first Aldermaston March on TV and read about it in the new CND paper, *Sanity*.

To Aldermaston

At Easter 1959 John and Guy were off to their first Aldermaston, squeezed into Aunt Bertha's pre-war Austin 7, on a tortuous journey to take part in the probably the biggest demonstration in Britain since the Second World War. John captures the sense of excitement, 'all we could see was the mass of people, a huge carnival. political parties and local Councils, students, mixed with those from different religious cultures, entertainers...Impromptu jazz bands blasting forth, groups of guitar players singing folk songs an d anti-war songs and everywhere banners, posters, the black and white CND symbol, TV, radio and press reporters closely watching for the outlandish or cranky marcher and

Aldermaston: Doug Jackson, Brenda Ingleby & Guy Falkenau

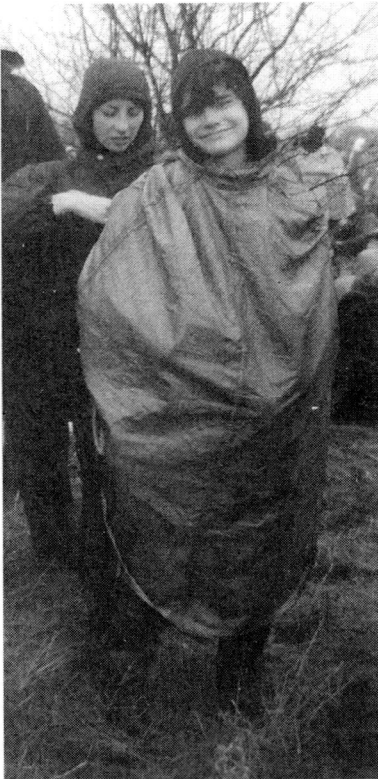

Margaret & John Creaby at
Aldermaston 1963

ignoring the huge mass. Jean Mortimer remembered, 'an apparently drunken Randolph Churchill hurling abuse from the pavement being met by good humoured repartee' and 'Birmingham necrophiliacs demanding a peaceful death'.[125]

The main banner, "March from Aldermaston to London" (had)...white lettering on black cloth, (and) always a bunch of daffodils tied to the top at the start...for a young teenager the anti-establishment feeling was intoxicating.'[126] Mike Down summed the experience up well, 'The marches provided an intense social and political education for tens of thousands of (mainly) young people – a kind of combined Glastonbury and 4-day seminar every Easter.'[127]

Local councils on the route were not sympathetic, so the hunt was on for on for friendly churches and trade union and co-op halls (also few and far between in the shires). So, 'we slept in tents. It was freezing outside in the morning queue to wash at the standpipes and the portable toilets. Once (1963) we slept in a big marquee, a thousand of us. There were groups discussing everything from anarchism to Zen Buddhism. The big buzz was about a leaflet. This was the *Spies for Peace*. Hundreds, including many north easterners joined a breakaway march to the Regional Seat of Government (RSG) bunker at Warren Row. A big campaign around the issue was to follow.

CND was not a membership organisation in the conventional sense. It was four years old before it issued membership cards. Its great strength lay in the fact that it provided an environment for action. Anyone could take initiatives like Nina Johnson's booking a bus. Wearing the famous badge made you feel a member. Talented organizers like Mike Worrall in the community, Walter Ryder in the University and Nina and Guy among the school students wrote and printed the handbills, booked the buses, collected the money and just looked after the contingents. Nobody chose the speakers. They just stood up and spoke like Mike Down and Dave Leigh from Kings College, John Creaby and Dave Douglass among the young people. On the marches and sit downs there were those who just took initiatives, like Marian Campbell who took a boat out at Holy Loch. In fact Mike Worrall believes 'the shift to bureaucracy, committees, cards, and annual conference [from 1962] probably contributed to its decline.' The spontaneity did have its downside. It was very hard to replace an unpopular leader. This was never a problem locally, but it was serious nationally where the movement's policy was decided. This was demonstrated in the big clash between Canon Collins and Bertrand Russell over direct action.

The actions of individuals locally were very important but they would have been meaningless without the regular influx of new people. Each school and college year seemed to bring fresh people into activity. Schools and colleges were the main source of recruitment. Determined individuals at the high schools, like Mary Feinmann, Fiona Scott Batey, Jane Owens, Pat Marley, Brenda Ingleby and Linda Potts brought little groups of contemporaries to meetings and activities. They often had to act subversively at their school and authoritarian attitudes from teaching staff may have increased their kudos with other students. Mary (Feinmann) Chuck remembered, 'an ever present fear. I could not believe the attitudes of people who didn't think it had anything to do with them. It did seem that getting rid of nuclear weapons was the most important thing we had to do. At school these views were met with disapproval from staff and pupils alike, which made it all seem a bit unreal!'[128]

When Fiona Scott-Batey was just 14, she and her friend Jane Owens organised a petition to send to Kruschev, urging him to stop Soviet nuclear tests. Fiona was quoted in the *Evening* Chronicle saying, 'This is a plea from the school children of Newcastle-we know of no other way to put forward our view...I don't want die, nor do my friends. This is only a tiny token; we cannot sit back and do nothing.' [129] A Tory Councillor, Mrs Muriel Sims, had attacked CND for 'political indoctrination in the schools' a charge which the Chairman of CND had called ridiculous, inviting the Councillor to debate the issue. Pat Johnson recalled that Mrs Sims may have felt specially sensitive since her own daughter was sympathetic to ban the bombers. [130] The episode is a reminder of how polarizing the issue was, even within families. Frequent ex-changes took place in the local press between CND and often determined anti-communists. Such people completely ignored the fact that the CP had only recently converted to unilaterialism and that the mass of CND supporters had virtually no affection for the Soviet Union.

Fiona Scott-Batey and her petition

Fiona said to the reporter, 'I don't want to die, and neither do my friends.' Fiona's view is a rather measured response for a 14 year old. Others were terrified by what they saw as the nuclear threat. Several people speak of bad dreams. Jean Mortimer remembered, 'a recurring nightmare…if I swam down the river, ran down the tunnels fast enough the bombs ranged along the river bank would not go off.' For a some years pictures of the Hiroshima disaster were filtering into public consciousness. Early in 1960 two powerful films reached Newcastle. *On the Beach* was a popular mainstream movie based on Neville Shute's best selling novel of 1957 relating the aftermath of a nuclear holocaust. Marge Wallace says, 'Jim Walker told me he was opposed to CND till he saw *On the Beach*. Alain Resnais's, *Hiroshima Mon Amour* was possibly more shocking with its seemingly documentary footage of the city after the bomb.

A drama which made quite an impact was the play, *A Climate of Fear* shown on ITV in early 1962. It featured a nuclear scientist whose daughter joined CND.

Maggie Anwell called it, 'Very bleak.' She rushed off a letter to the writer David Mercer. She says, 'He very decently sent me his rehearsal copy and said, "You mustn't feel too disillusioned. Human beings are complex and contradictory – and their motives in doing things are equally so. There is nothing wrong at all with idealism, only one should take enormous trouble to see clearly what has been achieved in relation to the ideals. Complete honesty with oneself is the only way to avoid being deceived by one's idealistic hopes into thinking that the world is easily changed.

Society will always try to resist those who wish to impose a moral view of human purpose on it. It will resist those who wish, who demand to live and love in peace ...creatively. It will distort the truth and parade its own lies in a semblance of truth – this is in the nature of things in a society where greed acquisition and competition are the basic motives and are accepted as legitimate values. But thank goodness there are hundreds and thousands of people who believe differently – who choose to live and work for a better idea of life.' She feels this was 'strong stuff when you're 15 and definitely nudged me into thinking that theatre and politics could talk to each other...'[131]

When he arrived at Kings College, Newcastle in 1959, Mike Down found CND activists but no CND Society. He wrote, 'I attended the freshers' events and was amazed to discover there was no CND. I phoned Peggy Duff in London and she sent up some literature, badges and membership forms. We organised a meeting in a small room on the first floor of the Union but had to move to a much larger room because too many people turned up. Barry Scaum wanted to know if 'unilateral' meant giving up the bomb even if the Russians kept theirs and was delighted to learn that it did. Barry later organised the silk-screen printing of hundreds of CND posters which we plastered all over the City one night. Some people were arrested. Kings College CND (KCNDS) became easily the largest political group at the university and remained so during my time there.'

'Canon Collins came up for the second meeting and we recruited dozens of new members, not only students but many lecturers and professors (including the artist Victor Pasmore). Because of our large membership we got lots of money from the student union so could afford to get speakers up from London including Konni Zilliacus, Michael Foot, Frank Allaun, and on one occasion, an apparently drunken Labour MP,[132]an ex-dentist, who had a son at Kings. He successfully alienated the thankfully small audience. Our main efforts went into leafleting, selling literature, recruiting members, raising money for central office, and mobilising for the Aldermaston march.'[133]

The University milieu became very important for CND. Harry Rothman said, 'There was a lot of support in the University and scientists, students and staff, were strongly engaged. It came out of interest in work done by Linus Pauling

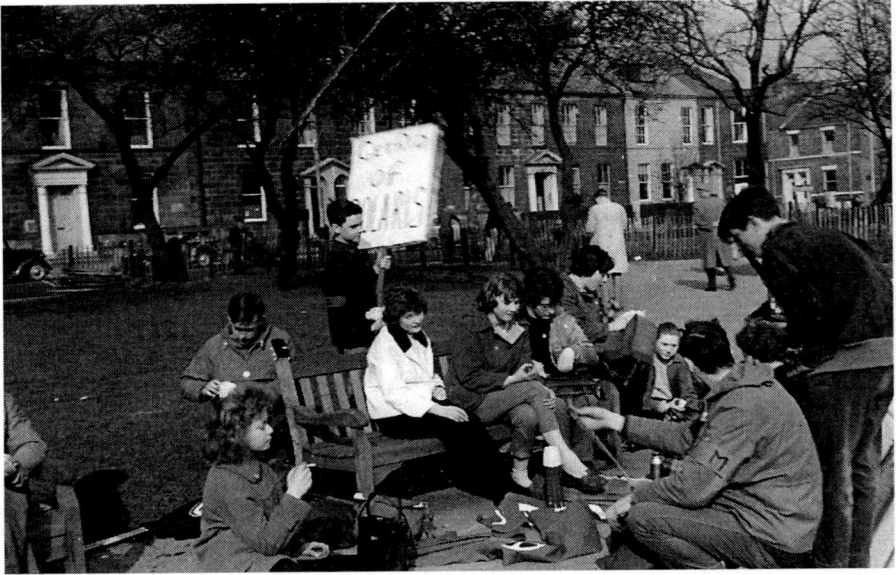

Picnic at North Shields on march to Newcastle. John Creaby with poster, Pat Wallace with cigarette,. On bench unknown, Jennifer Piachaud and Mary Feinmann. Mike Worrall and Alan Brown from behind

and others who researched and wrote up on the effects of radiation. We knew about the Voyage of the *Lucky Dragon*, the US tests at Bikini Atoll and then, nearer to home, the escape of radio active material from Windscale. There was a growing sense that we were not being told the truth by government or the scientists who supported their government.'[134]

Bill Phillips (guitar), Frank Wilson, Doreen Huddert & Pat Wallace

County Borough of Tynemouth

C N D

Protest March
from North Shields to Newcastle

Saturday, 14th September, 1963

Assemble in Northumberland Square, North Shields, at
10.45 a.m. for departure at 11 a.m. prompt
VIA Howdon Road, Wallsend, Shields Road
and Heaton, to Central Station
(Lunch break at Wallsend 1 p.m. approx.)

JOIN US

for all or part of the way. Our task is not easy. We do
not fool ourselves, or intend to fool you. Our leaders
are doing that, but history proves that ordinary people
can make changes for the better.

**DEMAND
NUCLEAR
DISARMAMENT
NOW!**

Local Group Secretary:
**Mrs. B. DAVIES
2 Tynemouth Terrace
Tynemouth**
Tel. North Shields 70897

● Please turn over

RodUm

Very peculiar clothes, some of these
youngsters

A local reaction to the Windscale affair demonstrates the climate of fear round nuclear issue. Pete Johnson, the journalist, got hold of aWindscale classified document on which a D Notice had been issued[135]. The problem was filtering the information out whilst protecting his source who had gone into hiding at Rothbury. Both Pete and his source could have expected serious consequences if caught. His daughter, Nina, remembers the tension around the house as they were expecting a police raid at any time.[136]

Tyneside CND took part in a large number of events, both local and national. Between the first March from North Shields to Whitley Bay in September 1958 and May Day 1964 there were at least 25 local events including marches, poster parades and vigils. A little further afield in July 1960, 'we struggled wearily in summer sun from Whitby to Fylingdales Early Warning Station, then on to Scarborough, converting only sheep.' In September 1960 Tynesiders were back in north Yorkshire. Mike Down recalled, '(that) a large group of us marched at the Labour Party conference in Scarborough and some of us were observers for the big unilateralist debate. The Labour Right was shattered by CND's albeit narrow victory and I clearly remember booing my way through Gaitskell's actually rather noble 'fight, fight and fight again' speech. We went to the Blackpool conference the following year, but this time we lost.

To this tally must be added several large meetings with national speakers including Canon Collins, J B Priestley, Emrys Hughes and Michael Foot. During this time several hundred local people came onto the street or into the City and Connaught Halls in Newcastle, the Town Hall and Westfield (ILP) Hall in Gateshead and the town halls in Wallsend and Jarrow. There were rather more informal happenings like slogan painting. Harry Rothman relates such a trip, 'Walter Ryder, Jim Walker and myself went on a bit of fly-posting in a village north of Newcastle. Walter had spent days practising painting slogans in a disused store in a cellar under the agriculture building. We'd designed, we thought, a very smart slogan – H-Gaitskell H-Bomb. When we reached the village in Walter's car – he was the only student I knew with a car – we found a great gable end on the Co-op and proceeded to paint, Walter from one end, Jim or me from the other, meeting in the middle. A local spotted us and called the police. When the cop arrived Walter and Jim had run away leaving me to face the bemused cop. He seemed unable to understand why we'd want to paint on the Co-op wall. Eventually he simply dumped me on the road outside the village.' [137]

Dave Douglass puts a similar experience more graphically, 'The Committee of 100, back from all neet at the Doonbeat [Downbeat club], gathers up reams of Peace Pledge Union posters (no sectarians us…) buckets of paste, and sets off through deserted streets via Heaton or roon by Jesmond, plastering oor any army adverts, any police adverts, any Tory adverts, any empty shops, blank walls, lampposts and the Tyne Bridge, so the poster could be read by those on the upstairs of a double decker bus.' [138]

Poster parades were another form of propaganda. 'Organised in a line or circle they were effective but may have just disguised small numbers turning up,' says Mike Worrall. The idea may have come from the US labour and Civil Rights movement where pickets moving in a single line skirted the law forbidding stationery groups of people.

There were CND 'groups' in Jesmond, Gosforth, Benton, Fenham, Seaton Burn, Wallsend, North Shields, Tynemouth and Whitley Bay, Morpeth, Blyth, Hexham, Prudhoe, Ryton, Gateshead, Jarrow, South Shields, Sunderland, Durham, Darlington, Stockton and Middlesbrough. There may have been more, as 'declaring a group's existence was very informal and may have entailed as little as having a contingent with a banner at an event,' recalls Guy Falkenau. It is hard to calculate 'membership' accurately as there are no surviving records but Guy Falkenau organised the north east Aldermaston contingent in 1961 and 62. He remembers seven full coaches from the north east which suggests about 300 marchers but several people made their own way there too. This would apply to a lot of students who had gone home at the start of the Easter holidays.

It is also true that many supporters did not go to Aldermaston due to parental pressure, work commitments and disability.

Guy gives invaluable information on the organisation to get people to the event and the event itself. Many have commented on the smooth running of the march. It should be remembered that it was an event with few precedents. Assembling tens of thousands of people in the English countryside, marching them in an orderly fashion, stopping on three nights, accommodating and feeding them and delivering them in good spirits and in reasonably good shape to a rally in Trafalgar Square was a great feat. The Jarrow March in 1936, for example, took much longer but was much smaller with a group of people, all male and all adults, who knew each other. This was also true of the Hunger marchers of the 1920s and 1930s. Those marchers were also much more used to enduring hardship.

CND marchers were more diverse in geographical origin. The marches brought together men, women and children. Many young people and children needed low level supervision. On the 1960 march Anna Tapsell was responsible for 'child care'. 'We had two buses set aside to take in children. I travelled up and down the march riding pillion on Mike's motor bike looking for parents with distressed or tired children who we'd take on the bus. It had a supply of nappies and so on.'[139]People with injuries or those taking too much alcohol needed attention and treatment. Nurses and doctors were available. Anna Tapsell remembers the formidable level of organisation. Then there was the problem of dealing with hostile responses from some antagonists along the route. This was usually no more than illiterate shouts like, 'Get back to Russia!' However it could be more serious. John Creaby and others recalled an attack in the night by members of the League of Empire Loyalists. In his Diary John recorded, 'Mike Down, semi-naked, shouting, "Let me get at them. I'm not a pacifist."`

One of the national organisers devised a grand plan. This was Russell Kerr, the future Labour MP for Rochester, who was a friend of Guy's father. He explained, 'They had been associated in the nascent package holiday travel business where Kerr had devised a methodology for getting people to airports in time, to reach the right group departure points, deposit their luggage, take the flight, pick up their luggage on arrival and get transport to the accommodation. Some of this involved pre-journey colour coding and labelling which we have all become familiar with as travellers. Kerr applied the same methodology to the Aldermaston March and mostly it worked.' Guy used these methods for the north east contingent and also for other events like the second Holy Loch March and sit-down in September 1961. He worked closely with Jack Lawther over the hiring and deployment of coaches. Lawther was the transport officer for the

NCB, a job which had become essential during the run down of the north east coalfields and the transfer of colliers. Guy kept a card index of supporters and their specific needs.

Aldermaston was an annual event with a long run up from New Year to Easter. While the 1961 March had a strong focus on that year's Labour Party Conference, the marches were not specially event related. They suffered the risk of lacking tension and becoming a ritual which was probably what happened after 1962. The big event-related episodes like the two at Holy Loch in 1961

Holy Loch May 1961. Brian Sharp, Kyran Casteel &
John Charlton

were much more dramatic. They were sparked by the arrival in the Clyde of the nuclear submarine supply ship, the *USS Theodore Roosevelt,* in January 1961. It aroused much anger and concern in the Glasgow area. We now know that the MacMillan government expressed its own, secret concerns to the US government that to present the Russians with a visible target within the Glasgow conurbation was at the very least tactless and invited civil disturbance.

Holy Loch

The Scottish Committee of 100 decided to take the issue to a British audience by mounting an Anti-Polaris march from Trafalgar Square to Holy Loch, 400 miles away, at the end of the Aldermaston March. The hope was to draw fresh marchers from the towns and villages passed through to add to the thirty who set off from London. They left London on 3rd April and entered the north east from Northallerton on the 25th. The *Northern Echo* mentioned it in one line, but printed a letter from the Secretary of Richmond Labour Party 'disassociating the Party from the Anti-Polaris March.' The paper made one further reference to the already notorious Pat Arrowsmith and '23 marchers passing through

Darlington carrying a canoe.' [140]

At Stockton the marchers stopped at the market cross where Pat MacIntyre, her new baby in a push chair, was thrust forward by friends to make her maiden outdoor speech. She must have impressed the audience because she was asked to speak at Newcastle when the marchers reached Tyneside three days later.[141] Meanwhile the little band made its way via Hartlepools, where they met a Regional YS conference, through mining villages to Sunderland where a meeting was held in the Town Hall on Sunday evening. It was supported by the Trades Council, the Confederation of Shipbuilding and Engineering Unions, the AEU, the Draughtsmen (AESD) and the Scientific Workers (ASSETT).[142]

Given the tensions in the trade union movement over unilateralism, the strong support of the leading north east trade unions was remarkable. In that very week, the AEU National Committee, though deeply divided, was narrowly aligning with Hugh Gaitskell on the question. This was to be a key decision when the issue came before the Labour Party Conference in the Autumn when the 1960 triumph of the left was reversed. Among those outraged by the manoeuvring of the Labour right wing were Pat and Vin MacIntyre who resigned from the Party in disgust. The March re-assembled on Monday 30th at Boldon Colliery. The marchers were joined by a Tyneside group including Mike Worrall. Buoyed by trade union support at Sunderland, and accompanied by Trade Union delegations, they went from Boldon Colliery along the riverside stopping for factory gate meetings at Palmers and Hawthorn Leslie's shipyards. The *Evening Chronicle* remarked that they had encountered 'some heated discussion' after 'the gates clanged warningly shut.' Subsequently they marched through Newcastle and held a meeting at Gateshead Town Hall before heading north for Morpeth and Scotland.

The march was joined in Newcastle by a small north east contingent including Marian Campbell. On 5th May the *Morpeth Herald* reported that, 'there was little interest as they (Anti-Polaris marchers) marched up the street led by a Methodist minister the Revd R A Kirtley. The Revd Kirtley met them on the outskirts of the town and took part in their meeting in Carlisle Park. Tea was served at the Howard Street Methodist Church and beds were found for them in Morpeth.'[143] They left Morpeth for Alnwick and arrived in Berwick two days later. The *Berwick Advertiser* reported, 'The marchers arrived in Berwick on the evening of Friday 5th May carrying a canoe on wheels, having walked from Alnwick on their way to Holy Loch. The twenty members of the Nuclear Disarmament Campaign walked through the town. The oldest of the marchers was a 70 year-old woman, the youngest was 18. Many of them had given up good jobs, one was a teacher, another a doctor. On the Friday night three of the party headed south to London by train to receive final instructions on their seaborne operation to the Polaris submarine tender on the Holy Loch. The marchers spent Friday and Saturday in St Mary's Hall at Berwick before continuing their journey north on Sunday. They were greeted at the border by spectators and supporters along with a pipe band.'[144]

Marian Campbell remembered miles and miles of open country on the way north and 'lots of singing and lots of sheep.' Staying overnight in Glasgow, before the final leg, she went leafleting in the Gorbals. Invited into a tenement flat by a woman with three children, she was shocked when shown completely bare kitchen cupboards, a level of poverty she had not seen before.

A bus load went from Tyneside to join the last day of the march on Saturday 21st June. Irene (Edwards) Lovell remembered the singing and laughter on the journey then, 'crossing the Clyde on the ferry from Gourock, reality kicked in as we saw the nuclear submarine and the line of grim faced American marines facing us from the deck of the (supply ship, ed) ship. These were people. We sang in their faces.'[145]Jean Mortimer thought, 'Holy Loch was altogether more dour and cheerless (than Aldermaston) not least because shopkeepers (counting American dollars) would not serve us. (Then) Pat Arrowsmith throbbed up and down on her motor bike yelling incoherently for us to jump in (the loch) and get arrested. Her friend Felicity, who wore red socks, made embarrassing speeches to the unimpressed burgers of Dunoon about two headed tadpoles. We sang, "Felicity has red socks on. We shall not be moved'[146]

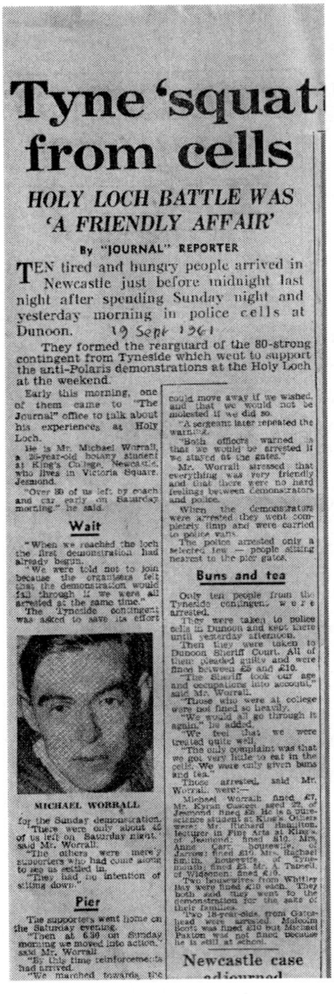

Tyne 'squat
from cells

HOLY LOCH BATTLE WAS 'A FRIENDLY AFFAIR'

By "JOURNAL" REPORTER

TEN tired and hungry people arrived in Newcastle just before midnight last night after spending Sunday night and yesterday morning in police cells at Dunoon. 19 Sept 1961

They formed the rearguard of the 80-strong contingent from Tyneside which went to support the anti-Polaris demonstrations at the Holy Loch at the weekend.

Early this morning, one of them came to "The Journal" office to talk about his experiences at Holy Loch.

He is Mr. Michael Worrall, a 20-year-old botany student at King's College, Newcastle, who lives in Victoria Square, Jesmond.

"Over 80 of us left by coach and car early on Saturday morning," he said.

Wait

"When we reached the loch the first demonstration had already begun.

"We were told not to join because the organisers felt that the demonstration would fall through if we were all arrested at the same time."

The Tyneside contingent was asked to save its effort for the Sunday demonstration.

MICHAEL WORRALL

"There were only about 40 of us left on Saturday night," said Mr. Worrall.

"The others were merely supporters who had come along to see us settled in.

"They had no intention of sitting down."

Pier

The supporters went home on the Saturday evening.

"Then at 6.30 on Sunday morning we moved into action," said Mr. Worrall.

"By this time reinforcements had arrived.

"We marched towards the ... could move away if we wished, and that we would not be molested if we did so.

"A sergeant later repeated the warning.

"Both officers warned us that we would be arrested if we stayed at the gates."

Mr. Worrall stressed that everything was very friendly and that there were no hard feelings between demonstrators and police.

When the demonstrators were arrested they went completely limp and were carried to police vans.

The police arrested only a selected few — people sitting nearest to the pier gates.

Buns and tea

Only ten people from the Tyneside contingent were arrested.

They were taken to police cells in Dunoon and kept there until yesterday afternoon.

Then they were taken to Dunoon Sheriff Court. All of them pleaded guilty and were fined between £5 and £10.

"The Sheriff took our age and occupations into account," said Mr. Worrall.

"Those who were at college were not fined so heavily.

"We would all go through it again," he added.

"We feel that we were treated quite well.

"The only complaint was that we got very little to eat in the cells. We were only given buns and tea."

Those arrested, said Mr. Worrall, were:—

Michael Worrall: fined £7, Mr. Kyran Cassen, aged 22, of Jesmond, fined £5. He is a pure-science student at King's. Others were: Mr. Richard Hamilton, lecturer in Fine Arts at King's, of Jesmond, fined £10. Mrs. Anne Carr, housewife, of Jarrow, fined £10. Mrs. Rachael Smith, housewife, of Tynemouth, fined £5. Mr. A. Tarrell, of Wideopen, fined £10.

Two housewives from Whitley Bay were fined £10 each. They both said they went to the demonstration for the sake of their families.

Two 18-year-olds from Gateshead were arrested. Malcolm Scott was fined £10 but Michael Paxton was not fined because he is still at school.

Newcastle case adjourned

Newcastle Journal report on Holy Loch

The march from Dunoon ended with a 20 hour sit down at the gates of the submarine base. Many of the Tyneside group took part and several were arrested including Ann Berg, John Gough, Walter Ryder, Ray Brown and Mike Worrall.[147] Marian Campbell averted arrest, though with Pat Arrowsmith she had crossed the Loch on a boat to be attacked with power hoses from *U.S.S. Theodore Roosevelt.*

Back again…

A larger Tyneside contingent of over eighty people went back to Holy Loch in September. They took part in a much bigger march. Irene catches another aspect of the Holy Loch events with the remark, 'as we marched round the Loch towards the base we were invited into the house of two elderly sisters who had their table set out with tea and cakes for the

protestors.'[148] This perhaps mundane event shows that there were local people who did not welcome the presence of the American navy at their front doors. It is a strange sort of echo of Harold Macmillan's concern voiced in the Cabinet at the news of the US State Department request for a base on the Clyde.

There were more arrests and convictions in September including Mike Worrall, Kyran Casteel, Richard Hamilton, all of Kings' College and Anne Carr of Jarrow, Rae Smith of Whitley Bay, Mike Tapsell of Seaton Burn and Malcolm Scott and Mick Paxton of Gateshead.[149] There were no prison sentences imposed on either occasion and the fines were token, raising the possibility that the local magistracy was not wholly unsympathetic to the protest. John Creaby was also arrested on the first sit down. He says, 'when those arrested were taken by bus and held in custody at small local police stations, they were something of an oddity. They sat in the cells with the doors open, singing folk songs to the delight of the local police constables on duty, who sent out for fish and chips. They even turned a blind eye to some of us just slipping out.'[150]

Most early protests appear to have been handled with relative moderation by local forces inexperienced in dealing with non violent protests. The media was also somewhat indulgent, largely using debunking humour rather than venom. This was to change.

The story of the 'Spies for Peace' and why they are important for your future

RESISTANCE SHALL GROW...
6d
SECOND PRINTING

ILP pamphlet

Spies for Peace

An issue the state and media took very seriously was the

Spies for Peace Campaign of 1963. A high level leak, let it be known that a shadow administration was in place. Developed on military lines to house members of the country's elite in the event of nuclear war, the scheme involved dividing the country into departments managed from underground sites. In April the Spies for Peace published anonymously, and distributed 4,000 copies of an 'official secret' on the opening day of the Aldermaston March. It listed RSG 6, an underground facility at Warren Row near Reading and encouraged marchers to head there. Forewarned, the principal organisers of the march tried to head off the splinter march. It was to no avail and hundreds of marchers took off down the lanes towards the site including several members of the north east contingent. The marchers swarmed around the bunker taking photographs and singing the Spies for Peace song. They were followed by squads of poorly organised police who attempted to take the leaflets but without arresting the carriers. After a few hours most of the marchers caught up with the main march. The remaining days of the March were taken up by lively debate and many press statements were issued by the organisers disapproving of the action and denying CND complicity.[151]

Many copies of the leaflet made their way back to the north east and over the days which followed copies were run off in hundreds for distribution across the area. On the 2nd May the Newcastle *Evening Chronicle* led with the story that, 'An anonymous document purporting to reveal the location of RSG2 described as the Regional Seat of Government for the North-East' had been received by the paper. The readers were titillated by a vague description of a site' surrounded and masked by thick woods and low hills...(an entrance) crudely but effectively disguised...(where) virtually every Government Department is represented with its staff and offices in the centre. The armed forces, police, civil defence...' The readers may have been comforted by the news that the Editor was forwarding the leaflet to the police and advising, 'any good citizen who gets one of these (leaflets) to send it to the police.' The paper could not avoid a bit of red baiting by getting from the Communist Party's spokesman a denial that they had anything to do with the leaflet 'Any statement we make of any kind, we sign.'[152]

Spies for Peace created quite a stir and a fresh focus for the movement. At the heart of it was a conundrum. On the one hand the government pedalled the idea that the independent nuclear deterrent kept everyone safe. Yet here was a growing body of evidence that the most elaborate preparations for a nuclear attack had been put in place. The idea that moles within the government were letting the population know the truth caused such a frisson especially since the authorities were making it known that they were in hot pursuit, not only of the leaker(s) but of everyone producing information leaflets, distributing them and even in possession of them. It all seemed hilarious and though there was some fear and caution about, laughter was the main sentiment expressed. A pastiche of the new Beatles song was on the street.

What have we here m'Lud?
A singing spy, m'Lud
"You mean he sings while spying?"
"No m'Lud he sings official secrets on the street.

"Well, I know a secret, a big official secret
But its not for the likes of you and me
Well, we all know the secret, the big official secret
Well, they call it the RSG.

That is a thing you cannae know
But we all know the secret, the big official secret
That's hidden in Warren Row.[153]

Everybody seemed to have a copy of the pamphlet naming the RSGs and their locations. There was an illicit thrill in hearing the Roneo or Gestetner whirr in the

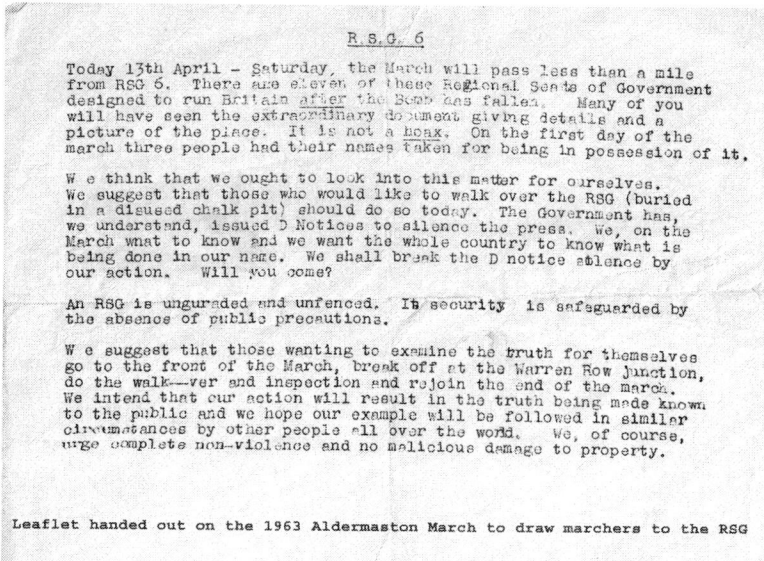

R.S.G. 6

Today 13th April – Saturday, the March will pass less than a mile from RSG 6. There are eleven of these Regional Seats of Government designed to run Britain after the Bomb has fallen. Many of you will have seen the extraordinary document giving details and a picture of the place. It is not a hoax. On the first day of the march three people had their names taken for being in possession of it.

We think that we ought to look into this matter for ourselves. We suggest that those who would like to walk over the RSG (buried in a disused chalk pit) should do so today. The Government has, we understand, issued D Notices to silence the press. We, on the March want to know and we want the whole country to know what is being done in our name. We shall break the D notice silence by our action. Will you come?

An RSG is unguarded and unfenced. Its security is safeguarded by the absence of public precautions.

We suggest that those wanting to examine the truth for themselves go to the front of the March, break off at the Warren Row junction, do the walk—ver and inspection and rejoin the end of the march. We intend that our action will result in the truth being made known to the public and we hope our example will be followed in similar circumstances by other people all over the world. We, of course, urge complete non-violence and no malicious damage to property.

Leaflet handed out on the 1963 Aldermaston March to draw marchers to the RSG

school office when everyone else had gone home. There was also misinformation. It was 'heard' that a local RSG sat under a civil service (Ministry of Agriculture Regional Office) facility at Kenton Bar. A leaflet was hastily produced and a thin line of YS and YCNDers set off to march up there leafleting on the way. This was a Saturday and the whole site was deserted. There were no police or security guards and no obvious 'secret' entrance, so to speak. What had been found was not an RSG but the operating HQ of Civil Defence (Northern). It has to be said, however, that the operations of civil defence were no less clandestine.

The sense of farce was never far away. Ludicrous instructions to seal all doors and cover your windows over with brown paper in the event of nuclear explosions were seriously offered by the authorities. Alderman Palmer, Chairman of the Wallsend Civil Defence Committee answered a CND 'interrogation' in the *Wallsend News* in January 1964 with a statement. CND's questions,'depended mainly on circumstances. Whether Wallsend would be a reception area or an evacuation area could not be answered until it was known where the Bomb had been dropped. In answer to the question which asked: Why is it assumed that the reception area is safer, Alderman Palmer said that this was obviously because the bomb had not dropped on it.'[154]

There appears to have been only one incident in the Tyneside area of actual police interest in Spies for Peace activity. Dave Douglass recounts a police raid on a flat in Heaton in 1964 where he and others were printing copies of the Spies for Peace leaflet. The officers impounded leaflets thrown from upstairs windows to the pavement below and arrested Dave and others. His autobiography gives a hilarious account of intimidation at Pilgrim Street police station but is silent on what the consequences were.[155]

Decline

Dave belonged to a group of young people who became active in 1963-64 when the mass movement, the Committee of 100 and indeed CND itself, was in decline. By mid-1964 Dave and his group, self-labelled flag-toting anarchists were centred on the ILP rooms in Byker. Initially the tiny ILP group of the elderly Barney Markson and the Secretary, the eccentric Douglas Kepper, must have been excited by the improbable arrival of droves of teenage activists but soon the wild and often drunken behaviour of 'the revolutionary youth' drew the unwelcome attention of the police and hostile neighbours. The premises' landlord brought the twenty five year old lease to an end and with it, effectively, the life of the ILP on Tyneside. The background to this was a 'debate' inside the group and round its periphery on the issue of violence. Non-violence was the *leit motif* of the Direct Action Movement and the Committee of 100 which it had spawned.

When the Committee organised a sit-down at Wethersfield in 1962 it issued a defining statement: 'We ask you not to shout slogans and to avoid provocation of any sort. The demonstrations must be carried out in a quiet, orderly way. Although we want massive support for these demonstrations, we ask you to come only if you are willing to accept this non-violent discipline.'[156] This attitude was to prevail whatever the provocation from police or political adversaries. This was a very tough demand for some of the working class kids from the pit villages and council estates of Tyneside. It tore the local group apart and activities were suspended. In June 1965 the national organisation of the Committee of 100 responded to the behaviour of the Tyneside contingent on a London demonstration and wrote to the Tyneside Secretary, as follows: 'I do not think you are suited to the job as secretary of a Committee of 100 group. You are inclined to go looking for trouble and an organisation that that believes in organised civil disobedience has to be careful not to allow that sort of thing. Your behaviour down here was disgraceful. I was deeply shocked that you should have smashed the windows of the Conservative Party Head Quarters. This is just proving to our enemies that we are exactly what they have always said we are and it solves no problems.'[157]

Desultory window breaking might be seen as symptomatic of a movement in decline. A measure of this is the number of activities taking place and the numbers participating. At its peak on Tyneside in 1960-62 there were over 60 recorded activities excluding regular meetings. From 1963-65 there were less than 20. The Aldermaston Marches peaked in 1961 with over 100,000 attending. 1962 was not far short of that whilst 1963 fell to less than 30,000 and was certainly damaged by the mass breakaway and descent upon the RSG at Ruislip. This decline in activity was compounded by the signing of the Test Ban Treaty in August '63. The movement at large did not recover. Many celebrity supporters resigned, including most of the original signatories of the Committee of 100. No Aldermaston March was organised for 1964. There was still some life in Tyneside CND. A long March from North Shields, via Wallsend, Heaton and Jesmond took place in September. Numerical weakness is registered by a November event in Newcastle being reduced to a poster Parade. There appears to have been only one local CND March on Tyneside 1964 though small local contingents went to Ruislip and London at Easter and Faslane in June.

By mid-1964 there was effectively only a rump of committed activists left. Anti-Bomb activity had mobilised several hundreds of Tynesiders since 1958. Many would never forget the excitement and the comradeship of the events, great and small. A sizeable number would take that enthusiasm into wider socialist politics in the decades which followed. Extraordinarily, of the many participants interviewed for this book none view that experience cynically.

Chapter 6: Some notes on youth culture

At some point in 1960 a fourteen year old lad from Blakelaw made contact with the 59 Society. He had recently left Secondary Modern School – well, he just stopped going – under a cloud, having had a sharp confrontation with a woodwork teacher. At 15 he had a boring job in Finneys, the seed merchants in Clayton Street, Newcastle. He was Tom Pickard. He quickly became friends with Jim Walker who was then working in the municipal parks, having graduated from King's College with a good degree. Jim had left his home in Byker and was living in a Jesmond 'commune' of poets, actors, artists and politicos. Tom was swept up into this Bohemian world. He was at home. He was already a poet, having been scribbling his free verse through adolescence.

Tom poked a knife into the sacks of seed and parted company with Finneys. In the potent mix at Buston Terrace, he met Connie Watson, moved in with her and soon became a married father. Connie was a teacher, an actress at the People's Theatre in Rye Hill, and a CND activist. They went to Aldermaston together and Connie joined the Committee of 100. As the Ban the Bomb movement started to decline, in Tom's words, 'Connie learnt the joys of a non-coercive communal activity round what she was most concerned with, poetry, and founded Morden Tower poetry centre.'[158] Tom describes, 'The Morden Tower, situated in an unlit alley, backing onto small factories emitting sulphurous fumes where prostitutes took clients for a quick turn, provided a focus for some of the finest talents in the region. Bryan Ferry, then a student at the Arts School under Richard Hamilton, was a regular visitor, and Alan Hull the singer songwriter of the folk-rock band Lindisfarne was to give his first public performance there. Hamilton was working in his studio at that time on the reconstruction of the Duchamp great glass (sculpture), *The Bride Stripped Bare By Her Bachelors* and we took Creeley[159] to see him and it in late 1964. The campaign to rescue Kurt Schwitters's [160]"wall" from the barn in the Lake District where it was deteriorating and bring it to the Hatton Gallery in Newcastle was also being organised by Hamilton.'[161]

The Morden Tower was a semi-derelict building on the western part of the Medieval town wall. It was to become a poetry venue of international repute but its real significance was surely to 'create a focus of poetical activity fomented by ordinary working class kids...sitting in smoky rooms discussing the merits of Wordsworth's writing, publishing and performing poetry every bit as sophisticated and highbrow as the poems I was reading by dead people.'[162] Maggie Anwell was 15 herself when she went along, 'I was really impressed by Tom Pickard. I was fascinated by his suitcase of carved figures and poems. He was the most surreal person I ever met. I heard Basil Bunting. It was amazing stuff. People were so imaginatively free.'[163]

Richard Hamilton, a lecturer in the Fine Art Department was an influential figure. He was an internationally famous artist, politically committed and active in CND. He was arrested and convicted at Holy Loch in 1961. Hamilton had been recruited to the Department by Victor Pasmore who had arrived in Newcastle in the early fifties. Pasmore had turned the Department upside down developing a general art and design course inspired by the 'basic course' of the Bauhaus, the revolutionary school of modernist art and design in Berlin, destroyed in 1933 by the Nazis. The course attracted adventurous students and was a breeding ground for the university left. Ann Berg enjoyed the space offered by the experimental regime where students could develop their own ideas. She was interested in the Constructivists in the early days of the Russian Revolution. She designed political leaflets and posters including the cover of the first Communist Society magazine.

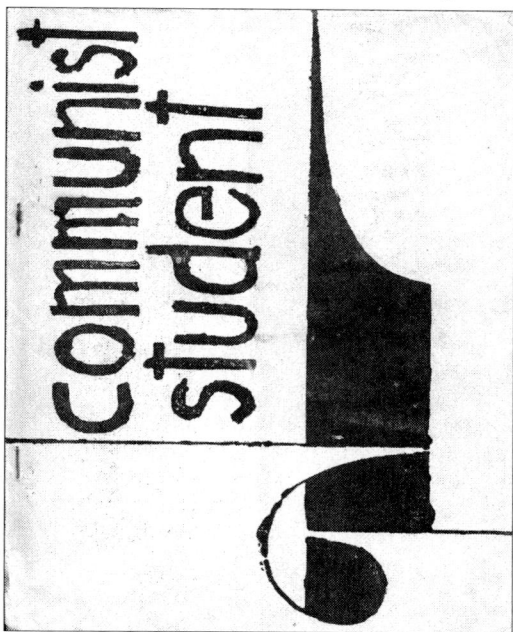

Cover design by Ann Berg

Barry Scaum was there from 1954 to 1959. After performing badly in their second year exams due to spending their time in the Dramatic Society rather than the Studio, he, Ralph Watson and Fred Pearson were all told to do National Service, after which they might be re-admitted to the course. For Barry, 'the Education Corps was an easy option served at Catterick, processing recruits at a rate of 200 per month.'

The Morden Tower was a focal point which brought students and town youngsters together with culture and politics. King's College Dramatic Society was another. Connie and Tom were involved there too. They played Viola and Sebastian in *Twelfth Night*, to a Durham audience, directed by People's theatre actor, David Prosser. Kyran Casteel, a geography student member of the Socialist Society and Labour Club did scene painting for this production and for *The Trojan Women* which went to the Edinburgh Festival.[164] Most of these people also acted at the People's Theatre. Barry Scaum is remembered by Jack Shepherd as the star of a 1961 review, *Four for a Season*, 'dressed like the rest of us in bowler hat, leotard and tights; (he) sported National Health spectacles and an enormous ginger beard. He was inspired. A working class Lytton Strachey on acid.'[165]

At 16, Maggie Anwell was playing Cordelia in *King Lear*.[166] Pat Marley and Mary Feinmann had walk on parts in *Richard II* and *The Good Woman of Setzuan*. Marge Wallace also worked backstage. Of course many young people went to the performances, like Moira Woods, dragged along by her socialist Dad.[167]

Poetry, Art and Drama also linked to the town's music scene. 'It's hard... to realise the straitjacket that was popular music in the 1950s. It was tenors and sopranos singing anodyne pop music and stuff from the shows, Alma Cogan and Edmund Hockridge, *Oklahoma* and *South Pacific*.'[168]When Jim Hutchinson went to Kings College, as late as 1959, the Union's Saturday night hop featured Henner Hudspeth's Dance Orchestra. Although Bill Haley and the Comets had appeared at the Odeon, Pilgrim Street in February 1957, it was the end of the decade before Tynesiders could 'rock around the clock.' The Oxford Gallery forbade jiving till 1960 but then introduced Saturday afternoon sessions for teenagers too young for the pub scene.

In 1958 Paul Robeson performed on Tyneside invited by the Trades Council.[169] It was arranged by the Secretary, Don Edwards, and his daughter Irene met Robeson. Pat and Kathleen Marley were taken to his dressing room. Their father's company Rediffusion provided the PA system for the Hall. Pat remembers asking Robeson why he needed loudspeakers and he replied, 'I have to keep my voice under control. Performing nearly every night, if I let it go I'd lose it.' She remembered him as very warm and friendly. The City Hall was filled to capacity.

The *Evening Chronicle* was lyrical in its praise for his performance, 'His deep resonant voice is intense and compelling whether he speaks or sings, and his smile is infectious. His repertoire varied from a transcription of the theme from the last movement of Beethoven's Ninth Symphony to *Old Man River*, plantation songs, chants and religious songs. He recounted an extract from *Othello* (whom he was playing at Stratford that year) joked and told the audience of his pleasure at being back on Tyneside.'[170]Irene remembered it being a great moment for the Trades Council and her father, who had also engineered to bring Joan Littlewood's Theatre Workshop to the town in 1957.[171] Robeson's visit and his reception was an act of solidarity since the US State Department had taken his passport away.

Louis Armstrong had played the contained setting of the City Hall in 1956. Jazz and folk, minority tastes, had put markers down with regular local venues in the mid-fifties. The New Orleans Jazz Club at Melbourne Street in Shieldfield, opened in 1955, the Marlborough Street Jazz Club, 1958, and the Newcastle Folk Club at 'the Sink,' the Barras Bridge Hotel, in 1958 before settling at The Bridge Hotel a year later.

The latter 'venue' was Newcastle's socialist and Irish republican watering hole from the early fifties. Folk music had a strong political strand. It was not surprising that the two worlds should meet at the Bridge. It was not straightforward, however. There were Folk enthusiasts who wished to keep politics at bay and for a time the Newcastle Folk Club did just that. This was not to the liking of the Elliot family of Birtley. They were firmly socialist and as we have mentioned, keen League of Youth activists in the first decade after the War. Coming from a similar political direction was the Young Communist League, some of whose members were strongly involved in folk music. Part of Lucy Nicholson's family were pit folk from Craghead, only a few miles west of Birtley. Lucy's grand parents' house was a cornucopia of music and musical instruments for a child with aptitude. Her aunt Dolly was 'a great boogy woogy player as she had heard a black American playing on big black records(78 rpm)...she knew how to roll with her left hand playing the base notes...she was breath of fresh air, dressed like a film star and smoked like Bette Davis and was a bit of a flapper.' Dolly also owned 'a small white accordion in a black case... She mastered it and handled it well.' Her husband 'looked like Errol Flynn and had a melodious voices and knew millions of dirty songs.' She also heard the pit band practicing at the Institute. 'You can learn all about harmony by listening to the way that two tunes can slot together in brass sections.' Someone left a mouth organ and Lucy took it out into the allotment 'till I perfected every tune I'd ever heard.' Then she heard the banjo'.[172]

As a teenager and young adult Lucy was part of a YCL group who were the mainstays of entertainment at socials and demonstrations. On Sunday nights, after politicking in the Bigg Market, they sang at The Old George in the Cloth market. Jim Hutchinson recalls Lucy and Bill Phillips singing, *'Does it take a soldier's pay, Billy Boy, Billy Boy, to die for Dunlop in Malaya, Billy Boy, Billy Boy?'*[173]

Alex Glasgow occupied a special place in this crowd. He was among the most explicitly political of the new performers. 'He had his own uncompromising style, writing his own songs. He was very popular with a discerning audience, demanding that people listen to his lyrics. He did fund raising benefits for

Alex Glasgow

political groups and strikers. He didn't always go down well with the latter used to pop music.' [174] Jim says, 'When I first met Alex he wore a black leather jacket which I later learnt was what all returning musicians from Germany wore.'[175]

John Creaby was also caught up with the Folk Revival. He said, 'I was a regular attender at the Bridge and Birtley Clubs...the Clubs were filled with (beer drinking and often raucous) young chorus singers. It was here that I learned a whole repertoire of traditional and contemporary songs. There were a lot of IWW songs like, *Union Maid*,

Solidarity for Ever, Joe Hill and *Which Side are you on?* I also learned from the US Civil Rights Movement, *Oh Freedom, If you miss me at the back of the bus,* and *We Shall Overcome.* These came mainly from Topic and Folkways Records.[176] Music seems to have run almost through John's veins. He also recalls being introduced by Mike Down and Mike Worrall to 'true blues artists like Big Bill Broonzy and Huddy Leadbetter and their songs, *Black, Brown and White and Bourgeois Blues*' from records and song sheets.

What Lucy and John may not have been aware of at the time was that they were part of a musical effervescence on Tyneside. If folk with its long roots led the way, newer (and older) genres of music arrived to excite the new generation. In Newcastle, to add to the new Jazz and Folk venues, clubs appeared, like the Downbeat, in a disused warehouse in Carliol Square, and the Club A Gogo on Percy Street. They featured an eclectic mix of trad and modern jazz, rhythm and blues, rock and pop: Alex Harvey, Spencer Davies, Eric Burdon, the Beatles, the Stones and Brian Ferry.[177] By 1961-62 the University Union had moved on too, to Howling Wolf, Ginger Baker and Dave Rowberry, the latter also tinkling piano at the Percy Arms.

The Animals and Lindisfarne emerged. They were the ones to achieve international celebrity but countless other groups were spawned, burned and died across the north east in this multi-faceted musical renaissance. And, like poetry, art and drama, it all somehow dovetailed with the new politics of protest.

Chapter seven: 'The fifty nine'[178]

In the Autumn of 1959 I started my first teaching job at Bolam Street Secondary Modern on a hill in Byker, a school dating from the 1890s. It was rough. And so was the staff room with a turnover of twenty seven in an establishment of thirteen in the one year I was there. Among the twenty seven was a most unpleasant figure, a prematurely grey haired, dark suited, smooth, posh talking Geordie, called Fergus Montgomery, 31 rising 50. I was then a very shallowly informed political lefty. Each morning as I entered the staff room, he would call out, 'so how is the left wing yellow press today,' a reference to my *Manchester Guardian*. I was usually too tongue-tied to retaliate. Montgomery was serving out his time waiting for the declaration of a General Election. He had been adopted as the Tory Candidate for Newcastle East. It came only a few weeks into the term. By the last week in September I was wreaking my revenge for his attacks by canvassing for Arthur Blenkinsop. Along with Roger Hall, I trudged the streets of Heaton and Byker asking people to support Good Old Arthur whom they had known since 1945.

The papers were full of the election, featuring simplistic and uncritical interviews with the candidates who appeared at meetings in Town Halls, Libraries and Church Halls. Horror was expressed by a Tory that his poster had been torn down in Gateshead whilst 'hotheads plastered the home of Rowland Scott-Batey,' Chairman of the City Labour Party. The correspondence columns zinged with letters warning the readers of a Labour victory. It was usually the threat of further nationalisation and communism but one cried of 'Nasser riding up Northumberland Street' if Labour was elected. Suez was not far in the past.

On Polling Day, Thursday October 8th, I was assigned to 'knock up' with the then General Secretary of the Boilermakers' Union, Danny McGarvey, who drove a big Rover, the largest car I had ever sat in. 'We'll be coonting on your support Mrs,' he announced on the doorstep with absolute conviction. 'Oh Aye,' the lady would reply. End of interchange and on to the next door down Grace Street. I think I was surprised at the time by the brevity of the interviews. 'No time for discussion,' was McGarvey's response. Indeed, that had been advice delivered on earlier canvassing expeditions. "We just want to identify our supporters. Don't argue. It wastes time. If there are any genuine (sic) questions take a note and Arthur will follow them up," said Bob, the

Agent's man. I guess this was my second lesson in Labour politics. The first also came from McGarvey. 'The workers are ungrateful bastards. We've given them a Health Service. We've given them jobs. If the buggers could be bothered to get out and vote there'd be a Labour Government for a century.'

McGarvey was a Tory hater from Glasgow. His savagery against Montgomery was almost shocking, though welcome to my ears, smarting from his staff room sneers. Had I been with him after the count it would no doubt have been sulphurous. For Arthur was out, by 98 votes after two recounts. The class traitor, son of a Jarrow Marcher, so McGarvey had it, had won. And, in a strange way he had won me for socialism. The atmosphere at the count was intense and very weepy. Roger and I tagged onto the 'official party' and were lifted across town to the Blenkinsop wake in Wingrove Road, Fenham. I remember Arthur as all sad grace and geniality, betraying absolutely no bitterness. He wrote in the *Evening Chronicle* a few days later that the election had been lost because of an excess of materialism in the population. What was needed, he said, was more socialism, not less. Bitterness was left to his acolytes. In a few short hours I had numbered myself among them and was determined to do something.

Labour Party secretary, Joe Eagles and Eric Walker

First step

I arranged to meet Arthur's son, David, a student at Kings' College, the next afternoon after work. We went down to Victoria Square where the City Labour Party had its offices to meet Joe Eagles and Roly Scott-Batey. Joe, a tall, gaunt and very shrewd man in his fifties was full-time Secretary and I think., though Catholic, probably a secret fellow traveller. He was an ex-miner from Lancashire via Workington or Whitehaven. He was taciturn, pretty good humoured and ready to assist the youngsters to try to get things moving. Scott-Batey was a large bluff ginger haired man turning grey. He was a key figure in the group which had recently wrested control of the City party from the truly unholy alliance of Catholics and freemasons. The front man was T Dan Smith, Chairman of the Housing Committee and promising the earth to the folks of Elswick and Scotswood. Also present was a young postal worker, Alan Elliot, who lived with his Aunt Bertha in a flat in that building. Bertha Elliot was the Labour Agent for Darlington and the daughter of Alderman Hancock a railway worker and one time leader of Gateshead Council.

In the inquest which followed what had been Labour's third successive General Election defeat, there was a big focus on the missing youth vote. One simplistic explanation was the absence of a youth section since 1955, when the League of Youth had been disbanded to stop 'Trot infiltration' in the shape of Gerry Healy's Socialist Labour League. Eagles explained that it would not be possible to found a Young Socialist group because of the ban but it might be possible to have a young socialist group. It may have been my non-Labour traditional mind which came up with the innocuously un-political name, *The 59 Society*.

Guy Falkenau came to the new group in a more obvious way. When only 12 he had attended a London demonstration in 1956 on the Suez question with his Aunt Bertha(Elliott). He says that 'I described to my father how demonstrators had been charged by mounted police in Whitehall. He asked why we hadn't scattered ball bearings under the hooves of the police horses as he'd seen striking miners do in Brussels before the war.' After a family crisis Guy had been sent to live in Gateshead with his grandfather, Peter Hancock. He was quickly pitched into political activity attending meetings, canvassing during local elections and going on demos, like the one above, with his redoubtable Aunt Bertha. Despite the embargo on local youth sections since 1956, some local Labour Parties, like Gateshead, did have youth sections. Guy joined and in 1959 he went to a summer school at Coleg Harlech, the Welsh labour college, where he met other young socialists.

Within months Gateshead youth section was thriving and rapidly shifting leftwards despite the vigilance of the party Secretary Agent, Harry Luxton. Guy was soon joined by John Creaby whom he saw as an exotic figure, 'John's bedroom was like entering a Bedouin tent. He was busy brewing exotic tea in an ornate kettle,

Jim Walker & Guy Falkenau

whilst a hookah bubbled away in the corner of the room.'[179]

If Guy's background was pretty much 'pure politics,' John's was cut with religion for he was reared in a strange mix, a Catholic-Communist home. He says, 'We, the children, went to church on Sunday and attended a church school...as an adolescent I became caught up in the ritual, the Latin liturgy, music, the culture and splendour of the church. From this developed an awareness of Christian ethics; concern for what was right and wrong, good or evil, the cause and consequence and accountability (to God) for your action. Religion began to have a real role in my life.' He even thought of joining the priesthood. In 1958 he joined the Young Christian Workers. It had a radical social ideology with links to the Labour Party.[180]

Guy and John went on the 1959 Aldermaston March, as school students. That exciting spring was followed by a summer and early autumn campaigning in Darlington by his Aunt Bertha Elliott. Guy was already a 'seasoned campaigner at 14 and was given the job of organizing polling day transport of 'almost 100 vehicles.' He recalls Alf Robens, MP of the Labour Shadow Cabinet and future butcher of the coal industry, committing a faux pas 'by arriving at Darlington Bank Top Station sporting a red rosette, the Tory colours in the north east. Labour's colour in the region, reflecting its origins in the Irish communities, was green!' Guy was to suffer his first political disappointment.[181] The Tories won Darlington and, indeed, the General Election.

Irene (Edwards) Lovell was another recruit from a socialist family. She was introduced to the new group by her dad, Don Edwards, the ETU official, who had been told about its appearance by Arthur Blenkinsop. Irene was 19 and a three year 'veteran' of work – at the Ministry of Pensions at Longbenton. She became one of the most committed of members involved in virtually every activity, political and especially social.[182]

After first meeting with Joe Eagles I had written to a number of friends about the new initiative. These included Jim Walker whom I had known from school at Heaton Grammar. He had also canvassed in the Newcastle East constituency. He wrote, 'John Charlton sent me a note (we didn't have telephones in those days) and I replied typically, with a pompous verse that ended: "Need you ask? /I know my task – for I live in Newcastle East." 'Jim was active in the Kings College Socialist Society. He was a magnet, with a lot of charisma, though he'd have denied that. He pulled several socialist students along with him including a second year Metallurgy student Jim Hutchinson, another old Heatonian, who was to become a stalwart of the Society and, indeed of the Tyneside socialist movement for the rest of his life. My other school friend, Roger Hall, had gone back to Manchester University after the Election. He was a final year student, and was to be a vacation member of the 59. Mike Worrall, who lived above the Labour Party office in Victoria Square was a post graduate scientist already active in both the Party and CND.

Mike Down arrived at Victoria Square (LP offices) independently. He wrote, 'I chose to go to Kings in 1959 because it was as far as I could get from the Isle of Wight while still receiving my grant from the IoW County Council (£80 a term plus the fare – I always hitch-hiked up the A1 and pocketed the cash). I thought Durham and Newcastle were the same place. I was billeted at Whitley Bay – a cold, bleak and windswept place after summer on the IoW. I quickly moved to Heaton and ate tasteless, soggy Sunday lunch watching *Bonanza* on TV with the landlady and her Alzheimer suffering mother. The first thing I did was visit the Labour Party rooms in Victoria Square. I met Joe Eagles, the local agent, and his tenant Michael Worrall. He became a close friend and ally. Joe Eagles was not a member of CND but neither was he hostile. He probably believed CND and all single-issue politics was a diversion from what really mattered viz. winning power in order to improve education, housing and so on. But these things never interested me very much. The world was about to be blown up and anyway people in Africa and Asia were suffering much more than people in Newcastle.

Mike Down, John Charlton & Guy Falkenau

I suspect most of the middle class angry young men of this time felt much the same.'[183]

The Marley sisters, Pat 18, and Kath 16, were also present at the first meeting. Both were pupils at the Church High School though Pat was about to go off to Darlington Teachers' Training College. They came from a fiercely left wing home. Their father, Fred, had been Konni Zilliacus's agent in Gateshead in the election after Zillie had been de-selected and stood as a independent socialist. By the end of the fifties Fred Marley, a very able organizer, was a key person in the local CND organization. The Marleys had also been to Aldermaston that spring.[184] Mary Feinmann was a sixth form student from the Central High School. Both sets of parents were long time Labour activists.

Marge Wallace was a 17 year old sixth form student from Dame Allen's Girls' School which gave the new society an unlikely foothold in all three of the Direct Grant girls' high schools in Newcastle. Her parents were also strong socialists. Her father, Peter, belonged to a group of radical blind people who had struggled against discrimination and patronizing attitudes to assert their rights. They took part in marches and were active in the Labour Party. Three blind men served as Newcastle city Councillors. One was Lionel Anwell the father of Marge's family friend, Maggie, who joined a little later. Several more girls from the direct grant schools followed this quartet into the Society over the following months.

Friday nights

By the end of October the new society had started to meet weekly on Fridays in Victoria Square. The first meeting was attended by over twenty people. The *Evening Chronicle* announced its arrival and reported: 'John Charlton (school teacher) elected Chairman, Margaret Pearson (clerk), Secretary, Walter Wilson (clerk), Treasurer and Jim Walker (student), Press Officer'. Margaret, from a Byker Labour Party family worked at the clerical workers' union office and was active in the union. Jim took his duties seriously and was soon in print attacking the 'fake' Tory trade unionist, Ray Mawby, who had called for the government to enact a contracting in policy for workplace Trades Union subscriptions. Jim thundered, "Can Mr Mawby deny that 'his' firm support for Conservatism comes out of the vast profits of big business? Socialist money as well as 'conservative money contributes to these profits—with NO option to contract out." '[185]

Walter Wilson was probably the only survivor in the new group from the disbanded League of Youth. He was a well established Labour Party activist in the Newcastle Central Constituency, perhaps the only one who had done National Service in the mid-fifties. He was on the upper end of what was to become the age limit of the new Labour Party YS. Walter was a clerical worker who always turned out immaculately in suit and tie. Correctly or incorrectly, he was widely suspected of being there to keep an eye on what were perceived to be a bunch of wild young people. The truth is his watch was limited for, though an amiable person who took jibes very well, he did not socialize with the group at all and exercised no influence. He was defeated when he stood for Treasurer at the 1960 AGM.

Though left wing, the new recruits were by no means Marxist entrists. Indeed the most likely 'entrists' at that time would have been Stalinists. The CP, although reeling from Kruschev's revelations of 1956, was still an active force on the left and many young lefties had CP connections. Irene Edwards, for example, was the daughter of Don Edwards an official of the Electrical Trades Union and a former local CP activist, soon to be investigated as the establishment Macarthyites closed in on the Electrical Trades Union leaders, the two Franks, Foulkes and Haxell. Don appeared to move right and survived, though remaining a friend to the left.

Fluid ideas

Over fifty people have been contacted about this project. They have usually been asked about their beliefs fifty years ago. It is a tough call to remember how one's mind worked in one's teens and twenties. Almost inevitably, old ideas are overlaid with subsequent experience. There are at least two further problems. The time frame is about five years and those five years of late adolescence and early twenties are probably the space in life when ideas change most and most rapidly. The second point, perhaps slightly easier to deal with, is the fact that many individuals are involved and there were perhaps as many perspectives as individuals.

The first port of call is memory. Subsequently we can look at papers and magazines to which people were in some degree attached. This is just a rule of thumb because we can't assume that readers necessarily either understood or completely agreed with what they read. Given all these caveats we can begin to look for an answer.

Ideas were in a very fluid state. Three electoral defeats in succession had seriously shaken up the Labour Party. The national leadership under Hugh Gaitskell was very ready to blame the left but this was often received unsympathetically at local party level. I made Joe Eagles very cross at our first encounter by quite innocently suggesting that Labour's best hope electorally might be to join up with the Liberals. I recall a snort accompanied by an 'invitation' to 'join them, then.' My comments were probably mis-borrowed from an article on Labour's future in the *Evening Chronicle* in that week. The author was described as 'an intellectual, a university member of the Fabian Society.' He was probably its Secretary, historian Ted (Edward) Hughes. He argued that Labour must free itself from socialist dogma in order to win back prosperous (sic) working class people who had voted Liberal in the election. At some point Bob Griffin, an elderly teacher and active NUT member of my acquaintance, invited Jim Walker and myself to Fabian Society meetings. It met at a house in Windsor Terrace, probably Ted Hughes'. Though it was welcoming and some of the speakers were interesting, it seemed a much older set, not interested in action. It felt very staid alongside the flighty '59.

Sam Dodds thinks that he, Jim Nichol and a few others were talking about ideas even before they came in contact with the YS. He says, 'my parents – they were Labour voters of course – just sort of accepted things as they were just sort of accepted things as they were, sort of apathetic. We wanted to change things and thought we could. We wanted better education opportunities, more equal shares, better welfare, world peace and so on…'[186]

What none of us had was any real grasp or context for the deep tides which moved society or for the very long project ahead. We sniggered at the patrician self confidence of Supermac with his cynical leer as he proclaimed 'You've never had it so good.' But there <u>was</u> full employment according to the definition of bourgeois economists. When I left my first teaching job after one year in 1960, my choice was enormous. The *Evening Chronicle*' Situations Vacant columns were ripe with opportunity. There was a growing access to consumer goods. My father, a co-op insurance agent since 1955, had his own car. He rented a TV. The house had just acquired 'a fitted carpet.'

The Midland Bank advertised in the *Evening Chronicle,* inviting the public to take a personal cheque book, 'So much easier. No pockets full of change. A safer and convenient way to handle your finances.' The much attacked wild-cat strike was pushing wage rates up. There was confidence in the working class. The Donovan Commission of 1968 found that rank and file shop floor organisation had burgeoned for over a decade to produce a force of 250,000 shop stewards. The paradox was that economic militancy did not lead into a drive for socialist politics. The Blenkinsop solution: 'More socialism. Not less,' with its millenial moralism plus nationalisation was washed up. Gaitskell's and Crosland's 'managed capitalism' conceding ground to the right was fatally flawed by its subservience to the Atlantic Alliance and the multi-nationals; in the eyes of the young socialists, at least.

Yet change was in the air. Young people did not like H Bomb diplomacy conducted by dinosaurs like Foster Dulles. The black and white image of the mushroom cloud over forlorn Japanese survivors of Hiroshima was a depressing part of our mental landscape. Scares about Strontium 90 in our milk supply made people very angry. The Bomb was the big issue of the day. Many young people truly feared imminent catastrophe. Almost everyone cites the Bomb as the single issue which had preoccupied them in their teenage years.

But it was not the only one. There was also a sometimes vague yearning for a socialist society. Few were attracted to the existing models: the Soviet Union, China and Yugoslavia. The image of tanks rolling into Budapest was a severe handicap for the Moscow model, though some hung on to the view that Hungary was an aberration and was nothing to do with the pursuit of communism for Britain. Harry Rothman felt that Hungary was viewed as 'over there.' It should not get in the way of the pursuit of justice and equality in Britain. It did not appear to prevent the Communist Society at Kings College recruiting some 60 members by

Jennifer Piachaud

Tricia Sorbie

1961.[187]Despite the impact of Krushchev's 1956 revelations and Hungary, young communists seemed confident and coherent, at least much more so than the new young socialists. The Kings College Communist Society published its own magazine full of articles on a wide range of subjects including international affairs and culture.

The members of *The 59 Society* came from a variety of different backgrounds of which the strongest was CND. The Labour Party was less than a year away from turning unilateralist at the 1960 Annual Conference. Tyneside CND, formed in 1957, was already a large organisation. The Ban the Bomb campaign delivered a wide range of young people. Mary Feinmann, Fiona Scott-Batey and Jane Owens daughters of Labour councillors, Jesse Scott Batey and Tess Owens came from the Central High School. Jennifer Piachaud, whose father was a consultant at the General Hospital, like her friends, the Marleys came from the Church High School and there was a strong contingent from Dame Allan's Girls' School including Brenda Ingleby, Tricia Sorbie, Margaret Anwell, Nickie Landau, Linda Potts, Pam Hepburn, Dorothy Simmons, Pam Garrett, Margaret Dick and Dan Smith's daughter, Gillian. Most of them had socialist parents.

There were fewer boys from private sector schools. They included the fifteen year old Jeremy Beecham, Harvey White, Chris Blue and David, son of Councillors Harry and Theresa Russell all from the Royal Grammar School and mostly with Labour Party backgrounds. These boys were from Jewish homes where the Labour Party was still relatively strong reflecting the anti-semitism and persecution by the British establishment before the Second World War. Prosperous middle class boys were destined for careers in the professions and business, the Jewish experience having a cross current of discrimination which might still lead to the left. Only Alistair Graham, from Morpeth, of the RGS boys, stood out with a non-Jewish background.

The large number of females perhaps suggest an early challenge to the patrician values of the fifties. Several of the women interviewed commented upon parental attitudes privileging their brothers' futures over theirs. On the other hand, several speak of more positive attitudes from their schools where university and career were promoted. These same attitudes contributed to the birth of the new women's movement a decade later. Some also remark on the arrival of the birth control pill in 1962 as a factor in opening out attitudes.

Ann Berg

Students

A year or two older than most of this coterie were the students from Kings College. Here the gender situation was exactly reversed. There was Mike Down,

Harry Rothman and his impressive array of athletics trophies

Jim Walker, Jim Hutchinson, Miles Hutchinson (no relation), Kyran Casteel, John Metcalf, Tony Corcoran and Brian Ebbatson. Mike Down, and possibly others, operated dual membership with the YCL which was also well represented among students with Harry Rothman, Dave Leigh, Ann Berg, Ann Kane and Lu Bell.

This influx to radical politics was associated with the widening of educational opportunities for the post-1944 Education Act generation. The classic image of students wielding staves for the establishment in the General Strike was replaced by college scarves on Ban the Bomb demos. Their parents were often working class or lower middle class and several had radical histories. Harry Rothman came to Newcastle in 1956 to study Zoology. He was born in Cheshire in 1937. His father was a second generation Jewish migrant from Eastern Europe who fallen out with his family after marrying 'out' to a woman cotton spinner. He was a skilled engineer. Benny and his wife, Lily, both joined the CP in the thirties and he achieved fame and notoriety by leading the Kinder Scout mass trespass in 1936. Harry was instrumental in organising a Communist student branch at Kings' College in the wake of the turmoil in the CP, following 1956.

Harry Rothman was joined by Dave Leigh, a determined and able organizer, well read in the Marxist classics. A research student in the Mining Engineering Department Leigh also came from a Jewish communist family. His were East Londoners, of whom he says, more than a dozen were CP members. His father was a working class east ender whose parents had arrived from Lithuania and Russia respectively in the 1890s. The CP Branch was formed from Kings College students and the Fine Art Department supplied several activists like Ann Berg, another Londoner, came from an affluent left wing family. She was to marry Harry Rothman and make a living as working artist. She was one of several art students and some teachers who gravitated to the left. The Kings' College Fine Art Department was perhaps the only academic department which could be described as radical in the mid-fifties. The relationship between 'modernism' and radicalism in the field of Fine Art created a more enduring basis for alternative thinking in the early Cold War era than was the case in other disciplines.

Mike Down was an undergraduate biology student. His father had gone to Charterhouse school and then Sandhurst. He wrote, 'He was a professional soldier, served in the First World War (the Somme) and later in Ireland. He left the army in the mid thirties, trained as a chef/manager at the Trocadero in London, married my mother in 1936, moved to the Isle of Wight. They sank their savings into Greengates Hotel, Seaview, just in time for the cessation of all business for years to come. My mother was Catholic and fell out with her family by marrying an agnostic/Cof E divorcee. My half brother was a fighter pilot. I learned much later that he downed six enemy planes the year I was born. Incredibly I knew none of this until after my parents had both died.'

Peer Groups

Ann Kane, a biology student, was the daughter of Jock Kane the South Yorkshire NUM leader. He and his wife Betty had been in the CP since the 1920s and had gone to the Lenin School in Moscow in the early 30s. Jock's brother Mick had been gaoled for two years after a celebrated strike victory at Harworth, Notts, in 1937.[188] So, Ann had been reared in a CP family rooted in the village of Armthorpe near Doncaster. She says,'I was devoted to my father who was very popular in his local community even during the Cold War period. We kept an open door for anyone with troubles... My closest friends (before University) were also in the YCL,' she reports, stressing the importance of the peer group in political outcomes. Her sister in a non-political school peer group did not become involved politically though she would consider herself left wing.[189] Ann had been to at least one Aldermaston March when she arrived at Kings' College in 1961 to study biology. She took her politics seriously as a student 'perhaps to the detriment of my studies. I sold the *Daily Worker* regularly on the Union steps.'[190]

The point about peer groups is well made. Peer group influence has been a persistent subject of inquiry. It has been of particular interest to academics and professionals interested in the causes of deviance, habit forming and school performance. Very few scholars have looked at its significance in building political association. It is relevant in the sense that Ann Kane uses it –

recruitment to politics, or indeed non-recruitment where other factors might suggest it likely; the different directions taken by siblings from a politically active home environment. Peer group theory largely supports the idea of adolescent contemporaries having more influence than parents on behaviour.

In this collection of individuals there appears to have been at least eight peer groups operating before the individuals became politically active, though in three cases individuals were thrown together because their parents were friends and activists (e.g. Ann Kane and her friends, the Feinmanns and Marleys and the Scott Bateys and Owens). These political affinities seem to have helped to act to draw other contemporaries round them. The Dame Allen's school students seem to have three separate peer groups and all were formed before active politics took hold though parental friendships were important in one case (Wallace and Anwell). The Heaton (Charlton, Hall, Denton and Walker) and Gateshead Grammar School groups (Sharp, Scott and Paxton) also pre-dated political involvement. Apart from the obvious cases (Feinmann, Marley and Scott-Batey Owens) none of the rest seem to have come from active or specially socialist home backgrounds (Ingleby, Sorbie/Potts, Simmons) though most parents were thought to have been at least, Labour voters. Though caution is always called for with small samples of people, the suggestion is strong that peer group pressure was an important ingredient in the growth of this movement. The literature on peer groups usually cites the importance of a strong or charismatic individual at the centre of a group. This was probably widely the

John & Margaret Creaby

case in these groups (Jim Nichol and the Westerhope Group/ Mary Feinmann/ Marge Wallace/Brian Sharp) though active politics is such a public activity that peer groups might draw together confident and articulate people anyway.

Outwards

From the town in the first tranche of 59 Society members there were few from manual working class families or working in manual jobs. Peter Wilton from Fenham, Frank Wilson from Westerhope and Peter Laing from Kenton were clerks. Roger Carroll also from the West End, one of the very few Gaitskell supporters, became a Fleet Street tabloid journalist. Terry Watson, who entered the library service came from a street in Scotswood where, 'everybody was Labour'.[191] A young apprentice electrician recruit from Gosforth, Eric Mirley joined too, but he died in his very early twenties.

A group from Gateshead and Felling started to attend the 59 Society, following Guy Falkenau and John Creaby. There was Doug Jackson, a Co-op undertaker, Gail Lawrence, who later became a teacher and Brenda Rankin. Brenda was the daughter of a Bakers' Union official. She became a journalist on the *Yorkshire Post*.[192] From Felling there were the Southern sisters, Margaret, and Ann who died young. Their brother Herbie was also involved. They were the children of long time Labour Party stalwarts in Felling. Mike Whitaker, also from Felling worked at International Paints and was a highly unusual young worker at that time because he owned a car. He was in great demand!

In late 1960 the social mix was further shifted a bit by an influx of young workers from Newburn, Westerhope and Scotswood including the fifteen year old national Coal Board clerk Jim Nichol, Sam Dodds, Mick Slatter, Jenn Scott and Val Nicholson. Jenn says that she heard about the Young Socialists from a leafletter in town. She was the daughter of Bob Scott, the first post war leader of Newcastle City Council. He was a railway worker whose active political history went back to the General Strike in 1926. He had died in 1947 when only 43. His daughter was just 2 years old. Jenn's cousin Val was a tough fighting woman who worked in the Co-op optician's Department. In her twenties she became a lay official of USDAW, sadly dying in her late thirties.[193]

Sam Dodds was part of the Westerhope group encouraged to get involved by his friend Jim Nichol. He says, our interest in politics started at about 13 or 14. We'd run round with flyers for the LP at election times but then we wanted to know a bit more. We'd go to the Bigg Market on Sunday nights to listen to all sorts of speakers on their soap boxes. We did some proper canvassing for Ernie Popplewell in the 1959 Election and heard about young socialists meeting in Jesmond.[194]

Meetings in the early days were lively and, largely, comradely. There was always a speaker. We heard Dan Smith. His vaulting imagination spoke of the new Newcastle, a 'Venice of the North,' Eric Walker from the Fabian Society gave us 'Comprehensive Education' and 'Hadrian's Wall', Dick Kelly from the BBC, 'Broadcasting and Free Speech' and Doris Starkey 'The Co-operative Movement.' A Polish immigrant, Fabian Koseda, from the National Council of Labour Colleges spoke on 'Economics' and sold books by GDH Cole and Tressall from a battered brown suitcase. There were several speakers on the Bomb and peace, Don Edwards on 'Trade Unionism Today,'just before the notorious ETU case at the High Court, Professor Neil Jenkins, from the Socialist Medical Association on 'A Socialist Health Service.' He was pushing fluoridation of children's teeth. Jack Cadogan, brother of the Peter, the socialist intellectual talked on'The Coal Industry Today.' The industry was just experiencing its first major assault after nationalisation. Northumberland and Durham were threatened with a 10% cut in labour from 243,000 mine workers! The railwayman MP, Ernie Popplewell, spoke pompously, lecturing us on our susceptibility to 'vicarious celluloid images'. He couldn't say, 'movies.' This was par for the course from a former Master of the King's Bedchamber in the Attlee government. There were no meetings on historical or theoretical topics apart from Koseda's incomprehensible one on economics. Strangely, not a single member gave a lecture to the group. Young socialists were still clearly tied into a paternalistic relationship with the Labour Party.

Meetings ended with a trail along Jesmond Road to the Royal Oak on Claremont Road where there was once a memorable pavement confrontation with the Tory MP for Newcastle North, R W Elliot. His urbane supercilious

ANTI-APARTHEID MARCH NEWCASTLE 1960
Tony Cortcoron, Madeleine Wise, May Smailes, not known,

calm ended with a threat to have us horse whipped when 'red' fingers wagged under his nose.

Marches ...

The sustaining activities were the marches. Apart from the great annual CND one from Aldermaston, there were many other marches. 'It was a Saturday, and there was a march through the town and we managed to get a chant going: "boycott South African goods". Quite a lot of Quakers participated, too. Regrettably 3 or 4 Africans showed up after the march had taken place so could not join in. We also had a stall in the Bigg Market with various speakers. I remember vividly that Guy[Falkenau] was one of them, and I also remember being very impressed that someone so young could speak so well (and for that matter, had the courage to speak in public!).'[195] This was the first march, in November 1959. It was organised by a South African Communist student, Tony Seedat and Ursula Massey, a former teacher in Nigeria. Planning meetings were held in her flat in Windsor Terrace. The *Evening Chronicle* carried overtly racist letters attacking the marchers in the following weeks. A further protest, partly organised by the 59 Society took place, following the massacre at Sharpeville in March 1960,[196] also emphasized the theme of boycotting South African goods.

May Day events were a great labour movement ritual. Members of its great sections, political, industrial and co-operative would turn out in droves. It was popular with young socialists who could indulge their artistic flare. From 7.30

Newcastle May Day March. Front: Ted Short MP, Arthur Blenkinsop MP, Will Owen MP, Manny Shinwell MP; rear: Kate Scott, Roley Scott Batey, Mary Shaw and Dan Smith

on the morning of the procession, numerous enthusiasts would turn up outside the Newgate Street Co-op store to decorate the floats with elaborate, themed tableaus. There could be twenty of them. In 1960, the 59 Society's theme was 'Ban the Bomb.' Doris Starkey, the march organiser in chief, would be scurrying around giving orders – sending people into the Co-op haberdashery to get more ribbon – someone else, to the garage to find out where the Coxlodge Women's Guild truck had got to – settling a dispute – responding to a message about a speaker for the final rally – organising pots of tea.

Sometime after noon the floats would make their way down to the assembly point outside the Central Station where they would form up behind the float carrying the May Queen. Between each series of tableau would be a brass band from the Northumberland collieries. In 1960 there were bands from, Ellington, Woodhorn, Newbiggin & Lynemouth and Pegswood and Wallsend shipyards and Blyth British Railways. The procession, growing to over 2,000 people would make its way through crowded streets to the City Hall for a rally, with speeches from figures like Nye Bevan, and in 1960, Harold Wilson, relayed to the crowds outside the hall. They would disperse round five o'clock and people would rush home to get into their glad rags for the May Day Dance in the evening at the Mayfair Ballroom where a figure like Dan Smith would lead off with the May Queen.

There was also an annual open air meeting on the Moor, in June, at the start of the Hoppings,[197] where some cut their speaking teeth dealing incompetently with various hecklers including the League of Empire Loyalists. 'Never offer the platform to a heckler. He might accept.' Again, this was Joe Eagles' advice. In 1960 the meeting was preceded by a Young Socialist march, again on the South African issue.

In the winter was the staid LP Annual Dance at the Mayfair. Some youngsters could dance, that is, ball room dance, and even took dancing lessons at places like Miss Newbiggen's Silver Swing ballroom dancing school on Shields Road. A lesson cost 1/6d. In fact it was the main pastime of Margaret Pearson, accompanied, on occasion by Irene Edwards. However this was the critical cross over moment for the young between the fox trot and the twist. The Labour Party had just painfully recognized it and a tiny corner of the evening's programme was turned over to wild cavorting.

Leisure time...

Coffee Bars, the very height of sophistication, were just on the agenda, like the Paletta on Clayton Street. They were important to a movement where so many of the new recruits were under 18. There were very drunken parties in houses, like the 'commune' at Buston Terrace so long as the police did not call by. You could visit the Theatre Royal and be spat upon for sitting during the National Anthem, the Playhouse on Benton Bank, and the People's Theatre, in Rye Hill. There Brecht was much in fashion, played by future TV actors, Jackie Shepherd: Ralph Watson, Fred Pearson and Jimmy Garbett.

A glance at the *Evening Chronicle* in election week 1959 shows that the Odeon Cinema offered Rock Hudson and Jean Simmons in '*The Earth is Mine*' whilst at Gateshead you could have *Oklahoma* in its 'second great year'. If you got there early you could hear Jack Glancey, or Con Docherty, live on the electronic organ. You did not have to travel too far for entertainment. 38 local cinemas on Tyneside offered programmes. If you stayed at home, TV started at 5 pm, and, the evening's high spot between 8 and 10 was the Horse of the Year Show from Olympia which followed Carol Carr, in person, singing and accompanying herself on the piano.

Some read a lot: Steinbeck, Upton Sinclair, Kerouac, Tawney, Cole, Robert Jungk, *Out of Apathy* and Raymond Williams's *Culture and Society*, pushed by Jimmy Murray, and Nye Bevan's, *In Place of Fear*. The latter was recommended to me by Joe Eagles, an action which, in 1959, located him accurately in Labour politics. When helping to clear out Newcastle West Constituency premises, an old butcher's shop on Denton Road, I found a mouldy box of books and papers which contained the Left Book Club edition of *The Road to Wigan Pier*. What I would later know to be an archivist's dream was dumped that Saturday by three young socialists and Bob Brown, the Party Secretary and future Labour Minister for the Army – an action which located Brown's politics as surely as Joe Eagles offering Nye Bevan.

John Creaby was an avid reader. He picked up a lot from his attendance at classes. He said, 'From the NCLC I acquired a deep interest in William Morris. I bought *William Morris: Selected Writings and Designs* and I also read Franz Mehring, *Karl Marx, the Story of his life* and developed my interest in Marx the man. Then there was A.L. Morton's *The British Labour Movement* and *A People's History of England,* with its the study guide.' He also read , 'Alan Paton's book, *Cry the Beloved Country*, which added to my knowledge of the plight of black South Africans. However, most significant was the great black novelist, James Baldwin. His *The Fire Next Time* gave a real insight into racism.' John also thought 'being different was like and addiction. Certainly I was different from my workmates, however the 'difference' did not seem to alienate them from me. In fact they were often interested in what I was reading or I had done, the previous evening or weekend.'[198]

Jean Mortimer's parents' bookshelves were 'crammed with poetry, philosophy, novels-the classics, whodunits – the ubiquitous Hansards, a set of Hansards.' She said, 'By 1960 (at 15) I was already well read, that is to say that as an avid, eclectic reader from an early age I read everything on the bookshelves at home and 'every' new book from the back of the Library', and 'was familiar with Hemingway, Steinbeck, Emil Zola, Graham Greene, and especially memorable, *The Ragged Trousered Philanthropist* and James Bark's *The Land of the Leal*. Many were disapproved of by my manic depressive head mistress but I was supported all the way by my parents.'[199]

For most in 1960, Marxism lay just around the corner. My own introduction was Deutscher's biography of Trotsky, *The Prophet Armed* but this came after our plunge into national youth politics. The specifically political books were *The Ragged Trousered Philanthropists* and *Homage to Catalonia*, the latter with its exciting opening evocation of workers' power in Barcelona.

Sexual attitudes

Although Philip Larkin felt that sexual intercourse began in 1963 the fledgling members of the 59 Society anticipated him by a few years. One of the intrinsic attractions of political gatherings in the late fifties was the opportunity and incentive to capitalise on meetings with the opposite (or same) sex. Sexual repression, condemnation of sex outside marriage and residential facts of life up to this time meant that opportunities for having sex were restricted. This might be expected at home at this time but Jane (Lu) Bell recalled the very strict rules at her Hall of Residence when she arrived at Kings College in 1959. Even fathers had to be out of the building by 6 p.m.[200] So, the freedom offered by nights away from home during CND marches and weekend conferences was an added attraction.

Not that social life after the 1959 General Election crashed through normative boundaries overnight. It was simply a conjunction of ideological and material circumstances that created the pre-conditions for more relaxed conduct. But the ideology of sexual freedom was appropriated by the left before the contraceptive pill and significantly also the green shoots of women's lib. The decade from the mid-fifties onward, celebrated in jazz, rock and roll (remember the banning of *Wake up Little Suzy?*), beatnik culture and films like *A Kind of Loving* and *Saturday Night and Sunday Morning*, pointed the way to a style of life in which sex would become one day as democratised as politics.

Subsequent generations must look back on it and marvel at the glacial pace of change but the 59ers certainly felt they were living at the edge. It was the end of the beginning really for the intersection of political and sexual identity.[201]

The social composition of this new young socialist body was firmly biased towards the children of the professional middle class with strong family connections to existing labour and socialist movement activists. Ultimately though, 'the red diaper babies'[202] were outnumbered by a continuing influx of new members who came largely from the growing mass movement of CND. Through 1960 and 1961 the 59 Society held regular weekly meetings of over thirty but more significantly had played an important part in creating and building new Young Socialist branches in Gateshead and Felling, Ryton, Newcastle East (Byker, Heaton and Walker), Newcastle West (Newburn, Throckley, Westerhope, Denton and Scotswood), Wallsend, Longbenton and Tynemouth.

Towards a YS Conference

Soon after the General Election debacle the National Executive of the Labour Party concentrated attention on the creation of a new Young Socialist organization with a national and regional structure. The project had been placed in the hands of a National Executive sub-committee of elderly men. Shocked by the election result they were keen to accelerate the process and in the spring of 1960 they issued a report advocating the establishment of an organisation 'to interest active young members of the Party and to attract to it the many young people now outside its own machinery of administration from local to national levels.' L P Conference Reports show that there was a very rapid rise in the number of branches so that by the first Y S Conference in 1961 there were over 700.

Regional youth officers were appointed. Locally the Party appointed a middle-aged, pipe smoking anonymous mouse-like figure called Ron Evers, who seemed to arrive from 'nowhere' to keep a quiet watch on the new incendiaries. The hope was to encourage orthodoxy, though a left veil was provided by the charmingly elegant presence of Anthony Greenwood on the Youth sub-committee. The 59 Society officers entertained him in the 'sophisticated' surroundings of Newcastle's first Chinese Restaurant, the Maykway, recently opened on Northumberland Street where you could buy 'authentic' chinese curries and feel adventurous!

The LP hopes of containing the YS for Gaitskellite moderation were dashed from the outset. In the case of the 59 Society it was built from CND activity. Those who were 'active young members of the Party' were in a tiny minority. Even those who came from homes where their own parents were active were likely to be unilateralists and hence oppositional. North East delegates to the first conference in the Beaver Hall in April 1961 were almost all members or supporters of CND. It was suggested that Easter week-end was deliberately chosen because it coincided with the Aldermaston march. As it was, some delegates doubled up their attendance at the Conference with visits to the biggest of all the Aldermaston Marches which was wending its way to London over that Easter week-end. The Conference itself was a maelstrom of sectarian battles quite opaque to the newcomers. The pubs and cafes round the Hall were occupied by knots of plotting or quarrelling delegates and their friends.

Trotskyism

For many the Conference was a heady introduction to the Byzantine maze of Trotskyism. Among those constantly at the microphone were John Palmer from Esher, Chris Davidson from the LSE, Bob Gillespie ('Geggie') and the future Labour Minister, the now *Lord* Gus MacDonald, from the ship yards of Glasgow. They were all 'state caps'[203] and members of the Socialist Review Group (IS). The Socialist Labour League (SLL) was represented by the rather sinister Gavin Kennedy, the future Lambeth Council leader 'Red' Ted Knight, Pat and Geoff Sirokin, the brash and angry Sheila Torrance and the future 'Real Ale' columnist of the *Guardian'*, Roger Protz. The Revolutionary Socialist League (RSL), as The Militant Group, to become the *bête noire* of Kinnock's LP twenty years on. It had the articulate Merseysiders, the Taaffe brothers and Dave Ablett from Nottingham. Its theoreticians, Pat Jordan and Ted Grant, were rumoured to be ensconced in a nearby pub dispensing orders. The north east contingent was totally naïve by contrast. Though the LPYS was barely a year old, these people were already versed in past internicene struggles and saturated in the texts of Lenin and Trotsky.

The Gaitskellite right wing was a small rearguard represented by Gaitskell's daughter Julia, a future South London MP, John Fraser, David Daniels from Dewsbury and, operating round the conference fringe, the future leader John Smith, who was rumoured to have contact with the CIA through the magazine *'Encounter.'*

It was a very intense experience. I knew only one other delegate from the north east. That was Doug Jackson from Gateshead. We stayed at a small hotel off Russell Square, allocated by Transport House. Before the Conference I was taking *Keep Left* which I may have picked up at a demonstration earlier. We had had it on the literature table at 59 Society meetings for a month or so but I had regarded it merely as a paper of the left, persecuted by the Labour Party hierarchy. At the Conference I had met Mark Jenkins, an affable comrade from Hendon North Y S, one of the groups I was informed was being investigated by Transport House. He invited me to go to a YS meeting on the Sunday evening after the Conference was over. Jenkins told me not to tell anyone as the Labour Party might use the information against him and, of course, me. This was my introduction to the Keep Left-SLL paranoia. I was to see a lot of it over the next few years when I was on the receiving end, but at that point I took his remark at face value. I returned to Newcastle enthusiastic about pushing and defending *Keep Left.* Initially, I guess, the smell of conspiracy was fascinating.

On Monday, Doug and I went off to the final day of the twin CND March. In 1961 it had started simultaneously at two points, Aldermaston and Wethersfield. I think we waited somewhere on Turnpike Lane for the Tyneside contingent to pass. It was really exciting to meet up with friends but I remember feeling a bit of envy at their obvious camaraderie. Neither was it pleasant to have to leave Trafalgar Square to catch the train back north rather than bundle on to the coaches exchanging anecdotes.

Within a few months of that conference the socialist youth movement in the North East had turned into a Trotskyist bear garden as new adherents of *Young Guard* (state capitalists), and *Keep Left* (workers' statists) engaged in sectarian warfare and intrigue. Old friendships were seriously damaged as we jockeyed for position, massively inflating our importance. Both the main groups treated the few followers of *New Advance,* the official youth paper, with almost total contempt. Supporters of *Challenge,* the paper of the Young Communist League, then a substantial organisation, looked down upon all with a superior disdain. The simplistic days of 59-60 were over. By the end of 1961 the 59 Society, whilst still meeting, was all but dead. Its members had moved on into local YS branches several of which became battlefields for the IS, the SLL and the YCL. The sixties had begun – with a vengeance.

Chapter Eight: 'The groupuscule'[204]

After the return from the Conference, an important change took place. There emerged a state of dual membership for many of the young socialists: the Labour Party and either the International Socialists or the Socialist Labour League.[205] The 59 Society was apparently seen as a recruiting ground for the Young Communist League as well. The visible evidence of this was the presence on the literature table at meetings, of *Young Guard* and *Keep Left,* the IS and SLL youth papers. The YCL paper *Challenge* was available in the pub after the meetings. *Challenge* was probably absent from the meetings in order not to attract the interest of Labour Party officers following the long standing proscription by the LP of all things Communist. The SLL had also been proscribed since 1955 but not *Keep Left.* This was ironical because the other papers were undoubtedly more dangerous to the Labour Party's integrity than *Challenge* was. However *Keep Left* rapidly became the target of Labour Party wrath. This came as the result of the Party's National Executive refusing to accept three elected members of the new Young Socialist National Committee and the resignation of Roger Protz, the first editor of *New Advance.* He had announced to Conference that editorial policy was entirely controlled by Labour Party officials. Protz was soon sitting in the editorial chair of *Keep Left.*

The SLL was the first of the groups to bid for members in the north east. Within days of the YS Conference Ted Knight came to the area in his guise as a representative of a publishing house, New Park Publications. I introduced him to friends in the 59. My naïvety was demonstrated when I took him on a tour of the city to see the exciting changes being wrought by the Labour Council. At that point my politics were what were called 'Labour Left', basically unilateralist, anti colonial and, and in favour of an extension of state and municipal reform.

That spring, just before the YS Conference, I had attended my first selection meeting for election to the City Council for Scotswood Ward. I was being encouraged by Dan Smith and Harry and Theresa Russell. Despite their influential support I committed a serious error. I was asked by Alderman Frank Butterfield what I would do if I disagreed with Labour Party Policy. To his pleasure, and my friends' disappointment, I said that I would resign. With Labour in control of the city council only by the Lord Mayor's casting vote, it was definitely not the correct answer. This turned out to be the end of my 'dramatic' rise in the Labour Party! It was the YS Conference that proved to be my *signpost for the sixties.*[206]

The SLL

In the week following Ted Knight's visit, Bill Hunter from Liverpool arrived. He was a veteran of 1940s Trotskyism and had originally come from the north east. He tried to recruit me to the SLL at the Maykway restaurant. I held out on the grounds that I was reading Deutscher's biography of Trotsky *The Prophet Armed* and needed to feel better equipped to argue with others.

The culmination of this flattering interest in me was the arrival of Gerry Healy on Tyneside. This turned out to be the end of my interest in the SLL. I travelled with Healy and Liz Thompson, his acolyte, from Wigan, to a meeting in a community centre in South Shields. This was to meet some YS members from Shields who I think included Wal and Gladys Hobson. I am not sure where Healy and Thompson stayed that night but on the following day he was to speak to a group of Newcastle and Gateshead young socialists whom I had invited. The meeting had to take place in the utmost secrecy I was told, by Liz Thompson, because Labour Party officials would be watching. I had booked the committee room at the YMCA on Blackett Street but was told to meet my friends at a pub and not to let them know the venue of the meeting till we assembled. Healy was to be spirited in by car after the rest of the gathering was assembled. Among those present were Jim Hutchinson, Mike Ingleby, Eric Mirley, Terry Rodgers and Ken Moffit, also a draughtsman from Parsons, whom Terry invited. Mike Wales, an articulate independent Marxist from South Shields was there, and possibly Roland Boyes from Houghton le Spring who was later to become a Labour MP. I was surprised to see Mike Ginsburg from Blyth who had been elected from our region to the National Committee for which I had been a candidate. I was unaware of his connection with the Healyites. Then there was Bob Todd, a Scots administrator from Newcastle University whom I did not know, and I think, never saw again, Liz Thompson, and a few others I can't remember. We amounted to about 15 in all.

Although no written record of this event was made, its timing can be easily established. It was at the beginning of May during the Bay of Pigs episode. A shambles of an army, backed by the USA, had invaded Cuba, in late April, to try to depose Fidel Castro. Healy made the issue the centre piece of his presentation. He was a squat, balding, pugnacious man. It was a warm evening on the top floor of the YMCA and he sweated profusely as he spoke, starting very quietly, then rising in pitch and level, hitting the table with his fist for emphasis. He said that the apparent failure of the Bay of Pigs adventure was a humiliation for US imperialism. They would be back, he warned. It was of the utmost importance to build a revolutionary leadership to take the class forward. This was all delivered with a rhetorical and brutal certainty. I found it deeply unattractive.

When he finished he asked for questions. As I recall, there were none. He then asked people to commit themselves to the SLL. When it came to my turn I declined, repeating the answer I had given Bill Hunter. He treated me with scorn, alleging that I had clearly not understood the gravity of the crisis. When the meeting ended I got out of the place as fast as possible, not wanting to risk further brow-beating. That was the end of my association with the Healy group.

In discussing the groups I am very aware of my bias. I chose the International Socialists (IS) and have been a member since then. That causes two problems. I may have rosy specs when I write of them and muddy ones when I consider the others. I try to keep my vision clear but hope that views from others will help to redress any distortions. There is yet a further issue. Many of the people who feature in this book belonged to none of the groups but their story also needs to be told.

International Socialists

The IS did not move with the urgency of the Healy Group. After all, they did not believe that capitalism was entering its death agony. When asked about the imminence of revolution, sometime in 1962, Tony Cliff replied with a wave of his hand, 'ah twenty years.' In retrospect he was a hopeless optimist! Humour apart, one of the IS Group's attractive features at that time was its relaxed attitude to people who passed by. It exercised virtually no discipline on its members and had modest expectations. The downside of this was that some of the most enthusiastic young people did not take the IS seriously.

Jim Hutchinson made the first contact with the Cliff group and was its first member in the north east. He probably met them also on a demonstration, perhaps at Holy Loch. Glasgow was one of only two branches outside London in 1961. Tyneside may well have become the third. Jim had gone to London in the summer of 1961 and stayed with a prominent member of IS, Chris Davidson, who was then a student at LSE.

At some point that summer Tony Cliff came to Newcastle. He had been once before in 1959 to speak at first meeting of the Left Club at the Bridge Hotel, probably invited by Jimmy Murray. The Left Clubs had been founded after a Conference at Wortley Hall, Sheffield, in the summer of 1957. The Conference had been called by a group of dissident Marxist intellectuals, most of whom had left the Communist Party in 1956. They were associated with the journals *New Reasoner* and *Universities and Left Review* which were about to merge as *The New Left Review*.

John Mapplebeck, newly arrived in Newcastle to work for the BBC, had been 'totally electrified' by E. P. Thompson and was a devoted reader of *New Reasoner*. He had been told there was a Left Club on Tyneside so he sought out its Secretary, Jim Murray. He wrote, 'The first meeting (with Jim), of course, was in a pub -The Crow's Nest, high above the Haymarket. Why, I wonder, does one say "of course" about meeting Jim in a public house? Principally, I suppose, because it was his home ground. It may have been responsible for his early and untimely death, but its culture was his essence.' [207]

Murray's main colleague on the non-CP left was Terry Rodgers. In 1961 he was 30 and working as a skilled draughtsman at Parsons. He had been in the League of Youth in Scotswood till its disbandment and then an active Labour Party member. Terry was a highly skilled organiser and quiet persuader. He was to become one of Tyneside's most respected rank and file trade unionists and a constant thorn in the side of union leaders and bosses. Perhaps his greatest skill was in carrying the members with him. He was antagonistic to cabals and a strong advocate of mass meetings. After the 1959 Election defeat the party leaders resolved to remove Clause 4 from the Constitution. Terry was the leader of the Tyneside Campaign to keep Clause 4. He was a worker intellectual, well read, and with a keen interest in ideas.

Terry Rodgers & Harry Blair

Although in other areas, Left Clubs tended to be started by dissident former communists it was not so on Tyneside. Both Murray's and Rodgers' inclination was Labour Party left. Tony Cliff had been invited to the first meeting to speak on Russia. In 1960 the attitude to Russia and the Eastern block was a defining feature of left wing discourse. Terry Rodgers had been very interested in Yugoslavia and was especially taken with the ideas of workers' control. By 1960 enthusiasm for Yugoslavia had waned somewhat, perhaps to be replaced in some circles by Mao Tse Tung, though not by Rodgers or Murray.

The Left Club was not the only forum for dissident ideas. Terry Rodgers' union DATA, and particularly the C.A.Parsons branch, sponsored both formal and informal get togethers where political ideas were exchanged. Week-end schools at Whitley Bay and a Friday night session at the Crows Nest pub in the Haymarket brought to Newcastle speakers like John Rex from Leeds, Robert Moore from Durham, Michael Barrett Brown, Mike Cooley, Michael Kidron and Bob Harrison the London WEA organiser, who spoke on topics such as Race in British Politics, Miners and Methodism, the Common Market, alternative technologies, the Permanent Arms Economy and workers' control. The latter topic led on to north east interest in the Institute for Workers Control, based in Nottingham.

Durham green shoots

Durham University also had an influx of people from outside the area who tried to build asocialist organisation. Brian Whitton had arrived as a junior lecturer in Botany. He said, 'By the time I was 7, I had my own garden and I could identify more than a hundred species of plants.' His background was firmly home counties middle class. His father was a senior bank officer in Wimbledon. There was no discernible history of political activism in his family though his mother would help the local conservatives. Searching for connections which might have inclined him to the left he recalled, 'evacuation to Stockport during the war to live with my aunt, the *Manchester Guardian* European correspondent.' He was one of the few new activists to have done National Service. He served in Cyprus from 1954-1956. His public school background meant he entered the army as an officer. At all of 19, called upon to give an education lecture to the men, he chose to speak on the middle east. 'I thought I'd done a pretty good job but then my Captain took over for ten minutes to straighten out what I had said.'

In the summer of 1956 whilst working for signals he was aware of 'British spy planes circling the Black Sea watching the Soviet Union.' When Anthony Eden stood up in Parliament to emphatically deny such activity, he was exposed (to Brian) as a complete liar. As suspicions grew of a pending middle east conflict, opinion among the soldiers was that 'we don't want to go to Egypt. Although I was six months short of completing my stint I was whipped back to England and discharged just before the Suez invasion.'

Brian describes his turn to the left as incremental rather than dramatic. He went on to Oxford that autumn (1956), attending the Labour Club then on to University College, London, where he joined the New Left Club and participated in several demonstrations. Arriving in Durham he found it politically dead and lacking any obvious radical roots. He joined the tiny Labour Club and helped to found a magazine *Durham Left,* 'terribly badly written and produced.' He was attracted to the International Socialists. Several students moved that way too.

Bob Heyes had arrived as an undergraduate in 1959. He was a maths student from Peterborough. His father was a skilled craftsman, an engineer, a firm trade unionist and Labour supporter. George Box was a true eccentric. A working class grammar school boy from Blackpool, he was extremely well read from Karl Marx to Kerouac. A tall, thin, spare shambling man he appeared to be held together by pieces of string, but his appearance disguised a sharp and witty mind. If there is a gene labelled 'opposition' he had it and exercised it with friend as well as foe. He was an improbable DJ on Nottingham local radio when cancer caught up with him at only 39. Ian Taylor was a working class lad from Sheffield who had joined the Sheffield Left Club before arriving in Durham to study Sociology. Ian is remembered by another slightly later arrival at Durham, John Smith, as 'earnest, but witty and very convincing in argument: reasonableness and radicalism combined.' [208]

This group looked outward from the University becoming involved with rank and file workers and not always comfortably. Brian Whitton shocked Jim Badger, a CPer from Bowburn, by saying, 'The only good thing to come out of the Soviet Union was Shostakovich.' They were engaged in strike support, perhaps the central activity which separated the IS from the New Left at that time. A steward at Thorne Electric, Spennymoor, asked the group to go in and argue their case with management. John Smith says we were clear that 'whispering sedition in a cultured tone was not the way forward.' Ian Taylor told the steward, 'It's for you to do it not for us.' This is all very early sixties stuff, a product of the coming together of the new far left, often university based, with a new rank and file militancy often a bit disconnected from the trade union bureaucracy and distant from the older union strongholds.[209]

Marxism on Tyne

This was all part the revival of Marxist ideas following the revolution in Hungary and its suppression. Although the CP was an important force in the unions on the Tyne and among young people, on the whole its members did not participate much in these sort of discussions. They probably could not for two reasons. Firstly, the party leadership still exercised enough discipline to check such interest in its members. In the case of DATA, for example, the formal discussions were deliberately suppressed by leading CP members and some of the dissident Marxists were removed from district union positions. Secondly, Hungary was still a raw topic and discussion of it and therefore of Russia and Eastern Europe was off limits for loyal CP members.

What this did was to leave the field open for Marxists from the Trotskyist tradition. In the north east this effectively meant the SLL and the IS. The RSL, soon to become the Militant Group, made no headway in the area before the mid-sixties. Their only activist was Herbie Bell of Wallsend, then in his late sixties, who had operated as a one man band through much of the fifties. The RCP, associated with the great 1944 Apprentices' Strike, had descended into factionalism and splits. Herbie was tireless, a teller of good tales and a friend to all, but he did not really connect with the new generation of socialist activists. He could often be found at the little café in Wallsend run by his friends, the former RCP members, Jack and Daisy Rawlings. The café was good for discussion about the 1930s and 40s but short on help on contemporary issues.

The 59 Society had an open and probably naïve culture which was inimical to the Healy Group but rather fitted the IS, or as it was known till December 1962, the Socialist Review Group. The Healyites regarded the Society as 'a petit bourgeois formation.' Yes, they really did use that language! As such it was regarded as fit for raiding parties who would deliver a contact to the luminaries of the SLL who would visit the area regularly to try to win the victims to their politics. 'Petit bourgeois' they might, be but suitably educated, they could be turned loose into the Young Socialists to sell *Keep Left*, manoeuvre for position and hopefully, win further converts.

Wal & Gladys Hobson, 1962

Healy was invited to speak at a DATA school at Whitley Bay in 1961. He failed to impress the redoubtable group of draughtsmen from Parsons: Terry Rodgers, Harry Blair, Ken Moffit and Ken Ternant who all subsequently joined IS. This may have been the occasion when he first met Wal Hobson who was working at Thermal Syndicate, Wallsend. Wal was 22 and had just returned from five years at sea, as an officer in the merchant navy. He was recently married and had begun activity in the union, DATA and in South Shields Young Socialists. He and his wife, Gladys, were attracted by what he calls, 'dissident Marxist philosophies.' He says, 'We got involved with Gerry Healy. They were strange days from 1961 to 1965. You were brainwashed into hearing a certain line. It was like being in a cult. The mechanism was to look for young idealistic people in the Labour Party and to persuade them that their group *(Keep Left)* was the only one which could lead to advances for the working class. Everybody else was not only rubbish but dangerous and had to be suppressed by any means possible. This led to unsavoury acts. Then the most able were selected to train as cadre who would be used as leaders.'

Healy would tell them at special training sessions for cadre that they, 'would be leadership material in any walk of life,' but now they could lead in the class struggle. 'He'd tell us there's the whole world. In it is socialism. It is the only thing worth dealing with. Inside it is the Labour Party. It is corrupt and useless, undermined by the ruling class. The Communist Party is the tool of the Russians and then there are the independent marxists. Inside that there are a number of groups. You know what they are like. Inside this is the only one worth considering, the SLL, and inside it is the cadre. You are the cadre. You are the leaders. You are the cream of the cream. He only said it once.'[210] Somehow this simple, indeed simplistic message, appealed to idealists and was probably quite flattering to young people who badly wanted to play their part in changing the world.

This inculcation of a sense of an individual's sense of importance to the struggle sat inside a political analysis alleged to be fully in the traditions of Trotsky. Capitalism was in its final throes, its 'death agony' according to Trotsky – writing in 1938. Every rise in unemployment and every international crisis was evidence of impending catastrophe. The two great Cuba incidents, the Bay

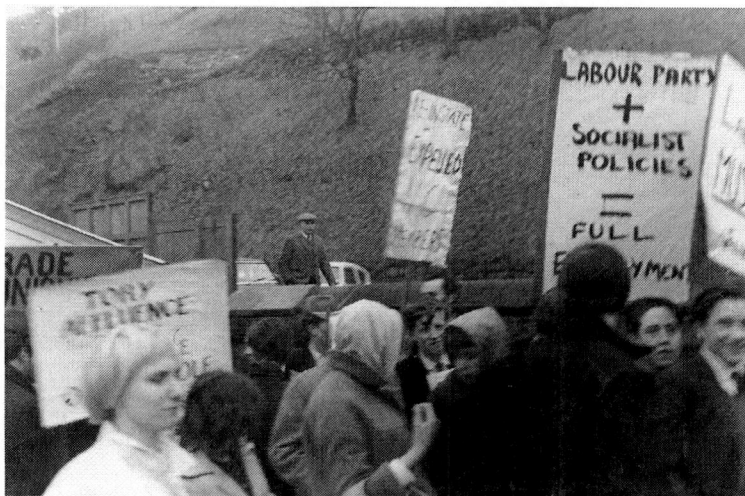

Gladys Hobson on Keep Left unemployment demo, 1963

of Pigs in 1961 and the Missile Crisis of 1962, prompted a massively heightened sense of emergency. Imperialism was leading everyone to destruction. Only the mass intervention of the working class could stop it in its tracks. The problem was entirely one of its leadership currently corrupted by base labour leaders.

The solution was to build, post haste, the world party of the proletariat. The Socialist Labour League, soon to be reborn as the Workers Revolutionary Party, was the only body fit to supply that leadership.

Once the newcomer became convinced of this proposition almost anything was acceptable including 'unsavory acts like packing meetings and fixing elections.'[211] Part of the process of convincing was carried out by Healy's leading lieutenants like Cliff Slaughter, Jack Gale, Michael Banda and Bill Hunter. Slaughter was the major party intellectual who wrote many of the pamphlets and documents. He commanded authority by seeking to smash people in argument. Trisha Fitzpatrick recalled a meeting when a young woman comrade from Prudhoe said that she could not understand the articles in the *Newsletter*, the weekly paper. Slaughter's response was to humiliate her angrily for her stupidity and demand that she struggle to understand, as her responsibility to the proletariat.[212]

Wal Hobson said he was very impressed by 'the personal sacrifice' of some leaders. 'I thought I was lucky to be associated with the right people at the right time. There were people who you could admire like Bill Hunter and Jack Gale, both close to Healy. They suffered for the cause. They were givers not takers. Bill Hunter would come and sleep on your floor for a week while he travelled the north east. They had no money. You would willingly feed them. Jack Gale was very intelligent. He gave his life to the ideas. He would drive up from Leeds on Friday night after school (he was a teacher) to sleep on your floor and drive back on Sunday for a week's work. They had nothing. There was no personal gain. When you are young and idealistic you can be very impressed by these attitude and behaviour. They seemed genuinely trying to do something for the workers with no personal reward.'[213]

The Healy Group were always very proud of winning people from other parts of the left especially the CP. For someone to break with Stalinism was a special triumph. The winning of Harry Rothman to the League was trumpeted as a terrific prize. In 1962 Rothman left the CP after a sample of bureaucratic treatment from Peter Kerrigan, the National Organiser, who later lost his daughter, Jean, to the SLL. Harry records that, 'We (Bill Hunter and I) met in a pub behind the University. He was very sincere and plausible. I read Trotsky's *Revolution Betrayed* which seemed to make a lot of sense, exactly explaining what seemed to had gone wrong with the Revolution. We held a meeting with Cliff Slaughter in our house in Eslington Terrace, taking half the CP branch into the SLL. Some members became very heavily involved. The problem was that their party discipline was not for me; and in any case keeping a family was proving hard work, Anne had a baby and was still a student, and starting teaching plus my long bus trip everyday to Consett (to teach). I remember at a camp, Healy putting his arm round me and saying 'we will have to put some work on these broad shoulders of yours.' I thought, I don't think so. I was never really 'in' the group, that is, thinking like them. I thought their permanent crisis theory a bit odd. Healy was a man of bizarre obsession, like ordering members to read Lenin's *Philosophical Notebooks*, devoting sessions of party schools to them and berating people for failing to make any sense of them. He was a man of some ability – though a bully. I hated his practice of deliberately humiliating people, like Bill Hunter, in front of young comrades. I guess he was creating a sort of religious cult.'[214]

Other former members are even less generous in their assessment. Trisha feels that once a member had graduated to cadre status he or she was expected to carry out orders unquestioningly. She gives an example of having been placed in an awful and humiliating situation. During the debates on defence policy in the early sixties, SLL members were sent to a large public meeting where Denis Healey was the speaker pushing the Labour Party's position against unilateralism. When Healey finished the Chairman invited questions. She put up her hand and was asked to put the first question. Here, in a meeting where large numbers of people were waiting to berate Healey on Labour's position on the Bomb, she stood up and attacked the speaker for his complicity in the decision to ban *Keep Left*! The speaker simply brushed the question aside. However such cursory treatment could reinforce certainty, as it did at this time, in her case.[215]

During the period 1961-65 the SLL members were busy in several YS branches north and south of the river Tyne. The comrades were instructed to endeavour to win the delegation to the annual Young Socialist Conference. The conference was an important field of activity for the League in its attempt to use the debate round *Keep Left* to challenge the Labour Party National Executive control of the youth organisation and discipline. The tactic was to pose as victims, hoping to win influence among the tranche of delegates not already committed to one or other of the factions at work. This cavalier behaviour with basic democracy infuriated many young socialists, making the SLL deeply unpopular in the wider movement. However, as ex-members say, such unpopularity was taken by the organisation as simple proof of the petit bourgeois, or, simply treacherous, attitudes of those parts of the movement.

Brenda Corcoron speaks of an even more sinister situation. She says she once had to fight off Jack Gale who attempted to rape her, arguing that it was her revolutionary duty to put petit bourgeois attitudes behind her.[216]In fact both Brenda and Trisha Fitzpatrick found themselves routinely facing sexual assault. Trish remembers being told that it was 'petit bourgeois' to insist on sharing a bed with her husband when attending a conference.

The term 'petit bourgeois' was routinely thrown round, as a term of abuse to justify appalling behaviour. When Trish's husband, Kevin Fitzpatrick, came to end of his tether and challenged the sense of a specific piece of political analysis, they were both summoned to the party HQ in Clapham to face a disciplinary committee. They were seen separately. When Kevin maintained his position despite brow-beating from Healy and others, he was expelled for 'petit bourgeois deviation.' He left the building to wait for Trisha in a nearby park. She was then told that she must leave her husband in the interests of the party and the struggle. To do less would be evidence of petit bourgeois tendencies. So inculcated into the mores of the group did she feel, that her first reaction was to agree and she went outside to tell Kevin. He responded with disbelief and she says that this was her moment of truth. She went back to inform Healy and she too was expelled. So they were both expelled despite the fact that they had both resigned!

Trish says that no one was ever allowed to resign.[217]

Trisha feels that they were seriously damaged by the experience, a sense shared by many. It took some years to recover. Very few survived the experience politically and felt able to redirect their political energies. This seemed to have applied to Jenn Scott who with Val Nicholson was recruited by Mike Ingleby. She was convinced by the serious commitment of SLL members, though occasionally prone to giggling at its intensity. She must have been considered

COUNTY BOROUGH OF SOUTH SHIELDS

WEST PARK WARD

MUNICIPAL ELECTION — THURSDAY, 11th MAY, 1961
Poll Open 8 a.m. to 9 p.m.

VOTE LABOUR

HOBSON

If you want an active Representative on the Council

VOTE FOR—

HOBSON, W. | X

Printed by F. & A. Tolson Ltd. (T.A.) and Published by A. J. Florence, 29, King Street, South Shields.

Wal Hobson's election address, 1961

cadre material by Gerry Healy because, at a point in 1964, she was being given a lift home by Healy along Scotswood Road when he pulled over and said he wanted her to go to London. She was shocked and asked when. ' Now, I want to take you right away.' She was terrified by the demand. Explaining that she would need to go home and tell her mother. In fact she walked away from active left wing politics and never returned.[218]

Wally and Gladys Hobson both left the League in 1965 and dropped out of active politics for over fifteen years. They re-joined the Labour Party in the early 1980's. Both were active and Gladys served for nine years on the Council. Kevin and Trisha eventually migrated to Ireland, largely staying out of Irish politics, though Kevin's instincts led him to fight his employers, the clerically dominated Galway Health Board, where he worked as a psychologist. Trisha's energies turned to cultural pursuits as an organiser of the successful Galway Arts Festival. Brenda Corcoron had a period as a socialist feminist activist on Tyneside in the late sixties and seventies and has played an active part in the Tyneside Irish Festival.

The 59 Society was a compatible target for *Young Guard*, the youth paper of the International Socialists. Its slogan, *Neither Washington nor Moscow but international socialism* encapsulated two ideas which meshed with the outlooks of most of the youth group, the exceptions being those attracted to the SLL, those close to, or in dual membership with the YCL and a few of those main stream Labour Party members suspicious of any outside influence. 'Neither Washington nor Moscow' was an idea with very wide appeal in the anti-Bomb movement, though very few of its adherents would have heard of the IS and many would not have extended their belief system to embrace socialism. Yet the IS would chime with the movement in that it stood wholeheartedly against the bomb. The SLL's espousal of the notion of the Soviet weapon as a workers' bomb was risible in the eyes of many. The IS had another practice which made it attractive. It had a very permissive regime which made very few demands upon its members and supporters. Its relaxed attitude derived at least in part from a reading of the economy which placed serious crisis a long way ahead. Tony Cliff spoke at a meeting at the Bridge Hotel in Newcastle during the Cuban Missile crisis. Asked if he feared a world war, Jim Hutchinson remembers Cliff laughing off the idea, saying that the system was not under threat, 'no one is throwing themselves off buildings.'

The IS started to hold meetings in Newcastle in the late summer of 1961 and a number of Young Socialists attended. The meetings were held in the Friends Meeting House on Jesmond Road but also at The Bridge Hotel and occasionally at the Labour Club in Leazes Park Road. These meeting points touched important constituencies; the former, of course the peace movement and the latter two, the trade unions and the Labour Party. They were soon represented in the IS meetings. Since it had no pretensions to replace the Labour Party as 'the leadership of the working class' it posed no threat and was much less likely to face hostility from LP organisers than *Keep Left*. It was therefore easy to sell *Young Guard* in YS meetings alongside, *New Advance*. The Bridge Hotel connection was also valuable for it was the virtual 'home' for left wing trade unionists including those associated with the Left Club, namely Jimmy Murray, Terry Rodgers, Harry Blair, Chairman of the Parsons Committee, Ken Moffit also from Parsons, Austin Tunney, the catholic Marxist draughtsman from Sunderland, Derek Bates, a young engineer from Pelton Fell and sundry other friends of Murray and Rodgers. There was also a group of journalists from the BBC including John Mapplebeck and John Taylor.

The Communist Party

The Communist Party had a complicated relationship with the 59 Society. There was interest from both university and town members of the Party, though in the latter case they may have seen it as a bit of a kindergarten. Curiously though, John Creaby and Guy Faulkenau, 16 year old young socialists, were invited to the CP District Committee to give their views on the 1960 Apprentices' strike. This was probably a reflection of the Party's anxiety with the health of the YCL, which had halved in membership after Hungary and Kruschev's speech in 1956. For university CP members, the 59 Society was very convenient, because the 2/6d per week membership charge did not confer Labour Party membership. Oddly perhaps LP vigilance did not extend to checking if the delegate to the City Party was actually a LP member. University CP members certainly participated freely in the 59 and its activities. Dave Leigh the leading CP organiser in the University does not recall if the 59 was *formally* an area of interest, as CND certainly was. There is no doubt that he was a much more skilled and systematic organiser than anyone in the 59 Society.

Dave Leigh had come to Newcastle in 1959 as a research student in the Mining Engineering Department. He had previously been at Imperial College, London and a member of the CP Branch there. He says, 'when I arrived the only left wing society in the University was the Labour Club and known communists were not eligible for membership though we did appeal to them. When at Imperial I had sheltered behind the experience and reputation of John Cox. I knew that in Newcastle I would have to assert myself

Dave Leigh, 1960

if the CP was to get anywhere. I decided that I needed to embark on a course of serious reading in the Marxist classics. When I was ready I started a course of public lectures in Marxist economics feeling ready to take on anyone.' He is remembered as a very formidable advocate of the CP line. With the lively, if more quixotic Harry Rothman, the Socialist Society (SocSoc) was founded, open to all, then within a year the Communist Society (ComSoc). SocSoc was a broad front which included genuinely independent thinkers like Jim Walker. He was imaginative, deeply sceptical, a debunker with a wide range of friends and admirers. It rapidly grew to 50-60 'members' from which Leigh and Rothman plucked the earnest and more committed to form ComSoc.

Mike Down was one of those. He had the sometimes overbearing self confidence of the public school boy. Extremely good on his feet, he became the most public and quotable face of north east socialist student politics. He wrote, 'I used to appear fairly regularly on the Tyne Tees TV show 'Youth puts the Question'. I wore my usual donkey jacket, grey striped drainpipes and purple suede shoes. I slanged off all the semi-famous guests and received 20 guineas per show, which was very welcome as I was quite poor and relied entirely on my grant and what I earned in the summer holidays. I never got any money from my parents as they didn't have any. The only show I remember in detail was about Scottish independence, which in those days seemed absurd. They were recorded on very wide 'Ampex' tape and we stayed afterwards for coffee and snacks and watch the recording with the guests. Geoff Denton tells me that one show had to be pulled because of my highly objectionable remarks but I cannot remember it.'

Ann Berg remembers the surprise at the number turning up for the first meeting of ComSoc. She burst into a rendering of the *Red Flag* but felt outdone by Dave Leigh 'who in his beautiful bass voice sang,

It's dark as a dungeon and damp as the dew
Where the dangers are double and the pleasures are few
Where the rain never falls and the sun never shines
It's dark as a dungeon way down in the mines.'[219]

The song's writer, the US radical Cisco Houston, had died that spring,

The profile of the CP was raised dramatically from the depths of 1956. Rothman explains the appeal. '(It) was, the idea, the vision of socialism as an egalitarian and planned society. In our blind faith & naivety we believe the USSR was the home of socialism and a worker's state. Further, our personal contacts in the CP were often with quite admirable and decent trade union workers who we saw fighting for their fellow workers at no little cost to themselves. We were especially impressed by the concepts of dialectical and historical materialism which we learned of mostly from a Soviet Manual *Fundamentals of Marxism – Leninism,* 900 pages, which we studied in 1962. I recall one fellow zoology student, later to become an outstanding ecologist and ethnologist, who was so impressed by the philosophical world outlook, he joined the CP.

We published a student magazine in which we attempted to develop our ideas, not always clearly. One article by the artist, the late Stuart Hodkinson, had its pages out of order but still seemed to make sense... So we tended to be involved in student affairs, and generally thought we could out argue other left students. Dave Leigh in particular seemed invincible. Issues such as Soviet Nuclear weapons, Hungary could be argued away. The Soviet Union was for peaceful coexistence; the US & other capitalist states were imperialist and so on. At the time we had had the Korean War, Malaya, Suez, Iran etc. The Soviet Union looked strong in technology and science, enough to scare the US.'

Mike Down explained the attraction similarly, 'We fell for the propaganda – Hungary was a Western plot and capitalism was actually on the verge of collapse, Russia was a potential paradise etc. etc. But many of my heroes at that time – Mao, Ho Chi Minh, Castro, most of the ANC leadership in South Africa, not to mention Pete Seeger and the London protest singers – were either communists or had communist connections. And The CP, unlike Labour to the right and the Trots to the left, had impressive international connections.'[220]

Down was attractive to would be acolytes and destructive to opponents. Rothman and Leigh, from CP families had a strong grasp of theory but, despite their endeavours, newcomers did not necessarily move beyond generalities. Mike Down said, 'Apart from the opening paragraphs of the *Communist Manifesto,* I remember reading no Marxist – Leninist theory whatever. The argument that capitalists wanted their workers to work harder for less while the workers wanted to work less for more did seem an irreconcilable contradiction and very powerful at the time. The nearest I got to reading theory was probably the Eric Bentley translations of all Brecht's poems and major plays and occasional pieces of theory in the *Daily Worker* or *Marxism Today.* I even got the *Daily Worker* when on holiday on the Isle of Wight – the only person in my village who did.'

Mike Worrall also joined the Party under Dave Leigh's influence. He was a scientist with a long peace movement connection. With Mike Down he was the student CP person in CND. Worrall was easily the most efficient of the younger CND fraternity. Clearly trusted and relied upon by the 'elders' who formed the regional committee, Mike made sure the bus left on time, that everyone registered was there, that the bills were paid and the banners ready for unfurling. Among the Post-Graduate students was Walter Ryder who was a bit unusual in being a working class Tynesider. His father was a shipyard worker at Wallsend

Slipway. Like Mike Worrall, he was a methodical and gifted organiser. Walter's involvement in left wing politics came from his interest in the Bomb's effect on ecology and the influence of fellow scientists like Harry Rothman and Dave Leigh. He worked closely with the CP students in CND though he only joined the Party after leaving University. [221]

Altogether this was an impressive and attractive core of political animals, possessed of sharp intellects. However their influence was to be short lived. Whilst several of the younger north easterners were drawn into their orbit, few followed them into the Communist Party. They did not have the messianic certainty, verging on the paranoid, of Gerry Healy and some of his followers. Their problem was the fundamentally rotten set of politics which underpinned their motivation and activity. One by one, they came to confront their own choices.

Harry Rothman was the first to break from the CP, initially at the cost of his relationship with his father. He says, 'I fell out with the Party after a piece of bureaucratic dealing at the Party Congress. The University Branch took a position on the Sino-Soviet dispute in 1962. I was a delegate and due to speak on it but was warned off by Peter Kerrigan who said the idea was 'very interesting' and would be considered but would I not raise it on the Congress floor? I grudgingly agreed but was very disappointed when it was just buried. I and others thought deeply about this treatment. We moved rapidly over the summer of 1962 from a sort of 'Maoist' sympathy to Trotskyism, in that very quick fashion that young people have.'[222] The SLL was his next, but, short lived, port of call. Walter Ryder stayed with the Party for less than two years allowing his membership to lapse, curiously perhaps, when he left for a four year working visit to Cuba. Dave Leigh worked for the NCB after getting his PhD then for a time at King Street.[223] He eventually worked for an import-export business with Eastern Europe which had been founded by Party veteran Phil Piratin. Witnessing at first hand the absurdities of the soviet economy did nothing to cement his attachment to the CP, but the Soviet invasion of Czechoslovakia in 1968 focused his disillusionment.[224]

Both Leigh and Ann Kane remember little contact by University CP members with the town YCL, except when organising transport for demonstrations. The newly formed Youth Campaign for Nuclear Disarmament (YCND), in 1960 became a very important field of activity for the YCL but this was a town rather than a University activity. Some YCND branches were formed and run by YCL members. Nina Johnson had been in the YCL since 1954 when, without telling her parents, she had gone to the People's Bookshop in Newcastle and joined. 'It became the centre of my life,' she said, 'I just loved the leafleting, the meetings, going to other Party households like Cecil Taylor the playwright's, seeing how other families operated and the avid reading of political books.'[225]

Lucy Nicholson's parents were both CP members. Her father, Ted, was Secretary of the Newcastle East Branch. Lucy was involved from the age of 12, delivering leaflets and helping her mother Grace at the *Daily Worker* jumble sales. She remembers Branch Committee meetings in the front room and being involved in discussions over tea and biscuits from a young age. Music grabbed her and she was soon singing and playing her guitar at Party events.[226]

Ann Green was 15 when she joined in 1957. Her Dad was the District Secretary, Horace Green. She wrote, '(He) was a self educated man with a huge library covering every subject. He was my best friend and friend and mentor to all the YCL. For many of us who left school at 15, the YCL gave us an education in Politics, Economics and History.' When Ann joined there were only about three other members, all a lot older than her. 'But it soon took off. Nothing to do with me, it was a result of Party members' kids reaching YCL age and the general political atmosphere of the times. YCND was also rising covering all political and religious points of view and there was also the fight against apartheid in South Africa.'[227]

Chapter nine: The Young Socialists and beyond

It is difficult to separate the early history of the Young Socialists from that of the Marxist groups. So much of the business of the YS branches was concerned with the activity of the far left groups and especially *Keep Left*/SLL. One example concerned Newcastle West constituency YS. In the spring of 1962 the YS branch was invited to nominate and elect a delegate to the second YS conference, subject to ratification by the Constituency Executive, in effect, by the Secretary, Bob Brown. On the evening in question a *Keep Left* supporter in the YS branch arrived at the meeting with up to ten new members allegedly signed up by the Treasurer in time for the meeting. None of the ten were known to the branch members who nevertheless accepted their presence in the meeting. When the time arrived for the ballot for Conference delegate the ten accordingly voted with the *Keep Left* supporters giving their nominee a narrow victory amidst intense bad feeling. Bob Brown was informed of the name of the nominee. Following a meeting of the Constituency E.C., ratification was denied and the YS Branch was informed. The matter came before the General Committee where the YS Secretary argued that the YS Branch should have autonomy over its selection. That position was defeated and the Branch had to run a further election. None of the ten new 'members' turned up, the *Keep Left* candidate who stood again was defeated and the nominated person was then accepted by the Party E.C. None of the new 'members' ever came to a meeting again. It is clear from the recollections of some of the *Keep Left* people of that time that it was SLL policy to acquire delegations by any mean possible. The business occupied a lot of the time and energy of the branch. It is impossible to know how damaging this was to the health of the Young Socialists. It certainly caused a lot of bitterness. The quarrel between *Keep Left* and the rest of the YS affected several branches in the area including, Newcastle East, Gosforth, Gateshead, Felling, Tynemouth, South Shields, Prudhoe, Houghton, Blyth and Stanley.

North YS

The only Tyneside branch not engaged with the dispute at all, was Newcastle North though one *Keep Left* supporter appeared there. It was actually started as a branch of the 59 Society but changed its name when the Labour Party officially constituted the Young Socialists. It is just possible that the branch was founded to escape from the ill feeling which marked the latter days of the 59 Society. It was probably the Labour Party's ideal YS branch. It met regularly, with no apparent acrimony between its members, and assiduously carried out canvassing work for Labour candidates in local elections. Despite its CND orientation it never got embroiled in the politics of the far left.

Jane Owens, 1959

The North Branch was certainly successful, holding regular weekly meetings at the Constituency offices at Winchester Terrace, Summerhill. Jane (Owen)Wadhams remembers that, 'an evening at Winchester Terrace would often involve an invited speaker. Sometimes we did our own thing with a dreaded 'Hat Debate' or someone from the group presenting a talk on a topical issue. We then used to process in an unthreatening horde down Westgate Road to the Bigg Market to listen to whoever was on their soapbox. Evenings often ended in the Wimpey Bar by the Mayfair.'[228] North branch also had a good complement of outside speakers. Jane said, 'we had Tony Greenwood MP and a woman who had been a suffragette who was still active in local politics (Connie Lewcock). Dan Smith did a *Desert Island Discs* session and there were speakers about a lot of topical issues including education and comprehensive schools, apartheid, unilateralism, regional development and local planning issues.'[229]

North branch had a membership of over 50. Jeremy Beecham, though only 15 at the outset, was very active and probably already considering a political career. He had joined the 59 Society but was apparently unattracted by either the left wing groups or CND, which he was 'thoroughly opposed to.' A founding member of the North Branch, he left for University in 1963. At Oxford he was Chairman of the Labour Club. On his return to Newcastle, and a legal practice, he was soon elected to the City Council, one of only three YS members from that period to do so. In the 1970s he was to become leader of the Labour Group and of the City Council.[230]

The branch was heavily based on the Jesmond Ward of the Constituency and hence socially quite middle class in composition. This meant that most members went off to University or college at 18. If they were to find their way into Labour Party activity it would be after University and quite often well away from Tyneside. They were unlikely to become involved with the YS again after campus politics.

Turnover of members

This held true for all the north east branches. In fact the balance in this young socialist organisation was always away from 15 or 16 year old school leavers and towards sixth formers likely to go to College. There were some exceptions, namely Newburn, Felling and Stanley and to some extent, Gateshead. Apart from the latter these were largely mining communities but coal mining was in decline and there was an anxiety among colliery families to have their youngsters pursue other occupations.

Though the YS membership in these branches might have a larger than average young worker composition, they were also vulnerable to rapid turn over and dissolution. Non-mining related occupations were likely to be outside the local community, involving travelling, day release or even full time college. Also marriage was likely to be earlier than for those entering higher education.

Across the whole of the membership of several hundreds in the period 1959 to 1965, only a few were sufficiently bitten by the politics bug to continue political activity into their twenties and beyond. Although we are looking at small number, most of those who did survive as political activists had joined groups such as the SLL, the IS or the Communist Party. The Labour Party seemed to hold little attraction, except for the few wishing to pursue a career in politics. For young people drawn into activity through opposition to the Bomb their idealism received an enormous boost in 1960 when the Party Conference went unilateralist. It was sustained through a year of demonstrations and exciting meetings. Hugh Gaitskell's success in reversing policy at the 1961 September Conference was a triumph for the party's old guard, but a disaster for the youth movement and the Labour Party's standing among politically motivated youth.

The Labour Party leadership handled young socialists very badly. The party was in decline as a membership organization. Many ward parties had become ageing husks. Rising wages, a lively job market, more comfortable homes and accessible entertainment contributed to political passivity and loss of membership without renewal. Yet the Party was willing to sacrifice the new upsurge of politically engaged youth to their obsession for control. Some Labour leaders like Tony Greenwood saw the potential and argued for giving youth its head. He was simply out voted on the National Executive Committee and brushed aside by bruisers like Bessie Braddock and Ray Gunter. They forced out Roger Protz their appointed Editor for New Advance at the first YS Conference in 1961, by denying him editorial freedom. Protz was replaced by 47 year old Reg Underhill, the Deputy National Agent. Bizarrely, Underhill resolutely refused to cover the issue of the bomb in the paper, even though it was the issue of most concern for young socialists. The Party appointed Regional Youth Officers, usually in middle aged, to watch over and report on YS branch activities.

In the Summer of 1962, *Keep Left* was proscribed but this simply increased its influence inside the YS. Many YS branches were reduced to sterile manoevring between the factions. By the 1964 YS Conference many *Keep Left* supporting members were suspended or expelled. In 1965 the Healyites took a fifth of the YS membership out of the Labour Party, declaring independence and forcing the LP to add 'Labour Party' to the name of its youth group. Wal Hobson describes the Healyite method. Wal had been elected to the YS National Committee in 1962. 'We (the SLL members) were encouraged to disagree on every issue in NC meetings, deliberately provoking the LP to take disciplinary action. Healy always wanted us to be expelled, to raise the question of democracy and take others out with us to build an independent Y.S.'[231] In this respect he was successful. The Hobsons were both suspended from the South Shields Labour Party in 1965. They were a little unusual in being fully participant in the Party. Indeed Wal had been a council candidate in 1961 and was popular among party members.[232]

The General Election of 1964

The General Election of 1964 brought Harold Wilson to office. In most of the YS branches the two years preceding the election were marked by sectarian battles and jockeying for positions. Yet conventional activity continued. The West YS members were busily involved in canvassing in council elections in Kenton and Newburn. The West YS branch turned out night after night in a Kenton by-election in 1962 where I was Secretary.

However, by mid-1963, I had married Marian Campbell and moved to live in Whitley Bay. Marian and I joined the local Party there which was in a sorry state. Meetings were small, never exceeding ten people, though the paper membership was larger. Soon I was elected Chairman and Marian, Secretary. The branch included John and Betty Mapplebeck, Benita Brown, a write, and Rae Fisher, the folk singer. There was one long term member, Councillor Bill Hutchinson, a CND supporter, who had been the General Election Candidate in 1955. The newly adopted Labour Candidate was Albert Booth, an engineering draughtsman and strong CND supporter. Although the Constituency had been won for Labour, by Grace Coleman, in 1945, it had been lost in 1950. With its wide swathes of owner occupied territory in Whitley Bay and Monkseaton, it was generally regarded as a rather hopeless case.

In 1964 most work went into the working class wards in North Shields and Percy Main. Whitley Bay was left to our small group. There were three areas of potential Labour voters. There was the mining village of Hartley, to the north, which elected Bill Hutchinson as councillor, a council estate at Hillheads and a small terraced area round the town centre which was thought to contain

Labour supporters. Since the latter contained a lot of bed and breakfast hotels we did not find many Labour voters there. A lot of dispiriting nastiness was encountered on the doorstep in what turned out to be my swansong as a Labour Party election worker, apart from a brief moment in Selby, Yorkshire in 1966. Albert Booth polled strongly but fell far short of the Tory harridan, Dame Irene Ward, on polling day.

However the 64 Election was to have one interesting moment, for me. After my failure to be adopted at Scotswood I had kept in touch with Dan Smith. I was flattered by his apparent interest in my ideas. We had discussed a *New Left Review* article on housing policy. He had accepted my invitation to speak in Whitley Bay for Albert Booth. The election was about a week away and the Polls indicated a probable national Labour victory. Smith offered me a lift home after the meeting. On the way he told me that great things were going to happen after the Election. I must have asked him what he was expecting to do and he replied that he expected a call from Harold Wilson to join the Cabinet as Minister for Regional Development. The call was never made. Many years later when relating the story to Paul Foot, Foot said that he had been told that Wilson had been warned, presumably by MI5, that Dan Smith would be a high risk appointment as he was being investigated for corruption. This was 1964, still nine years away from the famous court case.

John Mapplebeck encountered Dan in this period too. He wrote, 'I think I was always suspicious of T Dan Smithery. He use to give exclusive interviews to *Voice of the North* (out of respect for Dick Kelly). Usually by the time he came in, after some council meeting, shortly before we were due on air, Dick would have gone home and I would be producing. The interview would be recorded in one studio ...and it would sound dynamic. By the time I had rushed to the editing channel I used to find myself waiting in vain for an 'in cue.' I realized then that behind all the fashionable phrases, 'Venice of the North,' 'The new Brasilia'- there was very little substance. All this was confirmed, in the bar of the Trafalgar, when I heard from Jack Johnson the machinations behind the Crudens affair, later confirmed independently by John Dougray who for a brief period was a public relations man for Crudens.'[233]

Like other young socialists attracted by the International Socialists, the Labour Party was fast losing its charm for me. It was merely a venue for raising discussion, selling literature and hopefully, recruitment. This was the position in Newcastle East where Dave and Sandra Peers were active from their arrival in Newcastle in the autumn of 1963. They had joined the IS at Oxford. Dave was from Merseyside and Sandra from a mining village in Derbyshire. After Oxford they were briefly active in London but keen to move north. Tony Cliff suggested Tyneside, so Dave applied for a job at Charles Trevelyan College in Newcastle.

Some people in the movement assumed they had been sent by the organisation but that misunderstood the libertarian regime of IS at the time. People were not *sent* anywhere though Tony Cliff would suggest places which could benefit from new activists.

The group was small with around a dozen members: Terry Rodgers, Ken Moffitt, Len Clucas also a Parsons' draughtsmen (he had a whippet called Trotsky), Jim Hutchinson, Jim Nichol, Brian Ebbatson, Bob Heyes, and school students, Linda Potts, Dorothy Simmons and Pam Hepburn. Additionally there were perhaps up to ten others whose membership was much looser including Jim Murray, Jim Elder, Alex Glasgow and Guy Falkenau. But for all, membership was a rather informal business.

Building a group was a difficult task as some of the recruits were from school sixth forms and they were soon off to Universities across Britain. Dorothy Simmons, from Denton Burn joined the YS at about 16 and started to attend IS meetings with her friends Linda Potts from Longbenton and Pam Hepburn. For Dorothy it was both exciting and a bit scary. Excitement came from 'sitting in a pub in Whitley Bay gossiping with Paul Foot. From that time I loved him to bits. But then everybody did.' She also enjoyed the sometimes scary London trips, 'We went in a car load through the fog after school. We stayed on the Friday night in a suburban house in Wembley. I did think it was a bit off, going to London for a socialist meeting and staying in suburbia. The next day we went on to Chatterton Road, to Tony Cliff's house. This was different. Warm, cheerful, a terrific buzz, masses of books, ideas flying around, though the meeting in a cold church hall was oh so boring.' She said, 'Ideas were important. We struggled to understand our world. I once asked Jim Nichol what socialism would be like. He said, I think I know, but I can't prove it, 'cos you can't get into Albania.'[234]'They were both 17 at the time.

There was a downside. The IS made demands which she did not feel up to. A group of dissident communist Kurdish Students had got in touch with IS. At one of Dorothy and Linda's early meetings they were asked and agreed to go the Kurds' homes with leaflets and *Labour Worker* and to invite them to an IS meeting. They had a great discussion but she feels that this was too much to ask of 17 year olds. They felt used. She also felt appalled at what she saw as joy among the IS members at a meeting on the day that Kennedy was assassinated. She felt that these experiences led her to avoid student politics when she went to LSE in 1965.

Guy Falkenau also eschewed IS politics when he left for College in 1963. He writes, 'My involvement with IS was brief. I attended the odd meeting and the weekend conference held at Tony Cliff's house in London, but soon found it held as little interest for me as the SLL. My politics is essentially philosophic, not ideological. At the point at which ideology tips over into neo-theology I lose interest. Arcane debates over the nature of Soviet socialism may have provided fertile material for my college history main course dissertation, (I even made good use of Cliff's book), but as a guide to future action I found it as much use as astrology.

My politics have always been as concerned with the achievement of practical objectives, as with social transformation. Or put another way, temperamentally and philosophically I am a gradualist. It is an accumulation of small consecutive changes that produce social transformation, which I find more compelling. The easy part of revolutionary ideology is knowing what you are against. The problem is getting consensus about what revolutions are for. Lenin understood that, but achieving consensus about how the dictatorship of the proletariat should be exercised is unlikely to prove easier to achieve now than it was in the 20th century. Given the record of revolutionary movements in increasing the sum of human happiness I have preferred devoting my energies to the achievement of more immediate and practical social improvements.'[235]

Leaving town

In the summer of 1965 I applied for a teaching job at Selby in Yorkshire and in August the family moved away from Tyneside where I started a new political life in an unfamiliar area. On Tyneside, by that time, many of the people in this account had either reached or, were near reaching, the maximum age for the YS. Only a few graduated to activity in the Labour Party. Many moved away to college or work. For those who stayed and stayed in touch with politics the Communist Party, the YCL and the far left groups and eventually the women's movement provided a field of activity. On the broader front the Anti-Vietnam War campaign replaced CND.

Chapter ten: Where have all the marchers gone?

In 1974 the late Peter Sedgwick wrote, 'The story of the British Left from the 1956 split in the Communist Party up till the growth and disintegration of the Vietnam Solidarity movement is the record of a political adolescence. And who can review his own adolescence without an embarrassed blush or an amused smile at follies recognised as such too late? Not all of it will have been folly of course; but even what was ardent and delightful is now revealed as without issue, harbouring from its outset the contradictions that would dissolve or defeat its hope. *Where have all the flowers gone?* sang the marchers; and, in pacific elegy, *where have all the soldiers gone?* And, now, a few years later, *where have all the marchers gone?*[236]

Sedgwick's astringent comment holds some truths which might be recognised by some of those whose story is told in this book. It was written at the peak of the labour movement's success, when the miners had just brought down a Tory government. Whilst celebrating this achievement, he lamented the failure to create a new militant socialist party. He attributed this partly to the absence from the political process of the young people who had campaigned and marched in 1960 and 1968. It is hard to quantify the involvement in 1974 of the north east's participants in 1960 and 1968. One factor contributing to this difficulty was the dispersal of the participants from the north east to other regions.

Sedgwick died in 1983 so we don't have his comments on this generation fifty years on, after Thatcherism, Blairism, climate change, environmental disaster and serial international conflict. Politically, most people would see the contemporary situation as much worse than the one he commented on in 1974. Certainly there is no strong socialist party around which progressives can group for electoral purposes or campaign with on important issues. Oddly though, there is probably a much greater desire for such a party than there was in 1974 when there was wider belief in both the Labour Party and the growing organisations to the left of it. That is a discussion for another place. However, at an individual level, the 1960 cohort has fared quite well in terms of engagement with progressive causes.

A small number of the people who were drawn into activity continued at a high level of political commitment after 1965 and most people pursued an interest in causes or sought employment in, broadly, caring professions. To follow up in detail everyone's life after that date would involve a second book and is beyond the scope and intent of this one. However to satisfy possible interest in the future of the participants there follows a summary of what is known about the lives of some people who appear in the pages of this book. Not everyone could be reached.

Directory

Maggie Anwell, b 1947, joined the Peoples Theatre and read Drama at Birmingham University. She lived and worked in Interplay Community Arts Cooperative in Leeds, running theatre, film and women's projects in the early 1970s. She then moved to run similar projects in Manchester and with the Belgrade Theatre in Coventry . She married Tim Carlyle, an architect and had one daughter. She was active in the Rising Sun Domestic Violence Project in Canterbury where she now lives and is involved in therapy and outreach work with women, children and families.

Ken Appleby, b 1940, must hold a record for sackings for militancy. He lived and worked at Reyrolles, Hebburn, then in Kendal, Newton Abbot and Keighley followed by a period as Industrial Organiser for the SWP. Subsequently he worked in Loughborough and elsewhere in the East Midlands . He retired in 2007 and moved to northern France. He is still optimistic about the world changing.

Dave Arrowsmith, b 1946. After Gateshead Grammar School, he tried Art School (1963), adopted anarchism and became involved in Direct Action, travelling around Britain with a rucksack. Back on Tyneside he worked at Redheugh Gas Works, collected the Dole, worked at the same Dole Office, then spent seven years at Huwoods on the Team Valley. In 1974 he got a job in C A Parsons' office, 'collecting his union card and IS membership card on the way in.' In 1981 he moved south to begin 26 years in the Tesco I.T. Department. His IS (SWP) membership did not survive the move but he became active in the Anti-Cruise Missiles Campaign. In the early 90s he joined the Labour Party and served for four years as a Councillor. He goes to the odd demonstration, regrets that there is such a weak socialist response to the present crisis, but believes that 'the struggle goes on all over the World.'

John Baker, b 1940, has done an enormous number of jobs: labouer on a power station construction site, salesman (several times), taxi driver, barman, owner of small businesses, civil servant at the Ministry of Agriculture. He says. 'I have tried to wrest a living from a reluctant world.'

Jennifer (Piachaud) Bartholemew, b 1945, left Tyneside to do nursing training at Westminster Hospital. She married Mike Down and had 3 children plus two steps from a second marriage. In the seventies she completed a degree in psychology at University College, London and an MSc in Medical Sociology. She was a research administrator in General Practice at Kings College, London till retirement. Although she says she is not 'political,' she was a LP member for over 40 years till the Iraq War and a participant in demonstrations from Aldermaston and Grosvenor Grosvenor Square to the recent anti-war ones.

Jeremy Beecham, b 1945. He was elected to Newcastle City Council for Benwell Ward in 1967 shortly after returning to Newcastle having completed his qualifications as a solicitor. Over the last forty years he can truly be said to have been the leading City Councillor. He has been both leader of the Council and the Labour Group. He has been nationally known as Chairman and member of the Association of Metropolitan Councils and the Labour Party National Executive. He has been a stalwart of the Labour establishment, known for his probity and balanced judgement. He has never been a man of the Labour left. As a supporter of the State of Israel he has often been troubled by its behaviour towards Palestinians and has associated himself strongly, along with his wife **Brenda (Woolf),** Newcastle North YS), in an organisation supporting educational initiatives for both Arab and Jewish children.

Margaret (Dick) Brecknell, b 1943, went to Oxford ,joined the Labour Club and was briefly in the Labour Party. She trained as a Systems Analyst, working for the Greater London Council for 13 years, an electronics company, Distillers, Hatfield Polytechnic and a firm producing airline tickets.

Kyran Casteel, b 1941, graduated and married in 1964. He went Northern Rhodesia on a UNESCO/UK Government teacher training scheme just in time to attend Zambia's independence celebrations in Chipata. In he went to Harare (Salisbury) to do a PGCE. He did a bit of anti-Smith campaigning but failed to avert UDI which occurred during his final exams. He returned to Zambia and taught at two secondary schools before being transferred to a Geological Survey in Lusaka.. In 1969 he joined the copper mining industry. He returned to the UK 1972 and did an M.Sc in Information Science. After completion Kyran has worked in the minerals industry consulting and publishing, and, since 1995 as a freelance. He declined to offer his services as a Labour candidate for local council elections but hasn't changed his political views significantly, particularly not on nuclear disarmament . He supports various AVAAZ campaigns, Action Aid. He has three sons by his first marriage, and one daughter by his second.

Marian (Campbell) Charlton, b1941, was active in CND and anti apartheid until having children. She moved to Yorkshire in 1965 for her husband's employment. She worked in various part-time roles until graduating as a mature student at the University of Leeds in 1976. From 1979 has been employed in the teaching and development of programmes in youth and community development. In addition to teaching in HE she is a community and trade union activist, subscribing to the view that global action starts at the local level. This activism has included membership of Leeds Women's Committee and associated campaigns, Chairing of the Yorkshire and Humberside Low Pay Unit, Secretary of the Yorkshire and Humberside NATFHE Women's panel and active involvement in the organization and development of The Association of Lecturers in Youth and Community Work. Currently a Chair of Governors in an Inner City Primary School. She has ongoing involvement in various grass roots community organisations committed to the sustainability of urban communities. Marian is strongly

Dave Leigh & Barry Scaum, 1989

Jim Walker & Brenda Corcoran, 1999

committed to challenging social inequalities and supporting environmental issues including international organizations opposed to factory farming.

John Charlton, b 1938, left Tyneside in 1965 to teach at a High School in Yorkshire. He subsequently taught at City of Leeds and Carnegie College, Leeds Polytechnic and the University of Leeds. He retired in 1999, returning to Tyneside, where he has been involved in labour and local history. He has written on Chartism, New Unionism, Miners' strikes, Anti-globalisation struggles, Origins of the welfare state and the slavery business and north east England. He has remained a member of the SWP.

Marge (Wallace) Chryssostimidis,b 1942. After a history degree at York University, she went to the US where her fiancé was a graduate student at MIT. Tom (fiancé) never left MIT, becoming a professor of naval architecture, so she somewhat reluctantly stayed on in America, keeping a low profile politically to avoid compromising residence status. She gained an MSc in library science at Simmons College, Boston and worked in the MIT libraries for many years. Next she got a diploma in food and beverage management, wrote a food column for a local magazine, helped organize technical conferences at MIT and participated in four marine archaeology expeditions in Greece and Italy with Tom's technical team. She found local politics uninspiring, channelling her energies in the late 80s into volunteer work at a local Aids activist group, subsequently becoming very vocal in support of gay rights. Marge participated in MIT/Harvard anti-war demonstration in 2003, including sit-in on the Charles River bridge.

Mary (Feinmann) Chuck, b 1943. She went to Westfield College for Young Ladies in London – a bad mistake! (she says). She married, completed her degree at Queen Mary College, had two children, lived in Switzerland and America for several years, then moved back – to Coventry – to teacher training and divorce. Taught in Macclesfield and Warrington, where she spent 15 years as Head of a Comprehensive School serving the New Town. She thought there was enough politics, in every sense of the word, in the job, and always sought to ensure that the widest possible opportunities for achievement and excellence and culture were available to every child. She retired in 2001. Mary is still a paid up, but inactive, member of the Labour Party because it feels like giving up hope to resign. Content now with family, grand children, art, poetry, music – but hasn't changed her views and still believes we should try to save the world.

Fiona (Scott Batey) Clarke, b 1947, left Tyneside for Bedford College, London in 1965. After qualifying as a town planner she worked for Surrey and Berkshire County Council. She moved north to Manchester then back to Newcastle with her husband, Chris Clarke, in 1977. She did some part time work whilst her children were small then worked full time with the City Challenge regeneration project from 1991. Local government work limited her open activity for the Labour Party though has been a member since 1960, Secretary of Jesmond Ward and three times a council candidate since 2000. In Manchester and Newcastle she engaged in voluntary work for the National Childbirth Trust and in campaigns for a children's playground and to save and regenerate Jesmond community swimming pool. She says she has tried 'not to deviate from the values acquired in a socialist home, in the young socialists and CND and at Quaker meetings I attended as a young person.'

Brenda (Ingleby) Corcoron, b 1943, left the SLL after Leeds University, married Tony, had two children and taught English at Benfield Comprehensive School in Newcastle for twenty years. With Maggie Pearse and Maggie Gilfellan, she was a founding member of the Socialist Women's Action Group which supported the cleaners in dispute at Newcastle Polytechnic, the miners' wives in the great miners' strikes and campaigned against domestic violence. She was also active in the NUT and Rank and File Teacher. She says she has the same left wing socialist outlooks that she had in her teenage years.

Tony Corcoron, b 1941, taught in Further Education. He was active in the CP, IS and the Anti-Internment Committee in the 60s and early 70s after which he directed his energies into music as performer, teacher and promoter. He writes on his web site, 'At 28, I took up my bow again after being involved in the Anti-Internment Committee through the renowned 'Bridge Hotel' in the city. It was one of the earliest folk clubs and hosted everything from balladeers like Luke Kelly and Christy Moore to cultural and political happenings. It's still going strong today. Eventually music took over more from my politics. Through friendships forged with the flute player, John Doonan and the songwriter, Alex Glasgow, my mate Peter Kelly and I were inspired to start playing at Irish Feiseanna (set dancing festivals) in the mid-70s. I haven't stopped since. Around that time, I also started the Newcastle branch of Comhaltas Ceoltoiri Eireann, the network for Irish traditional musicians and events.'

John Creaby, b 1943, saw the YS and CND through to their mid-sixties decline. From 1965 to 1968 he worked at Vickers Armstrongs, Elswick. He was very active in the clerical workers union (CAWU) achieving 100% membership in the office. Whilst he was at Ruskin College in 1968, he was appointed to a full-time organiser's position in the CAWU which he held until retirement. He was a Labour Party member throughout though despairing of New Labour's performance. He always supported CND and Anti-Apartheid and was a founder of the Campaign Against Racial Discrimination on Tyneside. He says he owes a lot to the 59 Society where he learned the values of comradeship and openness of thought.

John & Margaret Creaby, 1999

Jim Nichol, Guy Falkenau & Jeannie Mortimer,
1999

Margaret (Southern) Creaby, b 1945, joined the Labour Party at 14 and was active all her life until the arrival of Tony Blair and New Labour. She heard him years before he became leader and thought then that she could have been listening to a Tory. Margaret worked in many clerical jobs, often for trade unions, the Co-op and local authorities. She is proudest of her work for welfare rights during the 1984 Miners' Strike. She has an abiding belief in the struggle for equality and responsibility for each other.

Sam Dodds, b 1945, left school at 15. He worked for 31 years for Dunn's the hat company in Newcastle and Carlisle. When he was made redundant his reward was – £9,000. He then spent 18 years in the furniture trade up to retirement. His working hourse – Saturdays included – made it difficult to participate in a lot of political activity but he always argued for socialism at work in a very difficult environment. He coached young basketball players for many years. He was been very disappointed in the record of Labour governments.

Mike Down, b 1940, see Addendum.

Dave Douglass, b 1947, left Tyneside for South Yorkshire in 1966. He worked at Hatfield Main Colliery till the pit was privatised in 1992 when he was blacklisted by the new owners. He was employed by the miners as the NUM Branch Secretary and Welfare Rights Adviser running the Mining Communities Advice Centre until 2004. He went to Ruskin College, and the Universities of Strathclyde and Keele (the latter by distance learning while doing nightshift) where he distinguished himself academically and then went back to work as a rank and file pitman. He has been in many different left wing parties (CP, RWP, Sinn Fein, Class War) up the IWW today. He has written two volumes (so far) of autobiography. He is a fine folk and protest singer widely respected in the labour movement as a man who has no price.

Brian Ebbatson, b 1945. Was active in IS through the sixties. He taught in Germany from 1972 to 1975. He joined the Labour Party after the Thatcher victory in 1979, seeking a practical outlet for his socialist politics. He taught German at New College, Durham till 1997. He undertook grass roots activity in communities, always his inclination. Elected to Durham County Council 1997, he has been closely involved with arts policy but considers his most important contribution to be in helping voluntary community based groups to mobilise themselves.

Linda (Potts) Ebbatson, b 1947, she went to Oxford to study archaeology, in which she is still involved. Active in IS, she married Brian and spent four years in Germany. Linda joined the Labour Party in 1979. She has been active locally and nationally in the Socialist Education Association and other progressive campaigns. A local Councillor in Chester le Street from 1997, she was latterly Chair of the District Council till 2009.

Guy Falkenau, b 1945, he qualified as a teacher in 1966. He taught in Gateshead and London till 1969. He returned to the north east in 1970, and taught for 16 years in Gateshead. From 1986 to retirement, in 2002, Guy was Deputy Chief Education Officer for Gateshead with a strong interest in refurbishing primary education in the borough. He has been a Labour Party member throughout, and was also very active in the second wave of CND from 1980.

Lucy (Nicholson) Faulkenau, b 1945. Lucy was active with the YCL and went to help build the Unity and Fraternity Highway in Yugoslavia in the sixties. She went to Newcastle Art School and Bretton Hall College (Yorks) qualifying as a teacher. She has been on countless demonstrations, which she prefers to political meetings. Music has really absorbed her – she plays six instruments and sings. She has been in several bands romping round the north east's pubs and folk clubs for forty years. She believes she is 'a natural socialist. When I see injustice I'll stand up and fight.'

Moira (Woods) Gray, b 1945, had a lifetime in Labour politics until the Blair era.

Alec Comb, b 1939 and **Ann (Green) Comb,** married in 1962. Members of the YCL and the CP till the split in 1991. Alec worked as an industrial chemist at several local factories including Formica. Involved in community politics on Tyneside, Melmerby (Cumberland) where they ran the village post office and cafe, and France where they now live.

Wally, b 1938 and **Gladys Hobson,** b 1943 were suspended from the Labour Party in 1964 and did not re-enter till 1980, inspired by Michael Foot becoming party leader. Gladys was a South Shields councillor from 1982 to 1991 and Wal from 2002 till 2006. Wal worked at Thermal Syndicate till 1974 then in the

Norman Ridley, Jim Walker & Dave Peers, 1989

Gladys & Wal Hobson

Careers Service, the Probation Service and drug rehabilitation until retirement in 2002. Gladys ran a series of small businesses including a market stall, along with care of their two children and has also served on the Health Authority. Both think their views have not changed much, seeing of themselves as left wing socialists.

Ann Kane, b 1941. After Newcastle did teacher training and embarked on a career teaching biology in High Schools in London. She stayed in the CP till its final split in 1991 but has remained as active as possible in progressive movements.

Dave Leigh, b 1937, worked for the National Coal Board's Operational Research Executive until 1972. He left after helping to publicise shortcomings in the Board's purchasing of powered roof supports which lead to a Select Committee enquiry and millions of pounds savings for the Coal Board. He was very active in the C P though opposed to the Soviet Union's intervention in Czechoslovakia in 1968. In 1972 he joined former Communist M.P., Phil Piratin, in a trading enterprise with Eastern Europe where he had close experience of the vagaries of socialist planning. He is active in CND and still marching.

Doreen Huddart, followed a nursing career on Tyneside and Sheffield. Left the Labour Party for the Liberal Democrats serving on Sheffield City Council and Newcastle City Council from her return to Tyneside in the 1990s.

Jim Hutchinson, b 1940. He joined the IS in 1962, the first member on Tyneside, whilst he was a metallurgy student at Kings College. He soon realised he was not cut out for a career in industry and after a Dip Ed in the mid-60s, he became a primary school teacher, mostly in South Tyneside, where he continued until retirement. He was an active member of the National Union of Teachers, usually in opposition to the official leadership of the union. From the mid-70s he was an organiser of Rank and File teacher in the north east and also of other attempts to bring together left wing members of the NUT. An active member of the IS-SWP, he has maintained a regular door to door sale of *Socialist Worker* and has usually

Roger Hall, 2008

sold the paper on the Saturday pitch at the Monument or Northumberland Street. He has been involved in support work for all the big, and many small, industrial disputes-miners, shipyard workers, engineers and countless public sector workers. He has been in all the great protest movements too, from the Vietnam War, to the Anti-Nazi League, the Anti-Poll Tax Movement and the current Anti-War movement. He has never sought office in anything. He also has a vast knowledge of the Tyneside music scene since the mid-50s.

Pat (Duffy), b 1935, & **Vin McIntyre,** b 1936, left the Labour Party in 1962, along with the entire Young Socialist branch, over the selection of William Rodgers for the Stockton Parliamentary seat. They joined again in 1972 after

Geoff Denton & Mike Down, 1999

Dave Douglass

they moved to Durham. Pat trained as a teacher at 18 but went to university in her 40s as an undergraduate and then as a doctoral student. She has taught every age group from nursery to university. Vin taught for 11 years before joining the Careers Advisory Service at Durham University, later becoming its Director. They joined the ILP in 1965 and both spent long periods on its national council. Pat was also on the executive of the Institute for Workers' Control. They have been active in many campaigns including Vietnam Solidarity, Chile Solidarity, Anti-Apartheid, CND (from 1958 to present), the campaigns against YTS and the Poll Tax and, of course the 1984 Miners' Strike. Pat was on the short list for several constituencies, including Sedgefield when Tony Blair was selected. They have remained strong left wing socialists and resigned from the Labour Party after the invasion of Iraq. They are currently active in the Anti-War Movement and the Palestine Solidarity Campaign.

Pat (Marley) Johnson, b 1941. After the CND and YS activity she went to Darlington Teachers' Training College, then taught in Middlesbrough for four years where she was active in the LP. After marrying the journalist Chris Johnson (and having three children), she went touring Europe and North Africa in a camper van. She was active in the Socialist Women's Action Group from the late 60s. She supported CND, second time round, in the 80s, joined the Labour Party and stayed till the Blair era. She still holds the views she held in her youth: 'a strong belief in social justice, democracy, women's rights and anti racism. You can't give up the fight. You can always change things if you make the effort.'

John Mapplebeck, b 1935, was expelled from the Labour League of Youth for supporting Richard Acland when he fought the Ban-the-Bomb by-election at Gravesend. He was readmitted a year later and, more through indolence than commitment, remains a member of the Labour Party. He writes, 'Having gained the battle honour of a Christmas Tree (the symbol on the BBC personal file which indicated that in the eyes of M16 I was politically unreliable) I left the Corporation in 1989 to work as an independent television producer. I produced and directed the Auden centenary South Bank Show in 2007 and currently (2009) am working on a profile of Lee Hall for one of the last editions of the programme.

John Metcalf, b 1941, after Tyneside did a Dip Ed but then went into housing and planning research in the civil service until early retirement after which he worked for the Rationalist Association until 2006. A secularist, he is a Board member of the Rationalist Association and of the Freethinker magazine. He has been a Labour Party activist since the fifties, serving on Hertfordshire County Council for over thirty years till 2009. He now works part-time as a cycling instructor and would describe himself as a green socialist.

Jean Mortimer, b 1945. After graduating in Politics, Economics and Social Studies and qualifying in social work she spent the next 10 years (1966–1976) as a social worker specialising in child care mainly in the London Borough of Brent. From 1976 to 1983 she formed various business ventures in central London. In 1983 she married an oil man, went to live in Norway and joined him on his travels throughout the world in his role as a trouble shooter. Jean has been an active supporter of the Labour Party from the age of 15 but resigned in 1997. Blair was the final straw. She has continued to support CND throughout and in latter years has become an active supporter of Palestine via the PSC and

Ken Appleby, 1990

Kyran Casteel, 2008

the Durham Palestine Educational Trust. Whilst in Norway she established a charity and led a campaign against the Iraq war and still holds the beliefs of her youth.

Jim Nichol, b 1945, joined the IS in 1962 and remains a member. He left Tyneside in 1964 to work for the IS in London for almost twenty years. During that time he was a key figure, founding and managing a commercial party print shop and acting successively as treasurer, national secretary and editor of *Socialist Worker.* He was also a driving force in the building of the Anti-Nazi League. In the early 1980's he changed careers. He studied law, did articles at the firm of Seifert Sedley then founded his own practice. Taylor Nichol became one of the best known progressive law firms in Britain, known for taking on and winning many of the miscarriages of justice cases over the past twenty

Jim Hutchinson, 1999

years including the celebrated Carl Bridgewater Case. In recent years he has worked on international projects including a UN one, monitoring of police practice in Nepal. He says he would want to be remembered as someone, 'who made a contribution to the world we live in and, a lawyer who defended the guilty.'

Maggie (Boyd) Pearse, b 1947. After College she taught from 1968 to 1973 in Wallsend. She was a member of IS and took part in Anti-Vietnam War and unemployment demonstrations. From 1997 to 1986 she did community work in Bradford, West Yorks. From 1986 to retirement she lectured in Youth and Community work at Bradford College. In that period she has been very active in the women's movement, miners' support (1984), anti-racist and anti-war campaigns (current). Maggie says, 'Although I don't belong to a party I am a Marxist. That has continued to give me a reference point through life.'

Dave Peers, b 1939, was the local organiser for the IS from the mid-sixties. He went to London as an organiser in 1974, leaving the SWP in the late 1980's. He worked as a Higher Education teacher, an ambulance driver and, till retirement, as a BBC producer and presenter.

Sandra Peers, b 1940, was Secretary of Newcastle Trades Council and the NATFHE Branch at Newcastle Polytechnic till leaving Tyneside, for London in 1974. She left the SWP in the 1980s. She taught at Croydon College, was active in the union at all levels and was Secretary of College Rank and File. She was also Secretary of Croydon Trades Council and regularly involved in strike support and in most major demonstrations, including Anti-Poll Tax, Stop the War and the Climate Control Camp. Sandra sees herself as 'still battling away.'

Harry Rothman, b 1937, finished his B.Sc and taught for two years at Consett Technical College. He then worked in the Unilever's laboratories in Bedford and Port Sunlight developing complex retrieval systems for scientific reports. He got a Leverhulme Fellowship to develop the study of Science and Society at Manchester University. He stayed for 12 years as a lecturer especially interested in environmental issues and in 1972, published, a highly praised book, *Murderous Providence*, a pioneering study on capitalism and the environment. He had a year in Fiji on a UNO development project then worked at Aston University and Bristol Polytechnic ending in 2000 as Professor of Science Policy. Harry has remained a left wing socialist but so far has failed to find a political party which he thinks has a prospect of helping to bring about a society based on democracy, equality and justice. He says he lives in hope.

Norman Ridley, b 1941, left school at 15 and after a year's general labouring secured an apprenticeship as a lithographer and member of the Society of Lithographers and Design Engineers. After the merger with the National Graphical Association, in 1982, Norman was Father of the Chapel at Thompson Newspapers till retirement. He is a life-long socialist.

Walter Ryder, b 1937, received his Ph.D (1962) and started work at May & Baker, Ongar, Essex. He joined CP, went to work in Cuba, then left the CP. He married, had three sons, then lost his first wife, Mary (1986). He worked

John Charlton, Brenda Corcoran & Harry Rothman, 1989

Jeremy Beecham & Ray Challinor, 1999

at Jealott's Hill Research Station (ICI), the Department of Biological Sciences, Dundee University and in Newcastle, as a freelance writer, translator and editor. He worked as an editor for the WHO, Geneva, from the 80s till the present. From 1973 he took up distance running and married again (1993). Walter moved to Cromarty in 1998. He says, 'I'm wary of labels but I suppose I'm a libertarian socialist. My basic feelings haven't changed. I'm not a member of any party and doubtful whether humanity is capable of living in a socialist way. I went to the "Make poverty history" demo in Edinburgh a few years ago with Harry Rothman.'

Barry Scaum, b 1936, is an actor, teacher and campaigner for community causes; 'great company, with a talent for friendship and a whacky sense of humour,' said one friend. When a Head Teacher asked, 'Do you think you are in the right profession, Mr Scaum?' He replied, 'Head Master, I'm not sure if I'm on the right planet.'

Brian Sharp, b 1942, went to Durham University to study physics where he remained involved in CND. After graduation he went to work as a social worker in North Shields. Four years later he qualified as a Social Worker at Newcastle and, after working in London and the north east was appointed to lecture in social work at Edinburgh University. Eleven years on Brian returned to Tyneside to work with the homeless. He founded the organisation Praxis and has run Elswick Lodge in Newcastle's west end for the past 25 years. He stayed in the Labour Party till the arrival of New Labour in 1997 and remains a convinced left wing socialist.

Tricia Sorbie, b 1942, joined the SLL while at Leeds University. She and her partner, **Kevin Fitzpatrick**, left the SLL in 1964. They moved to Tyneside in 1965 and were active in the Vietnam Solidarity Campaign and the Irish Solidarity Campaign before moving with their children to Galway in 1982. Kevin worked as a child psychologist while Trish became active in the Galway Arts community and was a co founder and organiser of the annual Cuirt International Festival of Literature. Trish and Kevin have participated in national campaigns such as the right to divorce, but their main political focus has been on organising within their local Connemara community on issues like the provision of mains water and services for the elderly.

Anna and Mike Tapsell came to Tyneside in 1959. They became heavily involved in CND. Anna was a Labour party member and former Secretary of the London Region CND. Mike had left the CP over the Soviet Union's treatment of Yugoslavia. In 1965 they moved to Bedford then Wandsworth where Mike was a town planning officer. Mike died aged only 49 in 1982. Anna has remained active in campaigns and community politics. She says she was pleased to be expelled from the LP in 1999.

Jane (Owens) Wadham b. 1947. After leaving Dudley College of Education in 1968 she married John, a fellow teacher. They have two sons. She spent her teaching career in the West Midlands, mainly in Walsall, retiring from the deputy headship of a community comprehensive school in 2006. Whilst teaching she studied with the OU, graduating in 1974. In 1982 she settled in Lichfield, Staffs. She is an active volunteer with Sands, the stillbirth charity, the National Memorial Arboretum and with the District Arts Association. She says, 'Although I've been away from the North East for so long, crossing the Tyne Bridge always feels like coming home..... You can take the girl out of Newcassel but you can't take Newcassel out of the girl.'

Nicky Waldy, b 1945, joined, then left the IS in the 'seventies. Since the mid-eighties she has been active for the Labour Party in Cornwall and is a County Councillor for a ward in Plymouth.

Jim Walker, b 1940. He followed his experience in the parks, factory and public library by working as a journalist on the *Northern Echo*, BBC Manchester and finally, for 15 years for Granada TV. He left active politics in the mid-seventies. He died after several illnesses in 2004. He had a dry, self deprecating sense of humour, 'I've never had a day's good health in my life,' he quipped.

Terry Watson, b 1939, and **Nina (Johnson) Watson**, b. 1941, moved from the North East to Buckinghamshire in the late 1960s and from there to London in the 1980s.Nina worked in Public Libraries and was active in many campaigning organisations (CND, AA, CAAT) and was a frequent visitor to Greenham Common Women's Peace Camp. Together with Terry she organised regular Marxist Education Classes and helped to run Uxbridge BSFS.Terry worked as a Film Preservation Officer for The Imperial War Museum. He was active in the Co-operative movement and for many years served on the London Education Committee. Both left the CP after the major split in 1991. They say, 'on retiring in 1999 we returned to Northumberland and are active in our local community and in the Berwick Justice not War Group. Currently we are not members of any party but still believe that the future lies with socialism.'

Mike Worrall, b 1936, taught in Newcastle (1965-1972) then Cumbria, retiring from teaching as Deputy Head of a rural primary school in 1991 followed by some part time lecturing in teacher education. He is married to **Kathleen Marley,** b 1943, an involved Quaker and radio journalist. Mike left the CP in the late sixties and found no political party which could embrace his independent progressive outlook. Has campaigned strongly to defend and extend public rights of way. He celebrated the mass anti-war demonstration in 2003 has a faith in 'a similar mass response to future government stupidities.'

Missing comrades

We would have liked to have kept in touch with several others. If this book reaches them and they care to get in contact via the publisher, or the North East Labour History web site: www.nelh.net, we will be very pleased!

They are David Blenkinsop, Ann Blyth, Roger Carroll, Isabel Fearon, Carol Flintoff, John Gough, John Hackworth, Brendan Halligan, Neil Hamilton, Miles Hutchinson, Howard King, Gail Lawrence, Carol MacDonald, Paula MacNamara, Doug Mitchell, Gail Nichol, Ann Paton, Margaret Pearson, Malcolm Purvis, Mick Renwick, Alan Rutter, Mike Slatter, Dave Smith, Walter Wilson, Frank Wilson and anyone else who thinks they should be on this list!

Conclusion: Taking account

If there was a motif for left wing youth politics round 1960 it would be direct action. It stretched from sit downs through large marches and small marches, long marches and short marches, to poster parades, wall daubing and fly posting. Conventional meetings and resolutions were almost a sub text. This took place inside a deep cultural shift embracing music, poetry, fashion and a loosening up of attitudes to sexuality and authority. This shift continued through the 60s and 70s but the direct action upsurge tailed off through 1963 as the General Election drew close.

The belief that there would be a Labour government was fuelled by the collapse of Tory morale as MacMillan, the magician, lost his wand. Mired in scandal and mercilessly assailed by the new satirists, the Tories reached fatally backwards for their saviour, the 14th Earl of Home, who, benefitting from Tony Benn's fight to renounce *his* peerage, followed suit to become Sir Alec Douglas Home. This enriched the tools of satire. It was such a retrograde step to take. Hugh Gaitskell had died suddenly in January 1963 and had been succeeded by Home's antithesis, Harold Wilson, a northern grammar school success. His public image, plus his undeserved reputation as a left winger, fed the illusion in the anti-Bomb movement that Labour's defence policy might shift leftwards towards a unilateralist policy. This illusion was enough for many to engage with the Labour Party's election campaign. This turn to parliamentary politics involved many anti-Bomb campaigners who were also LP members.

YS and LP activity gradually took precedence over CND/YCND. Mike Worrall's diary of events give an excellent sense of the rise and decline. He recorded, 4 events in 1959, 12 in 1960, 27 in 1961, 25 in 1962, 7 in 1963 and 6 in 1964.[237] Dave Douglas sees the 1963-65 period as the height of activity but what he is measuring through the eyes of a 16-18 year old is hyper-activity involving a squad of up to 30 or so young people of a similar age. There is a wide difference between 200 or so Direct Action Committee activists blocking the gates of Holy Loch in 1961 and 30 undertaking a ' mass' bill-sticking after the pub closed, possibly on a weekly basis. This is not to denigrate or patronise the anti-establishment response of those young people but to put it into proportion. Exciting though their rampages through town with a paint pot may have been for them, they would have little impact on the wider movement, or the public.

Certainly the anti-Bomb movement on Tyneside had fragmented by late 1963. To the political argument that attention had turned to electing a Labour Government, there are other points to be made. The key activists from 1959-60 had mostly finished their university courses at Newcastle and Durham and had moved away. Harry Rothman, Ann Berg, Dave Leigh, Lu Bell and Mike Down had gone to London. Mike Worrall was also to leave in 1964, though he returned in 1966. Nina Johnson and Terry Watson also went south. Jim Walker got a job on the *Northern Echo* in Darlington. Many of the school student activists of 1959 to 1962 were also on the move; Brenda Ingleby and Tricia Sorbie to Leeds, Jennifer Piachaud, Lindy Howard, Linda Potts, and Dorothy Simmons to London, Jane Owens to the West Midlands and Fiona Scott Batey to Nottingham. The Gateshead trio of Sharp, Scott and Paxton had also gone to University though the former two were active in CND at Durham though not in the YS. There is no sign of a new crop of school student organisers following them all into activity or drawing other school students round them. It is easy to underestimate the importance of key individuals especially when organisations or movements are small.

At the end of this period the Young Socialists were wracked with sectarian battles which came to an end with the secession of the Keep Left Group and the establishment of an SLL Young Socialist Group. This affected at least three of the Labour Party YS branches (Newcastle West, Newburn, South Shields and Felling) but their heyday of 1960-62 was over anyway. YS branches continued but largely with fresh faces who had not been much associated with the high point of CND. Very few of the YS recruits became active officers in the Labour Party or local councillors though some were to follow that route years later. Of the later crop of young socialists after 1964, this may have been different, but detailed research would be needed to establish the facts.

On the far left the SLL won and lost dozens of young people who were recruited in great enthusiasm but who soon became disillusioned with the Healyite machinations. The IS group was less successful in recruiting substantial numbers but more successful in keeping those who joined and in having an appeal for older workers. IS recruits were the most likely to have been in active politics at the other end of the 1960s and beyond, though Jeremy Beecham and the Hobsons in Shields became leading lights in their local Labour Parties and later on, so did Brian and Linda Ebbatson, John Metcalfe and Dave Arrowsmith. The YCL also lost student and school students activists who left the area and many did not make the jump from the YCL to the Communist Party. Czechoslovakia in 1968 was to take a fresh toll on CP membership.

Where did 'we' come from?

The project started in November 1999 at the forty year reunion of some participants in the movement on Tyneside. The event included a six hour discussion round a table at the Live Theatre. That was followed by a questionnaire circulated soon afterwards. Before New Year 2000 a dozen forms had been returned. They were valuable but had shortcomings. The main one was that the largely closed question format offered too many opportunities for one word answers! Open ended interviews changed the nature of the project. I had started by intending to tell the story of the YS, CND and the political culture in which they were situated. That has been the major focus of the book but an interview format which started with personal histories opened up other interesting themes. In trying to discover the motivations of the activists attention turned to family histories, childhood experience including community and schooling. It soon became clear that the impact of war had made a strong impact on both parents and children.

The First World War severely disrupted family life for many of the parents of this group of people. Their infancies and childhoods were badly disrupted. They were raised in the inter war world wracked by unemployment, poverty and the rise of fascism. As young adults they were pitched into a war of their own. This all had important consequences for their children. Firstly the parents created narratives out of their experience which their children imbibed. Elements of these narratives were frequently cited to explain their children's political behaviour. There were also more subjective forces at work. Parents' experience shaped their attitudes like, for example, the importance attributed to seeking security in employment. The condition of the post Second World labour market was at odds with such a sentiment and children often behaved with a nonchalance sometimes shocking to their parents.

Family background and internal family tensions are rather obviously an important key to understanding anyone's political behaviour. However by the time young people reach adolescence other influences impinge including school. The evidence from this group strongly suggests the peer group as a important variable. This seems to help to explain the involvement in political movements of those who families have no apparent connection to the philosophies and organisation of these movements. However there are some other questions to address which relate to the wider context – to the specific time or moment when a movement appeared and grew.

Was it a 'moment?'

Was there anything specially significant about this moment in time? It is normal enough for participants in an activity to regard their experience as deeply important. This tendency is even greater when looking back fifty years to one's youth. The sceptic will rightly ask for firm evidence. The first indisputable fact is that the frequency and size of political demonstrations rose steadily from 1956, to a peak in 1962. They declined again thereafter but never, for at least the next two decades to the levels, of the early fifties. Most large movements of protest rely for their size and impact upon young people in their teens and early twenties. This one was no exception. Nationally, tens of thousands of youngsters participated in anti-H Bomb, Anti-Apartheid and several other campaigns. In Tyneside and the north east of England there were thousands who marched, sat down, attended meetings and wore the famous CND badge. This contrasted sharply with the preceding years. Organisations sprouted. CND was the largest but Anti-Apartheid and the socialist political groups also emerged to hold many large and smaller events.

Then there was the impact of the arts. The Morden Tower, drawing dozens weekly to hear the poetry of the streets, would have been unthinkable only a few years before 1962. Though people had always attended musical events, a new music emerged and older genres experienced a revival, often with a specifically political content. Clearly the Fine Art Department at Kings College was an early influence on the student part of the new movement and the role of some University scientists should be taken into account, in the latter case by drawing attention to the alleged dangers of nuclear power.

In looking for a cause of this upsurge in activity, growing knowledge of the H Bomb and its effects must rank high. From the early 50s, the Bomb was frequently in the news whether it was ghastly evidence of its effects on Hiroshima and Nagasaki, the dangers of fall out from serial testing east and west or, just plain fear. Mature political activists disseminated information and organised events as many of them had done on other issues even before the Second World War. The people who provided the numbers to turn the protest into a mass movement were the young people becoming adults from the mid-50s.

Several participants remember the experience as being something special. Linda Ebbatson, referring to those involved calls it, 'the golden generation' and others echo this sentiment. Some may find this overblown; too self regarding. This was the first generation which could look beyond leaving school at 14, with the possibility of free post-school education, had the support of a free health service and the security of a booming labour market. These may have been the ingredients for low levels of anxiety about material security, providing the space to think and act on big issues effecting life's prospects. No issue could be bigger than the threat of nuclear war.

These factors may also have been the ingredients for a revolt against the values and practices of parents. On a wider stage, it was the period of 'the angry young man' in drama, fiction and film. Music was loosening up from the sentimental stodginess of the post-war years. Conventional authority was on the line. Tyneside was part of the vanguard of this deep cultural shift.

With regard to popular movements growth is not necessarily steady. It tends to move in fits and starts triggered by specific events.[238] The news of Pacific nuclear tests may explain the leap in numbers at Aldermaston from 1958 to 1959. The rise in the H Bomb debate in the Labour Party after the unexpected defeat in the 1959 Election may have energised the anti-nuclear movement. Almost certainly the victory for the unilateralists at the 1960 Labour Conference encouraged many to believe that a new Labour Government would shift Britain's policy. By 1963 many saw the Labour Party as a hopeless case, while paradoxically, the leadership of CND was seeing it as the only hope. Certainly by 1964, at the latest, the enthusiasm of young people for CND had much diminished.

After 'the moment'

The story of the Labour Party was similar. This was also paradoxical. By 1963 the Tories were in deep trouble, sinking in scandal. The prospects of a Labour Government in 1964 were increasingly strong. Yet most of the young people invigorated by several years of demonstrations were not enthused. The experience of Labour Party Ward meetings, the basic arena for members was not encouraging. Dave Peers went to the Benwell Ward meeting in Autumn 1964, to find a room with a few pensioners, 'delighted to see a young man.'[239] Kenton Ward meetings in 1963 were only a little better with two young people attending.[240] Others reported similar experience in Westerhope, Scotswood and South Shields. The revival of the Young Socialists and the large number of individuals gathered under the umbrella of CND appeared to have little impact on the Labour Party, apart from a negative one. The party seemed incapable of attracting and holding any but careerists to its ranks. Things were clearly not helped by the atmosphere of suspicion round the Young Socialists and its connections, real or imagined, with *Keep Left*.

The decline of CND and the failure of the Labour Party to win masses of young people was not the only outcome of this historical moment. Many stayed in left wing and protest politics either in the north east or elsewhere. By 1966 the Vietnam War was making an impact internationally. Many veterans of this phase of activity carried their experience into that campaign. The SLL continued to win numbers of young people but failed to hold on most of them. The International Socialists made modest progress in doing strike support work which won some credibility among some rank and file workers. It just did not have the numbers to convince lots of working class activists. Dave Peers remembered asking a Sunderland worker to join the IS in 1965. When asked how many members it had he answered about 300. 'Is that all, on the whole of Tyneside and Wearside?' Dave of course meant, in the whole of Britain.[241] Recruitment to the far left beyond would remain a problem in an area of high density trade unionism with an almost tribal loyalty to the Labour Party.

Some of the sentiment of the period carried forward into the new women's movement. Tyneside remained a male dominated area through this early upsurge. When visiting a NUM activist in Durham, Dave Peers was asked if he'd like a cup of tea. He replied that he would and was told, 'Hang on a bit. The wife will be in soon.' Dave jokingly asked if he ever made one himself to which the reply came, 'She does everything inside the house, cooking, washing mending, and I do it all outside, the garden and repairs'. Sandra Peers was warned off from talking politics to an activist's wife on the grounds that, 'she wasn't interested in politics.' Maggie Pearse from Stanley recalled that when she was accepted for College in 1960, there were uncles in the family who criticised her mother for allowing it.[242]Sandra faced similar attitudes in her colliery family when she was accepted for Oxford in 1959. From a middle class family, Jennifer Piachaud was offered nursing as a prospective career by her physician father, whilst her brothers were encouraged to choose medicine. Both Maggie and Sandra pointed out that their own parents were not discouraging at all, but proud of their achievements. So the situation was uneven.

The important point here is that many of the women who became involved in this period were determined not to accept the limitations the culture seemed to impose. Though few, if any, at the time, articulated the demands of the women's movement at the end of the sixties, in their own domestic situation they insisted on equality. Sandra, for example, shared all aspects of child care with her husband Dave, 'apart from breast feeding!' she said. She joked that she made a statement of intent by taking *Das Kapital* into the labour ward, though after delivery she was only up to reading *Women's Own,* like the rest of the mothers. There is no doubt many women on the left did not share Sandra's determination and that husbands or partners saw their public roles as taking precedence over attention to home and family business.

At the early national gatherings of the International Socialists at Caxton House Settlement, Finsbury Park, a few articulate women contributed though the meetings were heavily male-dominated. Many very able women and very few men were in the kitchen area cutting sandwiches and making tea. It was not till the birth of the new women's movement that such issues even appeared on the agenda of left wing political discourse.

Nevertheless there was a breakthrough for many young women in this period. Among the growing number who made it to college there were those who insisted on entering the work force and fighting for equality there. A smaller proportion who started without college education were forced to accept specifically women's work, pay differentials and profoundly sexist attitudes and behaviour. Several of the young women who involved themselves in the movement in the decade bridging 1960 went on to the women's movement at the end of the 1960s and in the '70s. That was true of Brenda Corcoron, Maggie Pearse, Marian Charlton, Maggie Anwell and Jane Bell at least, but that is part of another story.

Maggie Anwell was lucky enough to have both her parents living into their nineties, ready and able to talk about their lives. She thinks their generation on the left, had a view that 'they were there to try to make the world a better place. There was not much reflection on motivation.' This may be a fair generalisation but one that needs extending to some of their children's attitudes towards their own political lives. Maggie says she has never been satisfied by that position, ' I am a psychologically minded person, needing to delve the psychological depths. Straight politics is too cold.'[243] We don't need to agree with that view, to note that the left political community at large in our times moves in a world where psychological concerns are pervasive. One of the important contributions of the women's movement has been to bring to political discourse a concern for the manner in which those involved think and behave towards each other. This has consequences for political action. It has also contributed enormously to the confidence with which many women now freely participate in politics and trade unionism.

However, it is still important to consider the worlds in which each generation operated as political activists. The General Strike, mass unemployment, the rise of fascism and a world war are likely to have clarified views rather starkly for the parents. In a society like Britain in the post Second World War era things have rarely appeared so black and white for most people. The left has had no single clear road to follow. Adherents have had the luxury of choosing direction and participating in various fields: politics, community work, education, public service, journalism and the arts.

There are some striking features in the personal narratives. Many of those interviewed reveal themselves to have come from socialist families. Among them, conformity to family values is the norm. Antagonisms to parents usually turn out to be relatively minor, and, usually concerned with personal freedom. This affected female children more than male. Although attitudes might be conservative radical families probably behaved better than society at large. An opinion on what a daughter was permitted to do might be stated, but not enforced. Most daughters in this sample were able to express themselves freely and, largely to choose their life outcomes. The contrast with their mothers could not be more marked especially where education was concerned.

Some of this applied to men too. With a few exceptions most enjoyed childhoods relatively free from deprivation and the situation improved throughout the 50s.

Secondary education, again for all but a few, proved to be a boon, opening doors to higher education and equipping individuals with a degree of self confidence which they brought into the new movement. They had enormous advantages over their parents' generation, never fearing unemployment or the imminence of war. The downside of this might be that campaigning politics appeared almost a leisure activity for some. If serious engagement carried relatively little risk to life and well-being it could be easier to leave behind at particular moments, or perhaps in stages. This was the experience of a few of those interviewed for this book. It is likely to be true for a larger number of those who participated but dropped off the movement's radar.

Despite all ...keeping faith

The evidence is that the experience of taking part in the wide range of activities, political, social and cultural left an indelible mark on those who took part. Mostly people speak warmly of that time and of the people they met and made friends with. For many, life time friendships were made which have survived life's trials. Also several people acknowledge an intellectual debt, in that they developed a framework of ideas which have more or less stood up to the vagaries of history. Of course this is a broad framework. Today, of those interviewed only four remain members of the Labour Party. In 1964, apart from the YCL members, almost everyone else was a member of it. The1964-66 Labour Government's record disillusioned a few. They left. The arrival of Thatcher in 1979 and the accession to the leadership of Michael Foot inspired some to join, or re-join. The record of Tony Blair, his enthusiasm for privatisation and finally the Iraq War, caused almost everyone to leave. Faith in the Labour Party as a vehicle to bring a better world has almost completely evaporated, even among those few who remained members.

The YCL and Communist Party members also suffered enormous disappointment culminating in the final split in the Party in the early nineties. The few who trod the revolutionary road have also been disappointed as their organisations have failed to grow significantly. Those who stayed with the IS-SWP would say they are still optimistic; that the crisis in capitalism will ultimately lead to a revived labour movement. In any case they share with several others, the conviction that life is about continuous struggle.

That latter sentiment is probably the one that unites most people in this story. A glimpse at the little biographies – 'The Directory' – will show that, in the broadest sense, the left wing early sixties generation of north easterners have worked in the public service and continued to support progressive causes. Their life stories refute the widely held view that youthful radicals become conservatives in later life.

Addendum 1

A few people who appear in the above text contributed their own written accounts of the period and fragments appear frequently in the narrative. John Creaby gave a substantial chunk of his comprehensive autobiography and part of it appears below. Mike Down contributed a large autobiographical piece and part of it appears here too. Jim Walker and Roger Hall submitted short essays which were not so easily looted!

The shock of the '59, Jim Walker, 2000

"Oh; the Twenties were bad
And the Thirties were sad as the Dole
And the Forties were mad
But the Fifties discovered my soul."

Bear in mind that Alex Glasgow wrote that song in the Seventies and that distance proverbially lends enchantment. Take a silly but significant example: if you walked into Gateshead Public Library in 1959 and reached for *Ulysses* or *Das Kapital* you'd find yourself blushing, holding a block wood bearing the label: 'Present this to the librarian, who will decide if you are mature enough to read this book.' As for Lady Chatterley, she didn't even exist except in France.

More library stories. In Walker Library the racing pages of the newspapers were pasted over. In Quaker Darlington there was segregation – men and women were not allowed to read the same set of papers. The front page of *The Times* consisted of Classified ads. Ditto the *Liverpool Echo* and dozens of others.

I dwell on libraries because we practically lived in them. When kids ask me how we amused ourselves before TV, I talk about hours spent in the library, sometimes reading four books a day. And there were ten picture houses in walking distance, all changing their programmes every Wednesday and Saturday. As for radio, there were only three stations – Home, Light and Third. These were supplied by wire, rented from Rediffusion. Later we would discover the joys of *Radio Luxembourg* and play with a shining dial bearing the names of faraway places like Hilversum, Lahti and Praha, but that was when we got electricity. In 1959 our bit of Byker was still gas-lit, even though Joseph Swan had led the world by illuminating Collingwood Street with electricity half a century earlier.

If you lived in Byker you were woken up every morning at 7 o'clock by the ear-splitting shipyard buzzers. If you didn't work in the Yards or if you'd been up all night with a crying child, tough luck – Messrs. Swan Hunter, Wigham Richardson, Hawthorn Leslie and the rest had spoken. Byker, after all, was built as a barracks for the Yards – for housing their workers and breeding their apprentices. They weren't back-to-backs, they were one-up- and-one-downs, as in the song:

They'd skin a rat for its hide and fat
Wad the neighbours doon belaa...

and when 'upstairs!' had a party you knew about it – they were literally dancing on your ceiling.

The lavatories were out in the backyard – freezing for half of the year; especially at night. We had a little paraffin lamp to prevent the pipes bursting and to shed light on the squares of the *Newcastle Journal* (and *North Mail*) that served as kitten-soft bog-roll. And every house still had an air-raid shelter in 1959, very suitable for the aforementioned breeding and smoking the post-coital Turf.

All the streets were named in alphabetical order for the convenience of the rent man – we never saw the owner but I think his name was Fawcett. At the end of Canterbury, Cresswell and Cullercoats Streets there were short rows of council houses – with gardens. But of such Arcadian dwellings we could only dream. We were on the waiting-list for 20 years, by which time we'd moved away. All of the above is to paint the bitter grey background and to explain the shock when, in the Autumn of 1959, Byker voted Tory.

Amiable, apple-cheeked Arthur Blenkinsop lost Newcastle East to some bastard whose name I don't recall and the 59 Society was born. John Charlton sent me a note (we didn't have telephones in those days either) and I replied, typically, with a pompous verse that ended:

Need you ask? I know my task – for I live in Newcastle East.

I didn't know then that the Society would become Britain's first branch of the Young Socialists, which would eventually follow the fate of the Labour League of Youth, purged by the 'adult' party for leftward leanings. God knows how I got to meetings in Victoria Square. We had stately trolley buses gliding like illuminated galleons from Byker to Pilgrim Street. The rest of the journey to

Sandyford is a twilit blur. But I remember every detail of the Midnight Hikes, led by John Creaby into the black Northumbrian countryside for no purpose whatsoever. We would sleep wherever we could – in barns; in roadmenders' sheds or even under the stars. We once astonished a villager who looked out of her window at dawn and saw concentric circles of bodies draped around the steps of the Celtic Cross. Then the bodies began to move...

As I say; there was no purpose in these hikes, but the fact that there were girls in the group -- well-scrubbed angels from Church High School and Dame Allan`s – no doubt attracted the horny-minded sons of toil like myself. Not that I lived in Byker any more. I was no longer a Byker Bundler – I was a Jesmond Geordie, a traitor. Well, not really. Number 47 Buston Terrace was a hotbed of anarchists, dissidents and loonies (and still is; I'm glad to report, judging by the Meatloaf pictures on its front door). And one day there'll be a plaque saying that Paul Foot and (Lord) Gus MacDonald slept there. They were promoting *Young Guard* the youth mag of the International Socialists, edited by Roger Protz,[244] now a national expert on Ale. What else ?

Barry Scaum was the official tenant, while Ralph Watson, Jack Shepherd, (now DI Wycliffe on TV), Kyran Casteel and Martin Roots came and went. It was there that Guy Falkenau brought the news that Alan Brown[245] had died of leukaemia. It came as a stark surprise, somehow, to realise that 59-ers were mortal.

Barry was an art teacher at some rough school in Gateshead and, one Christmas, he threw a party to out-hooligan the hooligans. When they trooped in they saw no wallpaper, only hessian, painted luridly here and there. The 'decorations' consisted of squares of newspaper, threaded on twine and hung diagonally across the ceiling. At the height of the festivities, Barry set fire to the decorations and the kids gawped in amazement. They looked at him with a new respect as they ran for the door.

Naturally, I remember the Labour Agent, Joe Eagles, and how I quoted Tawney's *Acquisitive Society* at him in an attempt (pompous again) to stop his Labour Bingo sessions. Joe, a Scouser I think, was unmoved, arguing that his Bingo was a bit of fun for the old ladies rather than a bloodstained arm of international capitalism. He was eventually succeeded by a bird-like figure called Roy Evers who kept reporting us to the National Organiser, Reg Underhill for passing resolutions in favour of Fidel Castro and so forth.

I was reminded of this a few years later when I worked on the Northern Echo under the editorship of 'Hyperactive Harry'(Evans). We were taught to beware of the Skibbereen Eagle Syndrome. *The Skibbereen Eagle* was a local Irish paper which at the turn of the century printed on its front page the banner headline:

"THE SKIBBEREEN EAGLE CHALLENGES THE TSAR
To Answer These Ten Questions:
as if the Tsar read the *Skibbereen Eagle* every morning with his breakfast. Did Fidel take heart from our resolutions? Did Walter Ryder know? Did alarm bells ring in the Pentagon?

And yet, hilariously, I'm sure we were spied upon. Mike Worrall used to make phone calls arranging non-existent CND demonstrations and then watch the cops arrive. In King's College Labour Club there was a rain-coated bloke who was perpetually embarrassed by his own ignorance of Labour politics, labour history or even the purpose of our meetings. I remember using the phrase 'healthy class hatred' and seeing his face flood with horror. If anything, I'd guess he was a Tory, earning a few bob for taking notes on us.

In the 59 Society itself, there was a lad who helped to print pamphlets and obviously had access to some sophisticated graphics' kit – better than the John Bull Printing outfit I'd been using till then. Curiously, his surname used to change: sometimes it was Husband and sometimes, I think, Anthony.

Then, just before a Midnight Hike, we were killing time in a greasy plastic spoon opposite the Central Station when two huge gents joined us in conversation. They claimed to be electricians and volunteered to black out the whole of Tyneside if we asked them to. Provocateurs or what ??! We must have been dangerous characters after all, threatening to topple the turrets of world capitalism with our resolutionary politics, hiking fearlessly into the dark belly of the landed classes. If only the Special Branch had realised it, the Establishment became quite safe when we decided to tear each other apart – instead of the System.

This is not a happy memory, so I'll keep it brief. It started when the CND supporters, as the majority, decided to expel, rather than convert the minority. Then we had the Trots. Within the Trots, the Workers Revolutionary Party hated the International Socialists and vice versa. Four years later, when I was in the Manchester IS, I was in the 'libertarian' tendency and was quietly expelled (i.e. l got no notice of meetings any more.) Why were we so keen to expel each other when we were so overwhelmingly outnumbered in the first place?

Since capitalism seems more secure than ever, and since the Labour Party is so snugly in it's bed, perhaps it's time to form the 99 Society. But no schisms this time and no Midnight Hikes – how about Midday Drives to comfortable boozers. Anybody for Bingo!

Fifty Years Ago: looking back at the 59 Society
Roger Hall

Whatever the political centre of gravity of the 59 Society' (obviously left of wherever centre lay at that time), gravity itself was always diluted by a range of other diversions. We were authentically political enough, as the telegrams to Fidel Castro, Jack Kennedy and the regional agent of the Labour Party, among others, testified. But the spirit of the age was such that political revolt was only one of the stances which defined the movement. In addition there was also the class war, the gender war, the generational war, the race war, the last drinks war and so forth, all of these hotly debated in various licensed premises and meeting halls across Newcastle and its inner suburbs, mainly Jesmond and Sandyford with occasional forays into other parts of what would become stigmatised later as the 'inner city'.

This political complexion apart, the 59 Society was largely defined, by the social geography of convenient meeting places and public transport, the upward mobility very much in progress, of which we were beneficiaries, and by the reaction to the socio-political reality of the late 1950s. We were principally a grammar school phenomenon, I suppose, with top-ups from other parts of the meritocracy. Some people were already in jobs and were even trade unionists in the shipyards, the Post Office, British Rail (remember that) and some were scaling the Kafkaesque DHSS bureaucracy at Longbenton. Initially at least, most people were students of various descriptions and a heavily provincial tribe at that.

It is true some migrants from other parts of the UK would sign-up as part of their extra-mural studies at Kings College and brought confirmation that a wider Britain existed. This I had always doubted and even though most of my life since the early days has been spent in alternative worlds outside the North East, I was never convinced that they were anything other than pallid replicas of the life-style implanted North of the Tyne. Though many of its adherents came from across the river, incidentally, it was probably inevitable that the 59ers saw Newcastle as the homeland.

This was the social reality which spawned the 59 Society and though there may have been clones in other towns and cities it is possible that it was a freak combination of circumstances which made our sprawling, polymorphous organisation the force it was. The political context, of course, was the perceived irrelevance of the Labour Party in a world which we assumed, as youth does, to be changing rapidly but probably was not changing much at all. What mainly excited us politically was CND, the most potent expression of the new politics. The rest was largely, as it turned out, the dying stages of the old Britain, marked by terrible civic design, the comatose nature of night-life in the cities and the

bitter-sweet prospect of jobs in the few organisations which made sense to us
– schools, libraries, local government, the public sector generally. Nowadays
our successors move smoothly into the sort of occupations – the media, design,
voluntary organisations, political consultancy, the professions – quite beyond
our imaginations, never mind our reach. It was a rather repressive world that
has been memorably captured, for instance, in Stan Barstow's A Kind of Loving
or Keith Waterhouse's City Lights.

Regrettably there was no latter-day Jack Common in our ranks to pin it down
for the North-East and it if it was commemorated, apart from the folk history
ceaselessly recycled in The Bridge Hotel, this was a wistful climate of folk clubs,
re-union trips abroad,the People's Theatre and the rest. Not much set down in
print, in other words. Did it all matter save for its participants who must have
numbered hundreds in total? And, if it did matter, why did it and was there any
legacy of significance?

It mattered in our own lives, of course. It was the essential setting in which
political, sexual and psychological identities were established. Since it leaked
into other institutions too, it formed the hub of a slew of tentacles snaking
across the city's social map. I dare say that it was probably too inward-looking
and consensual. I remember going psychologically far away to university at
Manchester and meeting disturbing people who, unlike those in the 59 Society
on the whole, you could violently object to. I was even advised to seek out
periodicals that I would disagree with. In other words,not the New Statesman,
Peace News or Freedom. It was a harsh lesson and probably not one you would
ever face among the comrades as we were apt to call ourselves and (ironically?)
occasionally still do at the quiz and karaoke refreshers.

How much it mattered beyond this inter-personal world is hard to say. A
valid reflection of a world now gone, certainly. The society of the late fifties, or
the particular sub-system that we constituted anyway,was a weird blend of the
ascetic definitely and the aesthetic, up to a point. It was a culture largely shaped
by what was missing in contemporary Newcastle. Few thrilling intellectual
experiences, no great adventures in cross-gender sex or drug-taking, an absence
of meeting places to rank with Ken Tynan's Kardomah Cafe in 50s Birmingham,
and second-hand bookshops and repertory theatres which were strictly non-
Premier league. No wonder that our cathedrals were the old Central Library on
New Bridge Street, the ornate tea-room at the Central Station and those pubs
stretching out from the Bigg Market which tended to give us the shortest shrift
when it became clear that we wanted, alongside the quaffing, to sing the Red
Flag and debate whether President Kennedy was a fascist or not. Eventually the
suburbs necessarily hosted our brand of modest drinking spiked with radical
conscience. If other circumstances had not intervened in the late 60s, the chums

would no doubt have found themselves south of the river – or worse.

OK – so the bathos of the 1959 General Election and Labour's third defeat on the trot was the inspiration for the Society named after that seminal event. From the Labour Party rooms at Victoria Square in Jesmond, now appropriately and disastrously bisected by Dan Smith's inner-relief road, the message was sent forth. No third world war, no invasion of Cuba, no ambition to become a conventional political grouping and not yet much interest in the green and gender politics which in another time would have kept us rapping for hours and hours before the gloomy swede (lars torders) was called. The self-imposed curfew of eleven pm beckoned and yellow trolley-buses (yet to implement our vision of free public transport) ferried weary class warriors to the conservative outer limits of Walker, Heaton, Kenton, Denton Burn, Jesmond and other evocative dormitories.

The halcyon days were approximately 1959 to around 1967 or so, at least as far as I was concerned. For others it lasted longer and for some the torch is still carried in the bistros and palm courts from southerly Low Fell up to Forest Hall. Alumni were to be found be found in the great off-centre British institutions of the law, academia, the media and the DSS. Even if the bus pass calleth by now, we can safely say that few betrayed the cause by voting Conservative, driving a Volvo or laughing at Bernard Manning. We did not quite become the people we railed against forty plus years ago but a certain respectability was bound to break out. In the pluralism of the post-millennial year, most of the comrades are content with what they have become, are still easy in each other's company and take some satisfaction in not having suffered a recession into premature cynicism and defeat. A plaque where the Royal Oak used to stand on Claremont Road would be a fitting tribute to the birth-place of the 59 Society and surviving comrades could gather there each and every October, chant some of the great resolutions and points of order and finish off with *The Man Who Watered the Worker's Beer*. Magic!

We're not there yet, but we're getting there,
Mike Down, 2001

I was born in October 1940 in Liverpool – my parents moved there because of an expected German invasion of the Isle of Wight. But we soon moved back – dad was in charge of NAAFI there.

My father came from an upper middle class family of lawyers and clergymen. He went to Charterhouse public school and then Sandhurst. He was a professional soldier, served in the First World War (the Somme) and later in Ireland. He left the army in the mid-thirties, trained as a chef/manager at the Trocadero in London, married my mother in 1936, moved to the IoW and sank their savings into Greengates Hotel, Seaview, just in time for the cessation of all business for years to come.

My mother was Catholic and fell out with her family by marrying an agnostic/C of E divorcee. My half brother was a fighter pilot – I learned much later that he downed six enemy planes the year I was born. Incredibly I knew none of this until after my parents had both died – in the late 60s. Catholic guilt.

My parents voted Tory but were not party members. Dad was briefly an 'Independent' (then a cover for 'Tory') Isle of Wight councillor, but confessed to voting Labour in 1945. But he got the *Daily Mirror* – he said to help him do the pools. On Sundays it was the *Express* – he liked Giles. Mum got the *Telegraph* and finished the crossword every day. She was well read. Her family in Liverpool was very political – they backed Franco in the civil war, albeit for Catholic rather than directly fascist reasons but did succeed in getting a Liverpool anti-fascist prisoner released from a Franco jail, so they weren't all bad. My aunt regularly stood (unsuccessfully) for parliament against Bessie Braddock the (Catholic, right-wing) Labour MP for Liverpool Central.

The only books I remember in the house were mum's prayer book, a novel she had called *The Bridge of San Luis Rey* (which tried to justify the deaths of numerous totally innocent people in some disaster or other – a counter to *Candide*) and Arthur Mee's outdated, jingoist but nevertheless informative ten volume *Children's' Encyclopaedia*. I never saw Dad reading books but mum borrowed stacks each week from Boots' private library in Ryde – they had green covers with green shields on them. As for me, I read a lot – mainly *Eagle* comics, *Just William*, *Biggles* and Sherlock Holmes. Nothing serious.

We had no car (they did have one before the war, but business got so bad that they had to sell it the year I was born.) TV arrived around 1956. All 1 remember are sport and a crass Hughie Green quiz show. Plus ca change. Neither could they afford foreign holidays, although in 1954 I went to France to stay with mum's relatives in Cherbourg. They worked for Cunard. In 1955 I went with (French) school friends to Paris. I learned passable French and saw two great films – *La Salaire de la peur* and *Les Diaboliques* (with the body arising from the bath) at a cinema on the Champs Élyssées.

After five years at a truly ghastly prep school where because I was 'different' (Catholic, gay, studious AND anti-authority!!) I was bullied relentlessly – mainly it should said by staff rather than pupils. Dad wanted me to go to Dartmouth and become a naval officer but thank goodness I turned out to be red-green blind so did not even take the exam. I was finally expelled in 51. The headmaster, who owned the establishment with his brother (both ex-Army and both sadist paedophiles) told my parents I would end up in prison one day – a fate I have so far managed to avoid, although I have been fined for political protests (twice) and for growing dope plants (once).

I moved to a Catholic boarding school in Guildford. It was a much more liberal regime. The priests were OK and some of the Irish ones fairly progressive. Fr.Price, my housemaster, watched boxing on TV and sometimes stayed (free) at our hotel. I remember mum kicking me under the table when I started using Dad's stories about Ireland not helping us in the second world war (Dad got his OBE commanding Black and Tans). I discovered later that over 50,000 men from the Republic volunteered to join the English army and fight the fascists.

I remember taking part in a piss-take sketch based on Newbolt's jingoist *Play up and play the game* poem, given to me maybe because of an essay I wrote about my favourite poem – Kipling's *If*. I served at mass every morning (I still know most of the Latin texts by heart – very useful for following those beautiful masses by Mozart, Verdi etc. I was never seriously interested in Catholicism – I just took it for granted – and the priests gave up trying to groom me for the local seminary at Wonersh. They knew I was an unsafe bet. But I have never been particularly anti-Catholic and I have some regard for the recusant families (such as my mothers') who braved it out in Elizabethan times. One of the maternal ancestors was Christopher Wright, one of the gunpowder plot conspirators. And I definitely take the catholic rather than protestant line on free-will. I listened to the radio a lot at school and at home. I began listening with Dad (a great radio fan – exclusively Light Programme) to *Billy Cotton's Band Show* and *Forces' Family Favourites* on Sundays, *Friday Night is Music Night* (when the statutory opera singer came on it was 'She's off' and it was turned down. Dad was quite low-brow and liked music hall and dance music, especially the Crazy Gang (one of whom had a grandson at my school) and Max Wall. I saw one of his heroes many years later doing a brilliant version of Beckett's *Krapps' Last Tape*. Mum was more highbrow – she could play piano and admired Bach, although her favourite 78s were *Pedro the Fisherman* and Cole Porter's *Miss Otis Regrets* (I have a brilliant version by Kirsty MacColl and the Pogues). .

We had the best radios money could buy – our only luxury. We were the first in the village to get FM and I remember the first BBC stereo experiments using two radios tuned to different frequencies. As for me, I needed portable radios so I could take them to school. First was a crystal set using the iron bed frame for an aerial, then one which resembled a brief case, then a big white job. The Home Service – I remember listening to but not quite getting the *Goon Show*, *The Brains Trust*, and plays like Golding's *Lord of the Flies* (a radio play before it was a book).

I heard my first contemporary/protest folk music in the form of the Parker/ McColl/Lloyd *Ballad of John Axon*. The best lyric was *I may be a wage slave on Monday, but I am a free man on Sunday*. Not that I had ever actually met a wage slave. I also listened to a lot of American jazz and pop on AFN Stuttgart and Radio Luxemburg which the BBC did not play. I also remember a very funny play by Henry Reed on the Third Programme which featured a lesbian character called Dame Hilda Tablet, which took the piss out of the upper class snobs (although many listeners were probably precisely such types). I remain a radio addict although I am sure standards have declined since the 50s – the flipside of near universal higher education. The replacement of standards for style.

While at Guildford I started buying 78s (Gene Vincent, Frankie Laine, Guy Mitchell, Johnny Ray...) .The two that affected me most were *Rock around the Clock* (it now seems very dated and, after Howlin Wolf, incredibly bland) and Elvis' *Heartbreak Hotel*. The Beatles made no impression, although much later I admired John Lennon and remember his death better than either Kennedy or Martin Luther King. My first LP was Frankie Laine singing with Buck Clayton and Coleman Hawkins – my introduction to jazz. I also remember reading about the holocaust for the first time (we didn't do modern history) in a book by Lord Russell of Liverpool, and started reading James Joyce for the first time (confiscated). I was not actually expelled, but asked to 'move on' and went to a grammar school at Sandown on the IoW. A liberation.

Girls, non-Catholics, (some) working class, and (some) politically conscious people entered my life for the first time. This was when things really changed. I gave up Catholicism (though never dared tell my mother). I began to get into some serious jazz and blues: Leroy Carr, Blind Willie Johnson and McTell, early Armstrong, Bessie Smith, Mississippi John Hurt, Basie, Ellington, Morton and also some 20 Century music (Shostokovich's *cello concerto* was my second LP) ... Poetry too – I particularly liked Dylan Thomas and WH Auden. Still do for that matter. And Bertrand Russell's *History of Western Philosophy*. I doubt that I understood very much (I still don't) but I tried, and it confirmed my belief that God, like all superstition, is a con trick. I still have small picture books I bought of modern' artists like Klee, Picasso, Cezanne, Miro, Degas and Matisse. Up to then art had been a closed book and my grandfather, an amateur artist, thought Picasso was a fraud.

Most of my pocket money and what I earned washing dishes at a posh IoW hotel (not ours, which was more down market and not even licensed – dad was not a Freemason and only they got the licences in those days) went on folk music . I used to send off to Folkways in New York for LPs by Pete Seeger, Sonny Terry, Leadbelly, Spanish Civil War songs, the Weavers ... Music led me into politics, not vice versa. I was always a 'heart' rather than a 'head' person when it came to politics and music led the way and Pete Seeger's (now to me rather simplistic) lyrics undoubtedly influenced me more than any political philosopher.

I went with some sixth formers to the second Aldermaston march in 1959. Beforehand we went to the Partisan, the left-wing coffee shop in Soho run by *Universities and Left Review*, and sleeping in school halls and Quaker meeting houses en route. I met people who later became very familiar to me – Peggy Duff, Canon Collins, Bertrand Russell. It was intensely exciting. We believed nuclear war to be a real and present threat to mankind and were protesting not just against the bomb but against the core values of the society which sanctioned it.

Even before that Aldermaston march I remember arguing with my family about Spain (mum's family, remember, supported Franco), about capital punishment (it was the time of the Derek Bentley execution – Dad said he was a teddy boy and got what he deserved – an example should be set), about British colonialism (Suez , Malaya, Aden, Kenya, Cyprus) , and about the monarchy – in those days, at least on the IoW, people stood up for the national anthem – not just in cinemas. My elderly aunts insisted on standing for the anthem that preceded the Queen's Xmas broadcast. I refused to kow tow). Seaview, Isle of Wight was no revolutionary hotbed but I did my best. But I did steer clear of religion although by then I had decided that I was a humanist thanks to Russell.

I remember being particularly concerned about South Africa. I do not know why – I had never met a black – the nearest were two Japanese businessmen who stayed in the hotel in the 50s and who gave me a huge and totally unexpected tip for taking them out in my boat. Only one black lived on the IoW – he was a bus driver- although one did take over a neighbouring Hotel in the mid 60s. I had read Alan Paton and Trevor Huddleston on the iniquities of apartheid and remember annoying my parents by fiercely arguing with one of our hotel guests, a South African woman who thought blacks were like children and unready for democracy. Somehow I found out about *Drum* magazine (suppressed a few years later) and sent off to South Africa for a subscription, and later applied, unsuccessfully of course, for a scholarship to Cape Town University where I planned to join the ANC and fight apartheid.

I read a book about *Why I should be a socialist* by John Strachey. I learned later that he had well and truly sold out long before I read it. In 1957 I joined the IoW Labour Party (a lost cause then as now, although Labour did have a few councillors, mainly from Cowes where AV Roe made ships and flying boats and there existed a small working class community. A communist speaker went there during the Korean war and was thrown in the river by an angry mob. I bought *Reynolds News* on Sundays and *Tribune* and the *New Statesman* by post. My parents were remarkably tolerant of my rapidly left-shifting political views. Good people. They probably thought I would eventually grow out of them but

I never did – although some of them did eventually grow out of me. I was so much older then but I'm younger than that now.

I went to Sidcup in '57 to campaign for Peggy Reid, the mother of one of my new left-wing school friends who was standing for Labour against Patricia Hornsby Smith, the Ann Widdecombe of her day. We lost. Peggy later became a lecturer at the teacher training college in Newcastle, and my friend went to Sandhurst and joined the SAS.

During this time I began my lifetime interest in China. After writing to their London embassy I began receiving free copies of *Peking Review*, beautifully printed on extremely thin crinkle paper. I remember defending the invasion of Tibet – it was a corrupt feudal theocracy and always a Chinese province anyway. True sometimes – you can see it that way. Twenty years later I saw Tibetans begging on the streets of their own capital, their monasteries burned out, their mountains stripped of timber and erosion destroying their farmlands. But in 1958 socialism's appeal was its seeming internationalism and anti-racism approach.

I chose to go to Kings in 59 because it was as far as I could get from the IoW while still receiving my grant from the IoW county council (80 pounds a term plus the fare – I always hitch-hiked the A1 and pocketed the cash). I thought Durham and Newcastle were the same place. I was billeted at Whitley Bay – a cold, bleak and windswept place after summer on the IoW. I quickly moved to Heaton and ate tasteless, soggy Sunday lunch and watching *Bonanza* on TV with the landlady and her Alzheimer suffering mother.

The first thing I did was visit the Labour Party rooms in Victoria Square. I met Joe Eagles, the local agent, and his tenant Michael Worrall. He was an agriculture student at Kings and a pacifist, with connections with the Quakers and Unitarians. He became a close friend and ally. Joe Eagles was not a member of CND but neither was he hostile. He probably believed CND and all single-issue politics was a diversion from what really mattered viz. winning power in order to improve education, housing and so on. But these things never interested me very much. The world was about to be blown up and anyway people in Africa and Asia were suffering much more than people in Newcastle. I suspect most of the middle class angry young men of this time felt much the same.

CND, which itself grew out of campaigns against capital punishment and the Suez invasion, and which more or less died with the test ban treaties in the mid 70s (Greenham Common excepted) nonetheless lived on in the campaigns over Vietnam, South Africa, women's liberation, black and gay liberation, and so on.

The Aldermaston marches gave me the chance to experience left-wing London culture. I went to Brendhan Behan's *The Hostage*, Joan Littlewood's *Oh What a Lovely War*, and to a pub in Kings Cross where Bert Lloyd, Ewan MacColl and Peggy Seeger held their Singers' Club every weekend. When I moved to London at the end of '62 a skinny American turned up and sang about guns and sharp swords in the hands of small children and about hard rain, decades before Ruanda and Pol Pot, Bhopal and Chernobyl. I was to hear Dylan and twice more in the 60s – at the Festival Hall in 65 and at the IW Festival in 69. He electrified me. Ewan later dismissed Dylan as 'a youth of mediocre talent', a phoney and a sell-out.

In 60 a large group of us marched at the Labour Party conference in Scarborough and some of us were observers for the big unilateralist debate. The Labour Right was shattered by CND's albeit narrow victory and I clearly remember booing my way through Gaitskell's actually rather noble 'fight, fight and fight again' speech. We went to the Blackpool conference the following year, but this time we lost. We also sent coaches to a big demo at Holy Loch against the US Polaris submarines organised by Russell's radical CND breakaway group called Direct Action. We also went to the early warning facility at Fylingdales in north Yorkshire.

In the Easter vacations I worked at CND's central office in London. Aldermaston was a major logistics operation and Peggy Duff was a master of organisation. I stayed with her ex-son in law, who lived with his gay partner in Euston. I was naive enough about my own sexuality let alone other peoples' to realise that they were a gay couple. Not that I would have cared. One my Newcastle CND friends was Norman Harrod, who played French horn for the Northern Symphonia. He was extremely camp and at home wore a bright silk dressing gown. I knew he was different, in the way that Noel Coward was different (my mother liked Coward's plays but Dad made it clear to me that there was something odd about him of which he disapproved). And although I remember Geoff Denton, I do not remember him as gay. I wonder, does Geoff remember ME as being gay?! Anyway, I was far too busy immersed in collective campaigns for disarmament, colonial freedom and so on to worry about personal individual sexual politics. All that mattered was whether people were for us or against us.

In my second year I moved to the Feinmann's house in Osborne Avenue and was very happy there. I was part of a large and politically active family. They had been in the Manchester YCL with people like Ewan MacColl. They left the CP over Hungary and were leading members of the Labour Party and CND. On the wall of my small attic room was a large reproduction of Picasso's Guernica and an even larger Czech anti-war poster that said Ne.

We hand-painted most of the posters for CND and for other campaigns, at the house of a very enthusiastic non-CP socialist called Jim Elder which was in the middle of a golf course in Gosforth. One of his many student tenants was a Jamaican dental student called Willy Veitch and he became my first black friend. I also got friendly with an ex-communist Jewish Glaswegian guy called Cecil Taylor, who was a record salesman. He wrote plays in his spare time. He wanted me to tell him how young people were speaking – phrases, slang etc. I doubt if I was much help. He later had plays put on at the Royal Court in London.

In my second year and after constant nagging from Dave Leigh (doing a PhD in mining engineering at Kings) I joined the Communist Party. Mike Worrall also joined at this time. Strangely, this was only a few years after Hungary when thousands had just LEFT the CP! We fell for the propaganda – Hungary was a Western plot and capitalism was actually on the verge of collapse, Russia was a potential paradise etc. etc. But many of my heroes at that time – Mao, Ho Chi Minh, Castro, most of the ANC leadership in South Africa, not to mention Pete Seeger and the London protest singers – were either communists or had communist connections. And the CP , unlike Labour to the right and the trots to the left, had impressive international connections.

Apart from the opening paragraphs of the *Communist Manifesto,* I remember reading no Marxist-Leninist theory whatever. The argument that capitalists wanted their workers to work harder for less while the workers wanted to work less for more did seem an irreconcilable contradiction though very powerful at the time. The nearest I got to reading theory was probably the Eric Bentley translations of all Brecht's poems and major plays and occasional pieces of theory in the *Daily Worker* or *Marxism Today.* I even got the *Daily Worker* when on holiday on the Isle of Wight – the only person in my village who did.

I visited Russia several times in the 60s and believed that its grey misery was entirely the fault of the West and that things would get better as certainly as things here would get worse. In fact the reverse happened. As history was a predetermined sequence of slave – feudal – capitalist –socialist – communist societies. Like the first Christians we predicted an impending apocalypse and always managed to come up with excuses when it didn't happen. Recently, my friends told me that the 97 Asian recession would spread world-wide bringing about the collapse of capitalism by the millennium. Plus ca change. I now think that the significant eras of human history have probably been hunter-gatherer/ agricultural/ industrial and now information. The inegaliterian gaining of wealth and/or power has been present in all of them.

My political activity was concentrated in the university rather than the city. One already mentioned was the campaign to boycott South African goods viz. sherry and oranges from college facilities. The vice chancellor called me in to persuade me that I was 'bringing the college into disrepute'. We won the vote. Recently I saw the Market Theatre of Jo'burg's Robben Island and discovered that political prisoners worked as slave labourers in the orange plantations and vineyards. Who was it who brought the university into disrepute?

I took an active part in the debating society and was principal seconder on several occasions -including one with Barbara Castle on Cyprus and one with Canon Collins on CND. We won easily. Dave Leigh got me to stand for the SRC (student parliament) but when I got there I found it very boring and have loathed formal meetings ever since. One of the great attractions of the Gay Liberation Front in the 70s was its lack of formal structure.

I can just remember the pale, lanky and slightly creepy figure of T Dan Smith. He was showing Willi Brandt the Roman Wall (= Berlin wall). Being a good communist I believed that the Berlin Wall legitimately defended the people of East Germany from American imperialism and that Willi Brandt was neo-fascist. I learned later that Brandt had played an entirely honourable anti-fascist role in the war. I was neither surprised nor disturbed to read about the Smith-Poulson scandal during the Wilson years. I had left the Labour Party by then.

I joined Kings' Film Society and was turned on to cinema as a serious art form. Bergman's *Seventh Seal* (still my favourite film by my favourite director) made a deep impression. The final dance of death scene failed to make the Observer top 100 film moments in a recent poll. Also Kurosawa, Eisenstein, Vigo, Buñuel, Welles – I remember them in detail. As for theatre, I best remember Jack (then I think John) Shepherd's productions of *Death of a Salesman* and Strindberg's *Ghost Sonata*, and productions of Joan Littlewood's *Oh What a Lovely War*, and Brendan Behan's *The Hostage* at Stratford East following Aldermaston marches..

I used to appear fairly regularly on the Tyne Tees TV show *Youth puts the Question*. I wore my usual donkey jacket, grey striped drainpipes and purple suede shoes. I slanged off all the semi-famous guests and received 20 guineas per show, which was very welcome as I was quite poor and relied entirely on my grant and what I earned in the summer holidays. I never got any money from my parents as they didn't have any. The only show I remember in detail was about Scottish independence, which in those days seemed absurd. They were recorded on very wide 'Ampex' tape and we stayed afterwards for coffee and snacks and watch the recording with the guest. Geoff Denton tells me that one show had to be pulled because of my highly objectionable remarks but I cannot remember it.

During my second summer vacation at Kings I went to Kibbutz Manara on the Israel-Lebanon border and worked in the Hula valley fish farms. The valley is overlooked by the Golan Heights. The kibbutzim were socialists and communists whose families had survived the holocaust. On our way to work at 4 am each morning we passed deserted and bombed-out Palestinian villages, their inhabitants dead or displaced to refugee camps in Gaza and Beirut. It was there that I learned that both sides can be right in politics.

In my final summer vacation I went to an international socialist work camp in Velika Plana, central Yugoslavia and worked on the so-called Unity and Friendship highway. Communism's appeal was always its internationalism so what happened there subsequently was deeply depressing. It was in Yugoslavia that I met young people from Vietnam and Laos for the first time. After leaving Newcastle, Vietnam became the main focus of my political activity. I remember being charged by mounted police during the 68 demo in Grosvenor Square. Had we broken through, the marines would probably have shot us. The final victory, with the tank crashing into the US embassy in Saigon and the chaotic evacuation from the roof, gave me enormous satisfaction. It seemed at the time to be one of those rare things – a clear cut victory for peace, freedom and progress. I subsequently visited Vietnam several times and sadly it is one of the poorest and most oppressed countries in the world.

Politics was my main activity for the first two and a half years, and studying became my main activity only in the final six months and then under CP pressure in the form of Walter Ryder and Harry Rothman, both fellow zoologists ('the Party needs comrades with good degrees'!!). Luckily I scraped a second – teachers with seconds got the same bonus as teachers with firsts. Much later in my life I got an MSc and a MEd but they did little to help my career.

My experiences at Sandown grammar school and at Kings Newcastle dominated the rest of my life. That grounding developed the optimism and the confidence I needed to stand up for my beliefs through thick and thin. Bertrand Russell tells of his grandmother's additional commandment in the family bible – thou shalt not follow the multitude in doing evil . This has a sharper ring than Newcastle CPer May Smailes' anecdote 'the fish that swims with the stream is a dead fish'. She also bemoaned the fact that ' you could drag the working class to the gates of Eden (i.e. the communist paradise) and they still wouldn't go in', but I now think they were quite sensible.

After graduating I went to an international youth camp in the Caucuses, southern Russia, working on a Kolkhoz (collective farm). This was the time of Kruschev, with Gorbachev the local Party boss. He was the first to open Russian up to young communists, socialists and liberals from Western countries, unheard in Russia at the time. I remember long queues outside bookshops in Moscow for Solzenitzen's *Day in the Life of Ivan Denisovich*. On the way south we stayed at hotels where the electricity went off at unexpected moments and sand came out of the taps. Once I had to visit the dentist and moved to the front of a mile-long queue. There was no anaesthetic. The village near the farm was medievally poor and had a small library where nearly all the books were by

Marx, Lenin or Stalin. Yet – possibly because of Kruschev's wind of change – I do remember most people seemed quite cheerful. What is happening in Russia today beggars belief.

On returning to the UK I got a science job in a tough east London comprehensive. The head of science told me there were only three reasons for being a teacher – summer holiday, Easter holiday and Christmas holiday. The staff included one future MEP (Stan Newens) and Ken Livingstone's future deputy on the GLC (Iltyd Harrington). Everyone was very committed to dragging the kids upwards and outwards. We got a lot of support from the local Authority. All this disappeared from London schools under the Thatcher regime. So did the GLC.

After starting work in London I became engaged to Jenny Piachaud. We went to the folk clubs and theatre. We saw brilliant productions of Sam Beckett plays at the Royal Court, and Peter Brook 's productions of the *Marat Sade,* John Osborne's *Luther, Tell me Lies about Vietnam,* and the *Midsummer Night's Dream* at the RSC/Aldwych, and (Mrs) Brecht's Berliner Ensemble production of *Coriolanus* at the Old Vic.

I did voluntary work for the CP HQ in King Street. Fergus Nicholson, the student organiser, was a closet Stalinist but most of the people I worked with – Sammy Aaronovitch, Jack Woddis and Eric Hobsbawm – were genuine euro-communists. I edited the student journal and had an article in *Marxism Today* entitled 'satire, sex and politics' – David Frost's *That was the Week that Was* had just broken out on TV and *Private Eye* had started. We were in a broad left alliance with Labour students – our enemies were the trots. Jack Straw and Digby Jacks were among the people I worked who later made successful careers in the Labour Party.

The Falklands war also began around this time. Union Jacks were flying, Michael Foot and many of my left-wing friends joined in. Wasn't Galtieri a fascist? In despair I went to stay with friends in Amsterdam and was relieved to find not a single person who thought the invasion was right. I remembered Bertrand Russell's description of cheering London crowds in 1914 welcoming the start of war. He concluded that 90 per cent of the population 'anticipated the coming carnage with delight'.

Then came the miners' strikes. I remember the first one, during the Heath government. I was on the Isle of Wight and the lights went out every evening to save coal. But this time Thatcher was in power and she had prepared well. Coal stocks were high.

I had become friends with Maurice Jones during the 70s while on a communist delegation to Russia. Most of the YCL and CP delegates were Stalinists and hated us because we were euro communists, and me in particular because I was gay and because of what had happened earlier at the 73 festival in East Berlin. The KGB watched us all the time and bugged our hotel rooms. I made much of the fact that *Crime and Punishment*, arguably one of Russia's greatest novels by its greatest writer, was unavailable in Riga and Leningrad bookshops. They dug up a copy somewhere and ostentatiously presented to me on the final day, branding us imperialist dupes.

By the time of the 1984 miners' strike Maurice had been made editor of the *Yorkshire Miner* and was very close to Scargill. I was in London and being no longer a school teacher I had the time and energy to reflect on the political reality. I went to Barnsley about half way through already convinced that they/ we were going to lose and that it would be better to cut their/our losses and return to work. Scargill had lost the moral high ground by refusing to ballot his members and public opinion was with Thatcher. The grand old Duke of York was on a hiding to nothing. Heresy.

And so 'we' and 'our' now became 'they' and 'their'. I could no longer empathise with 'the Labour movement'. As my numerous trips to European and Asian 'socialist democracies' and 'peoples republics' had confirmed, communism was impractical, outdated, and unnecessary. Maurice, incidentally, thinks the whole thing was a MI5/MI6 set up – with agents placed in Scargill's circle, egging him on to certain defeat. This may be paranoia laced with hindsight.

I had become interested in Buddhist and Taoist teachings even before these sea changes and practised Tai Chi Chuan and meditation. After taking early retirement from teaching in 1992 I became a Theravada monk for a short period. And joined Amnesty and Greenpeace, smoking quite a lot of dope and catching up maybe on the 60s – which we 'missed' not because we were too drunk or too stoned but because we were too busy,

In the 60s we tried to change the way people think and to a large extent we succeeded – not on economic theory (Thatcher won that hands down) but certainly when it came to nuclear war, the environment, racism, and the rights of women, blacks and gays. Remember how reactionary mainstream views were concerning these issues?! Now even the *Daily Mail* has to pull its punches with snide references to 'political correctness'.

The Tiananmun Square massacre rubbed in the lessons of the miners' strike. I spent four days and some nights outside the Chinese embassy in Portland Square. One of 'our' embassies! It was clear that communism had caused more murder, misery and mayhem than Hitler, Mussolini and Franco added together. Indeed, communism now appears to me a form of fascism. I had visited China back in 81 and genuinely believed (as I had in Russia during my 62 trip) that things would get better. Now I found myself on a demo outside one of 'our' embassies.

My most recent demos involved the campaign to decriminalise cannabis (the least dangerous drug, legal or illegal, currently available). I was nearly caught growing it in the school greenhouse in 1970 and was busted with 16 plants in my back garden in 1984. I was fined £50 – most London magistrates were contemptuous of the law even then. Now even the police want it decriminalised. Fortunately my boss at London Zoo was entirely sympathetic and nothing happened. Since then I have strongly supported the legalise cannabis campaign. The millions of pounds saved could be used to educate young people how to use it sensibly. The Lib-Dems want a radical re-think on this while Jack Straw, the only 60s student never to smoke a joint, typifies New Labour Puritanism. They are Tories in pink.

I was also involved with Outrage's campaign to equalise the age of consent. A fair number of Labour peers and MPs voted with the Tories on this one with the Lib-Dems once again emerging as the more radical of Britain's two centre-left coalitions. This is mainly why I campaigned for the Lib Dems at the last election. We won the IoW (a Tory stronghold) by several thousand votes and I joined the party the following year. I do not attend meetings – I always hated meetings and I do not regret my decision.

Perhaps my old Stalinist opponents were right and I was a bourgeois-liberal all along! Bertrand Russell comes again to mind – throughout my life I have longed to feel that oneness that is experienced by members of enthusiastic crowds. The longing has been strong enough to lead me into self deception. I have in turn imagined myself a liberal, a socialist, or a pacifist, but I have never been any of these things in any profound sense. Always the sceptical instinct has whispered doubts to me and cut me off from the facile enthusiasms of others. While I was willing to accept the unpopularity and inconvenience belonging to unpopular opinions I would tell the pacifists that I thought many wars in history had been justified, the socialists that I dreaded the tyranny of the State.

What remains true is that without those political experiences back in the 50s and 60s my life would have been less interesting and a lot less worthwhile.

One of my sons has become quite active politically. He was on the Stop the City demo last year, lived in a tree to stop the Newbury by-pass, and was arrested (and escaped) on the Poll Tax demo (`riot') which signalled the end of the ghastly Thatcher era .. He collected aid for the Kosovan refugees and drove it out to Macedonia. He lives on a bus in Richmond car park. His heart remains, like mine, in the High lands. We are not there yet, but we're getting there…

In the Beginning....
John Creaby, 2001

Born into a working class district on Tyneside, Gateshead, on 15th December 1943, I became part of the traditional north-east extended family. My maternal grandparents, aunt, uncle and cousins lived on the opposite side of the street of terraced houses. Other members of my mother's family and their families lived nearby, all coming together on Sunday for lunch (or dinner as we called it) at my grandparent's home. With my two sisters, one older and one younger, we lived in a happy home.

My mother came from a mining family, where the trade union and work were synonymous. My father, during my early childhood, was a merchant seaman (bosun); my mother worked in our home. My father regaled us with stories of distant lands, the people and customs, and brought back presents. My mother was the mainstay of the family, with my father away to sea. Both were avid readers. There were always books around the house, both fiction and non-fiction. Books were given as presents and we all used the public library. The radio was the main source of entertainment, until my grandparents rented a television. It was a micro-community of discussions, play, singing and close family relationships.

Religion had not been a major influence in my early childhood, although I was brought up as Roman Catholics. That is we, the children, went to church on Sunday and attended a church school. Neither my father nor my mother (who *converted* so as to keep my father's family happy) had deep connections with the church, although my mother was the 'believer.' I was later to find that my father viewed the church as an anachronism, although he was freethinking enough not to influence me. As an adolescent, I became caught up in the ritual, the Latin liturgy, music, the culture and splendour of the church. From this developed an awareness of Christian ethics; concern for what is right and wrong, good or evil, the cause and consequence and accountability (to God) for your action. Religion began to have a major role in my life. Having passed the 'eleven plus' exam I attended a RC Grammar School and even had thoughts of the priesthood. The church was not only my ethical guidance; it was also a significant focus of my social life in my early teens. This was period of a developing 'teen sub-culture,' rock & roll, media attention and *teenagers*, a commercial market. The church youth club and school club was where I went to socialise with my peers.

My father had left the sea to work in engineering and the shipyard, when I was 12years of age. After just less than two years working on land, he had a serious accident at work, from which he was told he would never work again. But being the strong character that he was, he did obtain work after a long period of self-rehabilitating. The economic pressure at home must have been extreme, although I was not consciously aware of it. However, the class distinction amongst the grammar school students and often from the staff had an impact on my development of social awareness.

This whole period at Grammar School was not a happy one; nevertheless it did not undermine my unquestioning faith. It did, however, draw me to consider the arguments put forward by worker-priests in France in the late 1950s regarding capital and labour. Furthermore, puberty had put paid to any notion of the (celibate) priesthood. In 1958, having joined the Young Christian Workers (YCW), a RC youth organisation that had a working class radical social ideology and links to the Labour Party, I found my entrée to party politics. Of greatest influence was my membership of the Christian group of the Campaign for Nuclear Disarmament (CND), which I joined in the same year.

It was in this period that I had left school and commenced employment at Gateshead Co-operative Society. The Coop, as it was called, was very local and there were a number of socialists on the Board of Directors, elected from the consumer members. Although wages were poor, I had the opportunity to have time off for political and trade union activities. The five years of employment at the Coop were very memorable and happy. My fellow workers were great friends and the management was contained within the structure. I was to spend many happy times working within the union, USDAW, especially the clandestine collection of union dues at local anti-union retail shops and meeting workers whose jobs would be on the line if they were caught talking to us. It underlined my understanding of the relationship of capital and labour. The Coop also encouraged me to attend the Co-operative College at Loughborough. I was introduced to the writings of the early French socialists, Levellers, chartists, co-operatives and Marx and Engels. This was an introduction to analysing history from a very new perspective. Other subjects, such as the British Constitution, the growth of the British party system and perspectives on colonialism, remain in my memory as important signposts.

Late in 1959, I had become involved with the Gateshead cell (as local learning groups were called) of the National Council of Labour Colleges (NCLC), an independent (of the TUC) trade union correspondence course body, with a head office in Scotland. The NCLC had local organisers and held regular courses on economics, politics, labour history, labour and the arts etc. The cell met at the Railway Engineering sheds in Gateshead. Often the course would drift into discussions or enlightenment on geography, maths, literature and other areas as the participant's interests were aroused. I was now also involved in the Anti-Apartheid group and the Movement for Colonial Freedom. These campaigns were to a degree linked to CND, as the same individuals and organisation were involved. At the same time I was also developing a repertoire of political and folk songs and enjoying the Jazz and blues club scene.

The Marxist / Christian dialogue meetings and my father.

The Marxist /Christian Dialogue, was held under the patronage of *Marxism Today*, the theoretical journal of the CP. It opened up Christian theology to philosophical criticism and Marxism to a different scrutiny. These meetings for the Northeast were held in Newcastle. They were led by James Klugmann, a national organiser of the CP, who was later to be editor of *Marxism Today* and an Anglican vicar, who had lived here in the 30s. It was here that I first met Horace Green, Northern Regional Organiser of the CP. I did not know then that he would become, in many ways my mentor, in my trade union and political work, from the 1970s until his death in 1995. At this time, however, I was friendlier with his daughter Ann and her husband Alec Comb through the YCL/CND.

It was in these meetings that past oversimplification of complex situations was exposed. I was introduced to new perspectives that challenged previous concept of history and society's relationship to ethics, art, governance and nature. Linked to the Marxist perspective at the NCLC classes, many misconceptions were cleared. I was reading the usual Marxist tracts; *Manifesto of the Communist Party; Wages, Labour and Capital; Value, Prices and Profits; Socialism Utopian and Scientific* and others from the Little Marx Library. I was also introduced to the significance of other religions with comparable ethics, dogma and historic relevance. Much was put into context by reading Bertrand Russell's *History of Western Philosophy* particularly, but also others such as his *Has Man a Future* and *Why I Am Not a Christian* and Tawney's *Religion and the Rise of Capitalism*.

My Father never attempted to influence my religious beliefs or my political ideas, but when I approached him about his political and ideological position I was surprised at his strength of attitude. He was a communist of the thirties' school, more of a Russophile than a Stalinist, he idealised the Soviet Union. However this was not armchair polemics. In the Thirties he had been not only active in his union, the National Union of Seamen, but also in the breakaway Seamen's Minority Movement. Then there was the Anti Fascist League in Byker. Also he had met with members of the I.W.W. in the USA and Australia. His attitude to the church was further underlined by his involvement in the Spanish Civil War. During the Second World War he was on the maritime run to Russia and often had to wait there for an open return. He could also speak about apartheid in South Africa or racism in America as he had seen it. He could, therefore, talk from what he called 'the real history' and we were to have many discussions and political arguments all through my adult life. He would sometimes give me a difficult haranguing time, particularly after I had been appointed a full time trade union official in 1968. He was, however, proud that I had such a job. He always wanted to know about disputes and negotiations. In the early-60s he was a major stimulus to the process of change in my political awareness.

Although my political ideas had not achieved any real clarity, my religious beliefs had been shaken and shattered. I began to see why John Stuart Mill remarked that when a cause becomes too bad to defend on rational grounds, its defenders fell back on religion. However, the reading and discussion had created a utopian idea about working people. Joining the 59 Society was to help in consolidating the outcome of the old ideas jostling with the new.

I remember a discussion with my father about George Orwell, who he saw as an anti-Soviet pawn of the ultra-left, which always assists the right. He was a particularly scathing about *Homage to Catalonia*, which I had loaned him. I read *Spanish Diary* an account by the Northeast ILP socialist, John McNair. This gave greater insight and a more objective view of forces and parties on the Republican side. The account of his arrest by the communists for being connected with the Workers' Party (POUM) and the effect of soviet influence proved useful in discussions with my father. I found Orwell's novels very readable and entertaining. In retrospect, with information we now have on Orwell's links with the Intelligence Services, makes me wonder if my father was right.

Alan Paton's book, *Cry the Beloved Country*, added to the political documents on the plight of black South Africans. Steinbeck, *The Grapes of Wrath*, and Hemingway, were amongst the American writers I enjoyed. However, most significant was the great black novelist, James Baldwin. His *The Fire Next Time* gave a real insight into racism. His books, *Giovanni's Room* and *Another Country*, were about the taboo subject of homosexuality. Homosexuality was a subject of debate at this time, although it did not have any national lobby and was to the media (and religion) an abomination. Yet in working class communities there was tolerance.

For example, in that close community that was my society as a boy in the early 1950s, there were neighbours living in a gay partnership, Les and Jimmy. They lived with the latter's parents. I remember an adult's conversation as to whether they were brothers, to which the reply that they were 'Nancies.' I had not a clue what this meant at the time. They were market traders and other neighbours were more interested in that and the fact that they went abroad for a holiday, which was then, of course, most unusual in working class communities. There was no ostracism. In fact my parents had arranged for Jimmy to be my sponsor for my Confirmation Service at Church. I have since thought about the difficulties they must have faced before their religion and the law. It was not until 1967, with the passage of the Sexual Offences Bill, that homosexuals, or in the present parlance the gay community, were freed from criminal prosecution.

Addendum 2

From the local CND song book

It's a big bomb, its an atom bomb (Tune:Cushie Butterfield)

A'm a broken hearted Geordie, an aam worried as well,
With aal the talk aboot fall-oot, why ye nivvor can tell
Whether this year or next year, next month or next week
We'll get a dose of radiation and gan aal up the creek.

Chorus

It's a big bomb, it's an Atom bomb,
An aam scared oot ma wits;
If some feul pushes in the button ,
We'll be aal blown tae bits.

Aa've bein leukin at the papers an it isn't very good news,
There's a blather on aboot Skybolt an' Minutemen and U 2's
There's a rocket they caal Honest John, there's another they caal Thor
If they clart around with aal these missiles there'll be bloody war

Chorus

Noo aa divvnt knaa very much aboot deterrents an' defence,
But me mates an me are worried, like, with the terrible suspense.
If some feul should gan off his heed at an atom-bomber base
Its tat a to canny Tyneside, an aal the human race.

Chorus

Noo this musn't ever happen lads, it 'd ruin us for good;
If the Bomb didn't finish us, then the radiation would
So we're gannin to tell the Government, an the Party leaders too
If ye divvn't ban the bloody bomb, then we'll have to ban you.

The civil defence volunteer (Tune: Lambton Worm)

Wor Geordie was a canny lad, He tried to do his best
He felt inclined to lend a hand, So he joined up with the rest;
Now why can't we aal follow him, An use oor common sense
An' aal put on oor uniform, An' join Civil Defence.

> Fetch me up me dustbin lid,
> Me stirrup pump an some broon paper,
> Whitewash an bags o sand
> An aa'm ready for the Bomb

Noo Geordie lad teuk part one day in a C.D. exercise,
He was sent to man a Warden's Post, an' told to watch the skies,
He kept on leukin aal the day for rockets an' the like,
In case some foreign power should have the nerve to strike.

Chorus

When afternoon had turned to night, an' Geordie felt quite tired,
He thought he's been there lang eneuf, so to H.Q. he wired
He'd just got through to his Sector Boss and asked to be relieved,
When he heard a whistling overhead – 'twas a missile he believed

Chorus

It went at such a fearful speed, Wor Geordie hardly knew
Which way the thing was comin' from or where 'twas gannin to;
He flashed a message to Control an' yelled a loud LEUK OUT!
Hide from the heat flash an' the blast, an'divvent forget fall-out!

Chorus

When those in charge got word of this they aal went underground,
An' waited for the great gig bang but nivvir heard a sound;
Said the Big Brass Hat to the Brigadier – Our Geordie must have lied
The bang is a long time overdue, so I'll take a look outside.

Chorus

The Brass Hats came out one by one, An' to the Warden's Post
They went an found poor Geordie lad white, like he'd seen a ghost;
He said – aa thought it very queer, there was nee great bang,
Aa didn't knaa what was gannin' on an' aa'm glad you'd come alang.

Chorus

Now, listen, George, the Big Chief said, to me it seems quite clear,
You've contravened the Warden's Code and ruined your career
A false alarm is not allowed, its quite against the rules,
You made us hide from a harmless bird, and look a lot of fools.

Chorus

Now Geordie lad is very sad, they sacked him from the corps,
For sending oot a false alarm aboot a missile war;
So now yee knaa if ye're in doot, ye mustn't breath a word,
Until ye're sure the thing ye saw was a bomb an' not a bird.

Some further reading

Most of the primary material for this book is a collection of audio tapes and transcriptions. The tapes are unlike conventional oral history interviews in that the author frequently participates in a conversation with friends, which many of the subjects are. The transcripts are edited into a more conventional form as a record of the subjects' life stories. The tapes and transcripts will be deposited at the Tyne and Wear Archives [www.**tyne**and**wear**archives.org.uk] in 2010. The transcripts will be available but access to the tapes will require special permission from the author.

Local newspapers did not give extensive coverage to CND and even less to local young socialist events but the following papers have been consulted and some material gleaned: *Berwick Advertiser, Evening Chronicle, Morpeth Herald, Newcastle Journal, Northern Echo, Stockton and Darlington Times* and *Sunderland Echo*.

There are very few books which deal specifically with this period in the North East of England. Two exceptions are two volumes of autobiography by Dave Douglass who appears in this book. They are marvelously lively personal accounts of Dave's extraordinary life. His account of childhood and schooldays in Felling is both vivid and moving.

David John Douglass, *Geordies – Wa Mental*, Read 'n Noir, Hastings, 2008.

David John Douglass, *The Wheel's Still in Spin*, Read 'n Noir, Hastings, 2009.

Some of the background to the account in this book can be read in three recently published books and a fourth, published in autumn 2009, surveys the whole of the 1960's. Readers should also consult *North East History*, the journal of the North East Labour History Society. [www.nelh.org]

Anna Flowers and Vanessa Histon, *Water Under the Bridges*, Tyne Bridge Publishing, Newcastle, 1999.

Robert Colls and Bill Lancaster, *Newcastle Upon Tyne: A Modern History*, Phillimore, Chichester, 2001. David Byrne's essay, 'The Reconstruction of Newcastle's Planning since 1945'is especially interesting.

Alistair Moffat and George Rosie, *Tyneside: A History of Newcastle and Gateshead from Earliest Times*, Mainstream Publishing, Edinburgh, 2005.

Anna Flowers and Vanessa Histon, *It's My Life: 1960s Newcastle*, Tyne Bridge Publishing, Newcastle, 2009.

There is only an autobiography and two accounts of CND as a national movement. They are all strongly London based and say very little about the provinces, Scotland or the mass movement but are nevertheless useful.

Peggy Duff, *Left,Left, Left,* Allison & Busby, London, 1971.
Christopher Driver, *The Disarmers: A Study in Protest,* Hodder & Stoughton, London, 1964.
Richard Taylor and Colin Pritchard, *The British Nuclear Disarmament Movement of 1958-1965,Twenty Years On,* Pergamon Press, Oxford, 1980.

Notes

1 Jim Walker wrote, 'At that time (1964) I was doing occasional book and theatre crits for Richard (Kelly) and drinking with the crowd in the Trafalgar or Portland, that Alex and I discussed the impending Revolution, as we all did in the early Sixties and I, with typical cynicism, said, 'Oh yes, comrades, the revolution starts as soon as this pub closes.' Alex laughed and wrote the song, *As soon as this pub closes* which features in *Close the Coalhouse Door* and might be a suitable song to open the book, if it's not TOO cynical.' Personal letter to the author, 16/02/02.

2 Nick Howard, telephone discussion, 2009. In 1961 Joe Cocker, at 17, worked as an apprentice gas fitter and by night, became Vance Arnold, singing with The Avengers, in Sheffield pubs.

3 Mike Down, Personal Account, 2001.

4 Mary Phillips, telephone discussion, 2009 and ibid., Nick Howard.

5 Comment made in a WEA class on the 1950s, 2002.

6 A corrective to the picture of conservative renaissance is the fact that in 1951 the Labour Party recorded the highest aggregate vote of any party in British history before or since. The astronomical vote in most coal mining constituencies could not compensate for Tory superiority in the number of seats won.

7 This was Bill Ferguson, a school teacher, I think from Chester le Street, County Durham, who told me this many years ago. Unfortunately I have been unable to find him.

8 The Socialist League was founded in 1932 in the wake of the electoral disaster for Labour of 1931. It was an organisation of the Labour Left but much wider than that, supporting the idea of a United Front against fascism. Its tacit association with the Communist Party was unacceptable to the Labour Party. It was dissolved

in 1937 to avoid its members being expelled from the Labour Party. Its leading figure Stafford Cripps was expelled in 1939 for advocating a popular front with the CP.

9   Communist Party membership rose from 32,681 in March 1955 to 33,095 in February 1956 then fell to 26,742 by February 1957 and 24,670 in February 1958.

10   In the summer of 1956 the British Government connived with the French and Israelis to attack Eygpt. Led by Colonel Abdul Nasser, the Egyptians had seized the Suez Canal. Under pressure from Washington the Prime Minister, Antony Eden was forced into a humiliating retreat.

11   The Government, concerned by levels of unofficial strikes and wage inflation and by reports of economically damaging 'restrictive practices,' set up a Royal Commission under Lord Donovan 'to consider relations between managements and employees and the role of trade unions and employers' associations in promoting the interests of their members and in accelerating the social and economic advance of the nation, with particular reference to the Law affecting the activities of these bodies.' *European Commission for the Improvement of Living and Working conditions*[web site].

12   One aspect of this is the way that some of those failed by the system in the nineteen fifties and nineteen sixties entered expanded higher education as mature students in the nineteen seventies and eighties.

13   Announced in *Tribune*, November, 1959.

14   Modernism as an overall socially progressive trend of thought, that affirms the power of human beings to create, improve, and reshape their environment, with the aid of practical experimentation, scientific knowledge or technology. Modernising does not carry the same ideological baggage and may simply be applied to the replacement of any poorly functioning item with a new one. Dan Smith certainly was motivated by the former.

15   The Labour Party HQ.

16   This chapter is largely based on information on parents and grandparents given in interviews between 2000 and 2009.

17   John Charlton, after this, referenced as 'Author'

18   Pat (Marley) Johnson, interview, 2001.

19   Colin and Lillian Boyd, interview, 2006.

20   Jim Nichol, interview 1, 2004.

21   Margaret (Dick) Brecknell, interview 2006.

22   Harry Rothman, interview, 2006.

23   Lucy Nicholson, interview, 2004.

24   Wal Hobson, interview 1, 2006.

25   Maggie Anwell, interview, 2006.

26   Fiona (Scott Batey) Clarke, 2006

27   Jeremy Beecham, interview, 2006.

28   Author.

29   John Baker, interview, 2009.

30   Brian Sharp, interview, 2009.

31   op cit., Harry Rothman.

32   ibid., Harry Rothman.

33   Pat Johnson, interview 2, 2009.
34   Lionel Anwell, an appreciation, **North East History**, 37, 2006.
35   Marge (Wallace) Chryssostomides Questionnaire, 2001.
36   op cit., Colin and Lillian Boyd.
37   Maggie Anwell, interview, 2006.
38   ibid., Maggie Anwell.
39   Dorothy Simmons, interview 1, 2006.
40   op cit., Margaret Brecknell, interview, 2006.
41   op cit., Fiona Clarke, 2006.
42   Jessie (Ross) Scott Batey, interview 2004.
43   Mary (Feinmann) Chuck, notes, 2006.
44   op cit., John Baker.
45   Jim Hutchinson, Questionnaire, 2001, interview 1, 2004.
46   Wal Hobson, 2009.
47   op cit., Jessie Scott-Batey.
48   John Mapplebeck, Questionnaire, 2001.
49   Jim Nichol, interview 3, 2009.
50   op cit., John Baker.
51   Lucy Nicholson, unpublished memoir, 2005.
52   Author.
53   op cit. Lindy (Howard) Genton.
54   Irene (Edwards) Lovell, telephone interview, 2006.
55   Jean Mortimer, Questionnaire, 2001.
56   Nina (Johnson) Watson, interview, 2008.
57   Author.
58   Eric Walker, interview, 2002.
59   Jimmy Walker, **Of Rice and Men**, Stockport, 1997.
60   Author.
61   op cit., John Baker.
62   Roger Hall, interview, 2004.
63   Author.
64   op cit., Jessie Scott Batey.
65   Guy Falkenau, interview, 2006.
66   Jennifer Bartholemew, interview, 2001.
67   Jim Hutchinson, interview, 2004.
68   Albert & Joan Booth, interview, 2006.
69   Ronnie & Doreen Curran, interview, 2006.
70   Pete Wood, *The Elliots of Birtley*, Todmorden, 2008, p 103.
71   ibid., Pete Elliot,pp 43-44.
72   ibid., John writes of his father's 'set of Dickens which I still treasure'.
73   op cit., Harry Rothman.
74   op cit., Jesse Scott Batey.
75   Author.
76   op cit., Lindy Genton.
77   Pat Macintyre, letter to the author, 8 February, 2009.
78   Jim Nichol, interview 2, 2006.

79 Sam Dodds, interview, 2009.
80 Linda (Potts) Ebbatson, interview, 2009.
81 op cit., John Baker.
82 John Creaby, discussion, 2009.
83 op cit., Linda Ebbatson.
84 op cit., Brian Sharp.
85 Author.
86 op cit., Mike Worrall, 2009.
87 op cit., Mary Chuck, letter, 2009.
88 Pat Johnson, interview 2, 2009.
89 op cit., Brian Sharp.
90 Lucy Nicholson, interview 2, 2008.
91 Fiona Clarke, interview, 2006.
92 op cit., Pat Johnson, 2009.
93 op cit., Linda Ebbatson..
94 op cit., Jennifer Bartholemew.
95 op cit., Linda Ebbatson.
96 Nicky (Landau) Wildy, telephone interview, 2009
97 op cit.,Pat Johnson, 2009.
98 Wal Hobson interview 1, April 2006.
99 Ken Appleby, interview 2006.
100 Terry Watson, interview 2008.
101 John Creaby, Diary Note, no date.
102 op cit.,Brian Sharp.
103 Roger Hall, discussion with author, 2005.
104 Jim Walker, unpublished notes for a memoir, collected by his daughter Sally in 2005.
105 Author.
106 Jim Walker, see essay, *The Shock of the 59* in the Addendum.
107 In *The Hidden Persuaders*, published in 1957, Vance Packard explored the use of consumer motivational research and other psychological techniques, including depth psychology and subliminal tactics, by advertisers to manipulate expectations and induce desire for products, particularly in the American post war era. It also explored the manipulative techniques of promoting politicians to the electorate. The book questions the morality of using these techniques.[Wikipedia]. It was a very popular book in the late 1950s. It was one of the first hard back books I (the author) bought with my own teacher's salary.
108 David (Dave) John Douglass, *Geordies- Wa Mental*, London, 2008, p 56.
109 Lucy Nicholson, interview 1, 2006.
110 Jim Nichol, interview 1, 2004.
111 Irene (Edwards) Lovell, telephone interview 2, 2009.
112 op cit.,Terry Watson, 2008.
113 op cit., Sam Dodds, interview,2009
114 Marge Wallace, Questionnaire, 2001
115 ibid., Marge Wallace.
116 ibid., Marge Wallace.

117 op cit., Jim Walker, unpublished notes…

118 Ken Appleby, interview, 2006.

119 *Evening Chronicle*, August, 28th, 1960.

120 This telling phrase is borrowed from Emile Durkheim's writing on religion. It seems so apposite to describe the rapid involvement of youth against the Bomb.

121 *The Fellowship of Reconciliation (FoR or FOR*, founded in 1914, is the name used by a number of religious nonviolent peace organizations, in which Quakers are prominent.

122 Mike Worrall, interview, 2009.

123 Anna Tapsell, telephone discussion, 2009.

124 op cit., Nina Johnson.

125 op cit., Jean Mortimer.

126 op cit., John Creaby.

127 op cit., Mike Down.

128 Mary (Feinman) Chuck, letter, 2009.

129 *Evening Chronicle*, 2nd November, 1961.

130 op cit., Pat Johnson, 2009.

131 Maggie Anwell, personal letter to the author, 2009.

132 This was John Baird MP, a secret adherent of the Fourth International.

133 op cit., Mike Down.

134 Harry Rothman, interview, 2006

135 A D-Notice is an official request to news editors not to publish or broadcast items on specified subjects for reasons of national security.

136 op cit., Nina Johnson.

137 op cit., Harry Rothman.

138 op cit., Dave Douglass, p153.

139 op cit., Anna Tapsell, 2009.

140 *Northern Echo*, 30 April, 1961.

141 Pat Macintyre, interview, 2009.

142 *Evening Chronicle*, 2nd May,1961.

143 *Morpeth Herald*, 5th May, 1961.

144 *Berwick Advertiser*, 11th May, 1961.

145 op cit., Irene Lovell.

146 op cit., Jean Mortimer.

147 *Newcastle Journal*, 23 May, 1961.

148 op cit., Irene Lovell.

149 *Evening Chronicle*, 19 September, 1961.

150 John Creaby, Diary Note, nd.

151 *Resistance Shall Grow: The story of the Spies for Peace*, Independent Labour Party, et al, 1963.

152 *Evening Chronicle*, 2 May,1963.

153 Cited, Dave Douglass, p174.

154 *Wallsend News*, 31 January, 1964.

155 op cit., Dave Douglass, p 180-81

156 ibid., Dave Douglass, p 220.

157 ibid., Dave Douglass, p 220.

158 Tom Pickard, 'Morden Tower', **Mother Grumble**, June 1973.

159 Robert Creeley (1926 – 2005) was an American poet and author of more than sixty books

160 Schwitters worked in several genres and media, including Dada, Constructivism, Surrealism, poetry, sound, painting, sculpture, graphic design, typography and what came to be known as installation art.
     Kurt Schwitters (1887 -1948) was a German painter who was born in Hanover, Germany.
     He is most famous for his collages called *Merz Pictures*.

161 Tom Pickard, from Rough Music (Ruff Muzhik *Chicago Review*, 46, 2000.

162 Lee Hall, Archive Hour, BBC Radio 4, February 2009.

163 op cit., Maggie Anwell.

164 Kyran Casteel, Skype Interview, 2009.

165 Jack Shepherd, Foreward, C. Goulding, *The Story of The People's*, Newcastle City Libraries, Newcastle upon Tyne, 1991, p5.

166 op cit.,Maggie Anwell.

167 Moira Woods, Interview, 2009.

168 Pete Wood, *The Elliots of Birtley*, Todmorden, 2008, p 50.

169 A copy of the programme in Local Studies at Newcastle Central Library is annotated by its owner, 'Thanks to God for sight and hearing. Grateful the return of such a talented artist-7.30 p.m., 13th Novmber,1958.'

170 *Evening Chronicle*, 14th November, 1958.

171 op cit., Irene Edwards.

172 Lucy Nicholson, *Musical Chairs: A Craghead Tale*, unpub. autobiography.

173 Jim Hutchinson, Interview 2, 2009.

174 ibid., Jim Hutchinson.

175 ibid., Jim Hutchinson.

176 op cit., John Creaby Diary Notes.

177 op cit., Jim Hutchinson.

178 Much of this chapter is from the Author's recollection.

179 Guy Falkenau, discussion, 2009.

180 op cit., John Creaby, Diary Notes.

181 op cit., Guy Falkenau.

182 Irene Lovell, interview, 2009.

183 Mike Down, written testimony, 2000.

184 Pat Johnson, Questionnaire, 2001.

185 Jim Walker, letter *EC*, March, 1960.

186 op cit., Sam Dodds, interview 2009.

187 Dave Leigh, interview, 2006.

188 Jock Kane, an oral history, *No Wonder We Were Rebels*, Doncaster, no date.

189 Ann Kane, telephone interview, 2009.

190 ibid., Ann Kane.

191 op cit.,Terry Watson.

192 Guy Falkenau's recollection.

193 Jen (Scott) Holder, interview, 2009.

194 op cit., Sam Dodds, interview 2009.

195 Marge Wallace, personal letter, 2009.

196 On 21 March 1960 at least 180 black Africans were injured (there are claims of as many as 300) and 69 killed when South African police opened fire on approximately 300 demonstrators, who were protesting against the pass laws, at the township of Sharpeville in the Transvaal.

197 The Hoppings on the Town Moor of Newcastle upon Tyne is Europe's largest fairground and is back on the Moor at the end of June annually since 1882. A political rally took place there on the Sunday evening before the official opening.

198 op cit., John Creaby, Diary Notes.

199 op cit., Jean Mortimer.

200 Jane (Lu) Bell, interview, 2006.

201 I owe these paragraphs to discussion with Kris Beuret and Roger Hall.

202 In their book, *Red Diapers: Growing Up in the Communist Left*, 1998, Judy Kaplan and Linn Shapiro, define children of CPers, as 'Red diaper babies'. I extend it to include children of all left-wing parents.

203 It now seems a bit esoteric but then, how you defined the Soviet Union was crucial on the far left. Some argued that it was a degenerated or deformed (there was a difference!) workers' state where the workers owned but did not control the state (SLL, for example). A political revolution would be required to re-instate workers' control. The IS called Russia State Capitalists where state authorities, with similar priorities to western capitalists, dominated the process of capital accumulation. Nothing short of social revolution could dislodge them.

204 A **groupuscule** is a tiny political group. This is particularly common in anarchist, Stalinist and Trotskyist movements. This tendency was satirized in the film *Monty Python's Life of Brian*, in which various small groups (People's Front of Judea, Judean People's Front, Judean Popular People's Front and the Popular Front of Judea) spend more time and energy fighting and insulting each other than their common enemy, the Romans. Some readers may find this a little harsh.

205 The other significant trotskyist tendency the RSL (Revolutionary Socialist League), or Militant, was represented locally round 1960 only by the veteran Herbie Bell of Wallsend and made no significant inroads to the local YS or LP till after 1965.

206 *Signposts for the 'Sixties* was the Labour Party's pamphlet laying out its programme for the decade ahead.

207 From John Mapplebeck, *Jim Murray*, unpublished article, 2002.

208 Durham passages are based on an interview with Brian Whitton and John Smith, April 2006.

209 op cit., Brian Whitton and John Smith, April 2006.

210 Wal Hobson, interview 1, April 2006

211 ibid., Wal Hobson.

212 Trish (Sorbie) Fitzpatrick, interview, 2009.

213 ibid. Wal Hobson 1.

214 Harry Rothman interview, 2006.

215 op cit., Trish Fitzpatrick, 2009.

216 Brenda (Ingleby) Corcoron, discussion, 2009.

217 ibid., Trish Fitzpatrick.

218 Jenn (Scott) Holder, interview, 2009.

219 Ann Berg, telephone discussion, 2009.

220 op cit., Mike Down.

221 Walter Ryder interview, 2009.

222 Ibid., Harry Rothman

223 The Communist Party HQ was usually known as 'King Street.'

224 Dave Leigh, interview 2006.

225 Nina Watson, interview, 2008.

226 op cit., Lucy Nicholson, 2006.

227 Ann Green testimony, 2007.

228 Jane (Owens) Wadham, reply to author's Questionnaire, 2009.

229 ibid., Jane Wadham.

230 Jeremy Beecham, interview,2006.

231 Wal Hobson, interview 2, 2009.

232 Gladys Hobson, Interview 2009, says they were suspended rather than expelled, which may have reflected the friendships they had in the South Shields Labour Party. The disciplinary action was on the recommendation of the Regional Office.

233 John Mapplebeck, answer to the author's Questionnaire, 2000. Jack Johnson was a former friend and comrade of Dan Smith's in the ILP and on the City Council. He was deselected for his Armstrong Ward Council seat in 1962 for persistently raising questions in the Housing Committee about Cruden's building contracts.

234 Dorothy Simmons, interview 2006.

235 Guy Falkenau, reply to Questionnaire, 2009.

236 Peter Sedgwick, introduction to D. Widgery, *The Left in Britain, 1956-1968*, London, 1976.

237 Mike Worrall, Diary of Events, 1965 (in author's possession)

238 This point is discussed in, John Charlton, 'The archaeology of social movements,' in David Renton & Keith Flett, eds.*New Writings in Socialist History*, 2004.

239 Sandra Peers, interview 2009.

240 Author's recollection.

241 Dave Peers, interview 3, 2006.

242 Maggie Pearse, interview, 2009.

243 op cit., Maggie Anwell.

244 Roger Protz was not editor of *Young Guard* , but was later editor of *Socialist Worker.*

245 Alan Brown was the first casualty. A young worker from Washington, he died from Hodgkin's Disease in his late teens, c 1962. Soon afterwards, Eric Mirley, an electrician from Gosforth, died in his early twenties.